THE COURTROOM CONSPIRACY

ILLUSIONS OF JUSTICE

LARRY JAY LEVINE

The Courtroom Conspiracy: Illusions of Justice

First Edition
Printed in the United States of America

Publisher Information:
World Crime Media Inc
Sheridan, Wyoming
For inquiries contact help@worldcrimemedia.com

213.948.1069

ISBN: 979-8-9921484-9-7

Additional Notes:
All names, dates, and specific details in any examples or case studies presented have been altered to protect the identities of those involved. Any resemblance to actual persons, living or dead, is purely coincidental unless otherwise stated.

Dedications & Acknowledgments

Sarah Martin

Every project has a starting point, and most of them die there. This one didn't.

Thanks to the radiant Sarah Martin, the woman who bought the very first copy of my very first book Crimes That Never Happened when there was no audience, no media, no reputation, and no guarantee this would turn into anything more than a stack of pages and an idea. That matters – not emotionally, but factually. I find it fitting that I should honor her in my very last and final book.

People love success. Very few touch the work before it's validated. Sarah did. That puts her in the record whether anyone likes it or not. This is my last book, Illusions . So it closes the loop. The first buyer of the first book gets named in the final one. Not as a gesture. As documentation. Thanks Sarah for believing in me! xoxoxoxoxo

My Daughter, Jacqueline

You were a child of 14 when the Feds came knocking. One minute I was dropping you off at a friend's, the next I was gone—for ten long years. You didn't get a warning, a goodbye, or a chance to understand what was happening. That's on me. You bore the fallout of my choices, the system's cruelty, and a decade of silence I never wanted. You had to grow up fast, and you did it without the father you deserved. If there's one thing I want you to know, it's this: I never stopped thinking about you. I never stopped loving you. And every page of this book is soaked in the regret of a man who wishes he could've been there—for all of it.

My Grandchildren - Kalina, Lucas, and Joseph

You are my redemption. You represent everything that still matters in a world that tried to convince me I didn't. I write this for you so that when you're old enough to understand, you'll know that your grandfather didn't take the easy way out. I told the truth, even when it hurt. I stood up when it would've been easier to shut up. You'll inherit a world that's still broken, but I hope this book helps you see how to navigate it—with courage, with defiance, and with your eyes wide open. Never be afraid to ask hard questions—especially when everyone else is pretending they already have the answers.

Leticia – My Wife, My Constant, My Storm Anchor

We didn't meet in the middle of the chaos. We met after it – after the sentence, after the prisons, after the system took what it was going to take. You didn't see the worst of it firsthand, but you saw the aftermath. And that's its own kind of test. You stepped into a life that already had scars, noise, and unfinished business. You listened. You watched. You learned what the system leaves behind in a person long after the gates close. And you chose to stay anyway.

We married years later, not out of rescue or drama, but out of clarity. You understood who I was, where I'd been, and what I refused to forget. You never asked me to soften it, rewrite it, or shut up about it. You held your ground while I held mine. This book exists because you accepted the truth without needing to romanticize it. You didn't try to fix the past – you made sure it didn't control the future. That matters. And I don't confuse that with anything else.

My Parents – Ann and Ron

You didn't just support me. You fought for me when I couldn't fight for myself. When the headlines painted me as a villain, you reminded people I was still your son. When I was locked away, you showed up. Letters, visits, encouragement—you kept me tethered to something real. And when I started writing this, you pushed me to keep going. You believed in my voice when I didn't. You reminded me that surviving prison wasn't enough—I had to make something out of it. And here it is.

Eddie Dunne, Nadia, and family

You didn't just give me a place to stay in New York – you gave me a base. A home that came with laughter, conversation, and zero conditions. That matters more than hospitality. Eddie, the years of airtime on your station weren't favors – they were trust. *Street Justice* existed because you handed me a mic and let me tell the truth without interference. That kind of freedom is rare, and I don't forget who provides it. Nadia, your warmth set the tone, and your family made sure it never felt temporary. What you offered wasn't shelter – it was stability. That's loyalty in real form. And I don't take it lightly.

Holli Coulman

Holli, you didn't just do time – you used it. You turned Victorville into a proving ground, survived the SHU, and came out sharper and more disciplined than you went in. Instead of hiding your past, you put it to work, helping other women see life after custody and calling out hypocrisy most people are too scared to touch. As my partner in Pink Lady Prison Consultants, you don't sugarcoat. You tell the truth when lawyers won't, speak up when others stay quiet, and show up when it counts. That's loyalty, grit, and purpose in real form. There's no one else I'd want in the trenches with me.

Jacqueline Polverari

You did your time at Danbury, rebuilt your life, and didn't turn your back on anyone who needed a hand – including me. Opening your door in Connecticut wasn't charity; it was grounding. You brought stability when I needed it and didn't flinch when things were complicated.

You call out bullshit on sight, defend people with facts instead of feelings, and protect those you stand with. When my story was being twisted, you made sure the record was corrected – publicly and without hesitation. You've shown more loyalty than most people who share blood. That puts you where you belong.

Lynn Espejo

You walked out of Bryan FPC with your head up and your voice intact. You took what the system handed you and turned it into documentation, exposure, and pressure – not silence. You didn't just survive it. You challenged it. You're relentless about truth, allergic to sugarcoating, and solid when it counts. You stood up for me publicly and privately, louder than people I've known for decades. That's not common. You're smart, strategic, and unafraid – exactly the kind of person this system doesn't like. Which is exactly why you matter.

Keith Levey

You're not just a lawyer–you're a lifer. Not in the prison sense, but in the "ride or die" sense. You've been in my corner since before all this shitstorm began. You gave me counsel when I didn't want to hear it, and you gave me loyalty when others were cashing out. When I was released and had nothing but my name and a story, you stood by both. You never let me forget who I was before all this–and who I still had the power to become. You've practiced law with something most of the others forgot: heart. And I'm damn lucky to have had you in my corner through it all.

Sol Bash

Sol, you didn't blink. I came out of prison after a decade, and you didn't see a liability–you saw a man who needed a shot. You gave me a job when no one else would. You gave me dignity when the system tried to crush it. You've been there for over 50 years–long before the headlines, long before the courtrooms, long before the fallout. And when I hit rock bottom, you didn't ask questions. You said, "Get up." That's real friendship. That's what most people only wish they had. You helped me rebuild when all I had was broken pieces–and I'll never forget that.

Sid Blitz

Sid, we've done time together in more prisons than I can count. MDC Los Angeles. Victorville. The yards, the lockdowns, the late-night whispers between bunks–we've seen the underbelly of the beast together. You were there in the beginning, and you were still there when I got out. You handed me cash with no strings, no questions–just the look of a brother who'd been through the same fire. That meant more than money. It meant loyalty. It meant survival. We survived together, fought the same system side by side, and made it out without selling our souls. You're one of the last real ones–and I'd go to war with you any day.

WHY THIS BOOK

This book is not for the faint of heart. It's not for the lawyers who are too afraid to look in the mirror. It's for the people who've been screwed by their own defense team–talked into plea deals, lied to about options, and left holding the bag when it all came crashing down.

This is for the defendants who got a handshake in the hallway and a knife in the back inside the courtroom.

This is your warning shot.

They lied. I'm telling the truth.
 And I'm just getting started.

Why I Wrote The Courtroom Conspiracy:
Illusions of Justice

From *Crimes That Never Happened: Beating Federal Conspiracies* to this final chapter – *The Courtroom Conspiracy: Illusions of Justice* – this wasn't some overnight project. It took decades. Twenty-eight years of watching the system operate up close. Ten of them served behind razor wire, scribbling notes on yellow legal pads because that's all they'd give me. The rest typed out on whatever laptop was in front of me – free, but never detached from what I'd already seen.

This is the last book.

Over the years, I've crossed paths with every kind of person this system produces – the good, the crooked, and the ones who figured out how to smile while quietly selling people out. This book was born in the aftermath of betrayal – not just mine, but hundreds of others – by the very people who are supposed to protect your constitutional rights. Lawyers. Fixers. "Advisors." The ones who talk justice in public but negotiate surrender in private.

If you ever believed your attorney would fight – and later found out you were just another box to check on a plea deal spreadsheet – this book's for you.

I started shaping it during the COVID lockdown. Sick. In bed. Unsure if I'd even finish it. But the Chromebook kept clicking. I kept typing. Because silence is how this system survives. And I wasn't about to hand it that luxury.

The Courtroom Conspiracy: Illusions of Justice isn't a metaphor. It's a diagnosis. It's how the sausage gets made. How deals get cut. How loyalty gets faked. How your case gets decided long before a judge takes the bench. It's not theory. It's what happens when you finally stop listening to fairy tales and start reading the case docket.

This book is my final word.
 And it's the book your lawyer hopes you never read.

Now let me acknowledge a few people.

My Daily Writing Companion Hazel

"Crazy Hazy" is a purebred purple tongue Chow Chow that my wife Letecia and I rescued when she was a puppy just before Covid. If she's not busying playing or destroying her toys, she's constantly busting my balls banging on the door demanding to be let in or out, and can be found nearby as I write, trying to charm more nummies from me!

In Memory of U.S. Supreme Court Justices who consistently "stood for the people"!

Thurgood Marshall	William Dougals	Earl Warren	Hugo Black
Associate Justice 1967–1991	Associate Justice 1939–1975	Chief Justice 1953–1969	Associate Justice 1937–1971

I Dedicate This Book to the Last Justices for the People

Thurgood Marshall, William O. Douglas, Hugo Black, and Earl Warren did not sit on the Supreme Court to protect institutions – they sat there to restrain them. **Thurgood Marshall** came to the bench straight out of the trenches, having dismantled Jim Crow brick by brick through *Brown v. Board of Education*, carrying with him a lifetime of defending people the system had already written off.

William O. Douglas treated government power like a loaded weapon, defending privacy, free speech, and the Fourth Amendment with open hostility toward surveillance, police overreach, and moral busybodies who thought authority deserved automatic respect. **Hugo Black** read the Bill of Rights the way it was written – not as suggestions, not as guidelines, but as hard limits – enforcing free speech and due process even when the defendant was unpopular and the politics were ugly. And **Earl Warren**, presiding over the Court during its most defendant-protective era, forced the system to confront its own abuse through decisions like *Miranda v. Arizona* and *Gideon v. Wainwright*, recognizing that rights mean nothing if only the rich can afford to invoke them.

Together, they believed the Constitution was designed to protect people from the government – not excuse it, not balance away its obligations, and not bury citizens under procedure. Their legacy stands in direct contrast to the modern courtroom, where rights are negotiated, fairness is conditional, and justice is filtered through convenience, careerism, and institutional self-preservation. Their era proved the system *can* be restrained. What followed proved it chose not to be.

Introduction

The Courtroom Is a Stage

Let's get something straight before you start romanticizing this place: courtrooms aren't where justice happens. They're where justice gets *acted out* – in costume, under lights, with a script already written before you ever stepped on the goddamn stage.

The prosecutor? That smug bastard's not here to find truth – they're here to win. The judge? Just another overpaid referee protecting the illusion that this whole charade is "fair." And your defense lawyer? Half the time they're a glorified usher making sure you sit down, shut up, and take the plea before the lights go out.

This isn't justice. This is **performance art with prison time**.

I've watched people get steamrolled for crimes they didn't commit – or better yet, crimes that never even happened – all because the system needed a body and you were dumb enough to still believe in due process. I've seen defense attorneys tank cases just to keep their club membership in good standing. I've seen judges phone it in while people's lives got buried under paper. And I've seen defendants learn – too fucking late – that trusting the process is like hugging a rattlesnake and hoping for warmth.

This book isn't about getting screwed by bad luck. It's about getting *engineered* into failure. It's about how the system manipulates your fear, uses your own people against you, then tells you it was "justice" when you lose everything.

This ain't a reform manual.
It's a ***post-mortem.***
For what really happens when you walk into federal court thinking truth still matters.

You won't like everything you read.
 But you'll recognize every word of it.

Now sit down.
 The curtain's about to rise.

About the Author

Larry Levine didn't stumble into the federal criminal justice system – it hunted him, caged him, and accidentally trained him.

In 1998, a federal task force hit Levine with racketeering, securities fraud, obstruction, and conspiracy. Translation: stack charges, scare the defendant, and let the guidelines do the dirty work. He got ten years. And a front-row seat to a system that doesn't care who's guilty – just who's easiest to break.

Eleven federal prisons. Multiple states. Every security level. And the same dirty pattern every time: prosecutors inflate charges, judges rubber-stamp, defense lawyers whisper damage control, and the Bureau of Prisons buries the wreckage. Justice is the sales pitch. Compliance is the real hustle.

Inside, Levine became the guy people went to when the lies stopped working. He didn't sell hope – he sold clarity. That made him dangerous. He exposed sentencing scams, plea traps, and legal half-truths most lawyers were too gutless to admit.

From a Texas prison cell, he filed a habeas action that forced the Bureau of Prisons to fix mass misclassifications. Over 100 inmates were re-designated to lower-security yards. The BOP never said thank you. Bureaucracies don't like mirrors.

After release, Levine weaponized his experience and founded Wall Street Prison Consultants. Not to play nice – to teach people how to survive. He works with defendants at the only time it matters: before they screw themselves. Before the plea. Before the surrender. Before the BOP shreds what's left of their sanity.

He's written a stack of blunt, unsanitized books: *Crimes That Never Happened*, *Prison Politics 101*, *Lies My Lawyer Told Me*, *The Art of Dealing with Two-Faced People*, and now *The Courtroom Conspiracy: Illusions of Justice*. These aren't motivational reads. They're warning labels.

The media calls him not because he's polite – but because he's right. Levine's been featured on CNN, Fox News, MSNBC, Bloomberg, Court TV, NewsNation, Inside Edition, and quoted in The New York

Times, Forbes, The Wall Street Journal, The Washington Post, and Newsweek. He doesn't tell people what they want to hear – he tells them what's coming.

This book isn't a redemption story. It's a battle map.

Larry Levine isn't here to fix the justice system. He's here to make sure it doesn't fix *you*.

Behind the scenes, Larry's a husband, a father, and a grandfather, fiercely loyal to the people who stood by him when the system tried to wipe him out. His family is his real wealth–the reason he keeps swinging, exposing the lies, and pushing for a future where the next generation won't have to live through the same bullshit.

Table Of Contents

Dedications & Acknowledgments

Why I Wrote The Courtroom Conspiracy: Illusions of Justice

My Daily Writing Companion Hazel

Introduction

About the Author

Play the Game or Get Played

EXHIBIT ONE

    Federal Courthouse Conspiracy 1

EXHIBIT TWO

    Grand Jury Conspiracy 16

EXHIBIT THREE

    Federal Indictment Conspiracy 40

EXHIBIT FOUR

    Federal Arraignment Conspiracy..56

EXHIBIT FIVE

    Pre Trial Services Bail Conspiracy 70

EXHIBIT SIX

    Pre Trial Motions 94

EXHIBIT SEVEN

Public Defender Conspiracy..104

EXHIBIT EIGHT

My Lawyer Promised Probation..119

EXHIBIT NINE

Paid Lawyer Conspiracy..130

EXHIBIT TEN

Federal Prosecutor Conspiracy..151

EXHIBIT ELEVEN

The Unholy Triangle of Lawyer, Prosecutors & Judges............................169

EXHIBIT TWELVE

Federal Judge Conspirator..182

EXHIBIT THIRTEEN

Clerks and Stenographers...213

EXHIBIT FOURTEEN

Fighting the System...235

Play the Game or Get Played

There's no such thing as a fair fight in federal court. Everyone's lying, everyone's protecting something, and the only person who actually gives a damn about your freedom is you. So you've got two choices—either play the game like a hustler or get played like a rookie. You think your lawyers on your team? Think the Prosector's honest? Think the Judge gives a shit? Think Probation wants you to succeed? Well guess again stupid. They're all on the fucking payroll.

The law isn't justice; it's a machine, a marketplace. Everything's for sale—pleas, motions, reputations—and freedom, and you're the one footing the fucking bill. The only leverage you've got is pressure. Apply it relentlessly. Make them earn the money by pushing, because if you stop pushing they start cruising. And once they start cruising, you're on your way to prison for sure. So don't play nice—play smart.

They designed this game to drain you, but if you learn the rules, you can flip the board. Because the only real defense in America isn't in the courtroom—it's **in knowing the hustle better than the hustlers.** You want control? Then you gotta **take it**. Ask questions that make them uncomfortable. Be the nightmare —the one they can't bullshit without sweating through their suit.

Larry Levine

EXHIBIT ONE

Federal Courthouse Conspiracy

Where Everyone's Dirty and Justice Is a Scam

Alright, I'm gonna skip the handshake crap. You know who I am – Larry Jay Levine. And if you don't, you will. You're about to get dragged through the circus we call "justice," step by filthy step. I'm not here to hold hands or whisper fairy tales about fairness. I'm here to show you the beast while it's chewing. You might

find this book loaded with metaphors, and guess what, it's intentional. Although you might find it entertaining, my goal's to make sure you didn't waste money buying it and fully get a grasp on how to deal with a system that has you by the balls.

Courthouse Or Whore House?

So let's jump in. While the structure is purported to be a "Courthouse", you could just as well say "Whore House", because inside lots of money changes hands, dirty deals are cut and people get screwed inside it every motherfucking day. In reality, much of the shit that goes down is all a scam, with a cast of characters starting with your lawyer as your pimp, but rest assured you'll soon meet everyone as they bend you over, demean you, and make you feel like a cheap teenage slut on prom night! That being said, let me tell you about the building.

First off, it ain't some symbol of freedom but a monument to every lie the system ever sold. It stands out like concrete tombstone squatting in the middle of the city, staring you down like it knows your secrets. You look up at it and feel smaller already. That's the point. It wasn't built for people like you. It was built to remind you who runs the show: lawyers carving the stone, prosecutors polishing it, judges blessing it like priests of punishment. You step inside and the air gets thick, like the building's holding its breath, waiting to ruin another life.

That's where we start. **The Courtroom Conspiracy.** The house always wins, and "innocent"? That's just the first joke of the day.

The Courthouse: A Monolith of Fear & Misery

Now I'm gonna dissect the bitch and tell you what it's all about. Have you ever *looked* at a building and know it hates you? Kind of like an old girlfriend who caught you with your pants down doing her sister. That's this one. It's a big gray block, sitting downtown like it lost a bet with God and decided to take it out on everyone else. Nothing about it says justice – it screams *paperwork and pain.*

See those windows? Yeah, those aren't windows. They're eyes – dead, soulless, judgmental eyes. They don't let light in, they just stare down like, *"We already read your charges, buddy. Don't waste our time."*

The whole thing feels alive, but not in a Disney way – more like it feeds on bail money and broken promises. You can almost hear it burping up indictments.

And up there? That metal bird they call an eagle? Please. That thing hasn't meant "freedom" since disco had a heartbeat. It's a vulture with better PR – wings out, waiting for another defendant to drop dead and flip the bird at, so it can start picking at what's left of their reputation.

The flags? Oh, they love to wave – all proud and patriotic, flapping in the wind like they're cheering on the hypocrisy. Red, white, and blue – the holy trinity of "good luck with that." Those poles stab the sky like they're filing an appeal with heaven, but trust me, heaven stopped taking courthouse calls a long time ago.

You don't *enter* this place. You *get swallowed* by it. It's not a temple of law – it's a vending machine for guilt. Drop in a plea, hit a button, and watch the sentence fall.

Entering the Beast: Cold Metal and Dead Faces

Ok, so now grow a pair of balls, quit fucking around and follow me inside. Keep your guard up, because you're about to learn that the courthouse greets you like an ex with a restraining order. The second those glass doors swing open–bam–ice-cold air smacks you in the face like the system itself. It's not air-conditioning; it's attitude. It's the building saying, *"Welcome to hell, please enjoy the chill of hopelessness."* That's your first clue this isn't a place built for people–it's a morgue with better lighting.

Take a look around. The first thing you'll notice are the paintings. Wall-to-wall fancy portraits of long-dead judges, every one of them looking like they were born constipated and stayed that way through their whole career. You can almost hear them whispering from their fancy gold frames: *"Guilty, guilty, guilty."* These guys spent decades ruining lives from a high chair with a view, signing away futures with the same emotion you'd order a sandwich. Their eyes follow you down the hallway, cold, smug, and half-daring you to beg.

Then you spot it–the big, shiny government seal on the wall. The one they pretend means freedom. Let's be honest: that eagle isn't soaring anywhere. It's hovering over your case file, waiting to pounce. Talons out, eyes wild, clutching arrows like it's ready to turn your plea deal into target practice. And right beneath it? The flag. Limp. Colorless. Hanging there like a participation trophy for tyranny.

And if the décor wasn't enough of a joke, look at the plaques. *Justice. Honor. Liberty.* Real cute. Words carved into marble by the same system that crushes you for sport. They might as well replace them with *Bullshit. Hypocrisy. Fees.* Because that's what this place actually runs on. You can feel it in the air – the hum of a machine that's been grinding up people for generations. Doesn't matter if you're guilty, innocent, or just bad at parking – everyone gets chewed up the same.

You're not walking through a courthouse, you're walking through the government's idea of recycling: people in, paperwork out. And by the time you realize it, the doors have already shut behind you.

The Security Theater: Stripped and Prodded

Did you really think you were gonna just stroll in, flash an ID, and go about your day? This ain't the post office. This is *the People's Palace of Fear and Compliance*, and you're about to be stripped, scanned, judged, and silently humiliated before you even hit the courtroom carpet. Because nothing screams "justice" like a federally sanctioned TSA cosplay with badges and inferiority complexes.

First is the line. It snakes through the lobby like a human centipede of panic, late child-support payments, and unpaid parking tickets. And standing in it? A mixed bag of public defenders, baby mamas, nervous defendants, and shell-shocked family members holding manila folders like prayer books. Everyone's got the same glazed-over look—like they're waiting to get tagged, processed, and shrink-wrapped by the State.

"Take Out Your Shit and Place It in the Tray"

Okay, now you've hit the front of the line, and here comes the ritual: shoes off, belt off, wallet, keys, coins, cell phone, vape pen, your last shred of self-respect—all dumped into a cracked-ass plastic bin like offerings to the Gods of Paranoia. And standing over you? A marshal who looks like he bench-presses spite and takes pride in making eye contact with your belt buckle. He doesn't talk. He grunts. You are meat. Move.

Step through the metal detector and *beep*–oh shit, rookie mistake. Maybe it was your underwire bra, maybe it was a titanium knee, maybe it was that sliver of hope you carried in your pocket that today might go okay. Doesn't matter. The alarm sings, the line halts, and suddenly every head turns like you just confessed to 9/11.

You get waved back and forth like a busted Roomba, arms out, palms up, until they're satisfied you're not smuggling a bazooka in your rectum. And God forbid you *look annoyed*. Because now you're a "problem." A "noncompliant subject." A potential threat to the integrity of the sacred marble halls. You're a side-eye away from getting pulled into the little room with the rubber gloves.

What Not to Bring: A Survival Guide for the Legally Screwed

Walking into a federal courthouse isn't a pit stop–it's a goddamn minefield. If you show up with the wrong shit in your pockets, you're not just getting delayed–you're getting *detained*. So here's your crash course in *not being a dumbass*.

Metal = Mistake. Knives? Samurai Swords, Nope. Bottle openers? Nah. That ninja-star keychain you thought was quirky? Congratulations, you're now a security threat. The metal detectors here are like angry exes–they remember *everything*, they overreact, and they'll absolutely ruin your day over a belt buckle shaped like a grenade.

Guns, Tasers, Pepper Spray? You Want a Bonus Charge? This ain't a Call of Duty lobby. Unless you're a badge-flashing Fed, leave your heat at home. Showing up strapped is like lighting a flare and screaming, "Arrest me, daddy!"

Drugs & Vices: You Ain't at Coachella. I don't care how "medicinal" your weed is or how "forgotten" that bump of coke in your jacket pocket was–if they find it, you're not going to court, *you're going to jail*. Vape pens? They'll sniff those out too. This ain't their first rodeo.

Leave the Liquid Courage. Zippos, flasks, nips, and matches–ditch them all. Booze at court isn't rebellious, it's fucking suicidal. You can get hammered after. If they let you out.

Phones, Laptops, and Other Electronic Paranoia Machines

Now, they might let you bring your phone, but be prepared to have it go through the X-ray machine like a suspected terrorist device. And whatever you do, *turn it off*. The last thing you need is your phone lighting up with a string of inappropriate texts while the judge is talking. You might as well have brought in a bullhorn screaming, "Look at me, I'm an idiot!"–that's how much attention you'll get.

As for laptops, tablets, and any other electronic paraphernalia–you better check with the courthouse rules because some of them will treat your MacBook like it's a damn landmine. Unless you're some hotshot attorney, you probably won't need it. They've got enough wires and microphones in those courtrooms already, and believe me, the walls have ears.

In short, treat the courthouse like you're walking into an international airport run by humorless federal agents who didn't get enough sleep. Strip it down to the bare essentials. Bring your ID, your paperwork, and maybe a bottle of aspirin because, trust me, after spending a day in the courthouse, you're going to need it. Anything else? Leave it in the car.

You're Already Guilty of Breathing Funny

You're finally clear. Next stop is you'll shuffle barefoot to the other end of the conveyor belt like a broke-ass refugee at a Greyhound station, trying to scoop your life back together while the next unlucky bastard steps into the humiliation zone. You grab your shoes, your belt, your phone, your last trace of pride–oh wait, scratch that. Dignity's still in Bin #3, curled up next to someone's burner phone and a Ziploc full of expired fucks.

And then it hits you: *you haven't even made it to court yet*. You haven't seen your lawyer, locked eyes with the judge, or heard the word "Your Honor" used without irony. And already, you've been stripped, scanned, and downgraded to *state-approved livestock*. That's the brilliance of the security circus. It ain't about bombs or safety. It's about showing you the pecking order. And guess what? You're not even on the damn chart. Now it's time to meet the family of characters who will shape your future

Who Works at the Federal Courthouse

If you're to fucking dense to figure it out yet pay attention, because these people are what this entire fucking book is about. The players in the game who have the power to set you free or conspire to ruin your miserable life! In subsequent expanded chapters you will learn about each one of these assholes who keep this carnival of misery running, so let's jump right in!!!!

This ain't a cast of angels. It's a factory floor full of bureaucrats, actors, and legal hitmen – all pretending they're making the world a better place. But what they're really doing is playing parts in a system that eats people alive and calls it "justice."

Exhibit 5 - The Probation Officer: You might not see them today, but they're watching. Lurking like a future hangover, ready to swoop in with rules, curfews, drug tests, and threats of revocation. Their job is to "monitor your reintegration into society," which is code for "make sure you screw up so we can lock you back up." Don't worry – you'll meet them soon enough.

Exhibit 6 - The Public Defender: Overworked, underpaid, and running on pure caffeine and quiet despair. This poor bastard is juggling 80 cases, a broken printer, and your shattered dreams. They probably care deep down – or they did 500 clients ago. Now? They're just trying to get you the "least worst" deal before the judge throws the book at your head. Your legal savior? Maybe. More likely just another cog in the plea bargain machine.

Exhibit 7 - The Paid Lawyer: Think of a used car salesman with a law degree and a moral compass that spins like a roulette wheel. This is the one you *chose* – which makes it worse. They show up in thousand-dollar suits with twenty-dollar ethics, shaking your hand like they're doing you a favor. They'll promise you miracles, bill you for hope, and vanish the second your check clears. Their sacred text? *The Invoice.* Their holy ritual? *The Retainer.* They speak fluent bullshit – words like "strategy," "leverage," and "relationship with the prosecutor" – all code for "I'm about to sell you out politely."

Exhibit 8 - The Prosecutor: The courtroom's golden boy (or girl), armed with smugness, a federal badge, and a deep belief that you're guilty because their report says so. This is the power-humping sociopath who takes your messy life and turns it into a "narrative" – polished, weaponized, and usually half true. They smile in court like they're curing cancer, but they're just trying to pad their conviction stats so they can run for judge in five years.

Exhibit 10 - The Judge: Think of God in a black robe – but pettier. This is the one who gets to decide whether you go home or get sent to the meat grinder. They sit up high like they're presiding over Mount Olympus, sipping coffee and pretending they're burdened by your case. They're not. You're background noise to their daily crossword puzzle. They pretend neutrality, but they've got a soft spot for prosecutors, a hard-on for "order," and zero patience for your side of the story. Their motto? "Guilty until my lunch break."

Exhibit 11 - The Clerk: Gatekeeper of paper. Their desk is the last stop before your case either moves forward or vanishes into administrative limbo. They've got all the power of a DMV employee on a power trip – and the same level of give-a-shit. File your motions wrong? Lost in the void. Speak too loud? Instant side-eye and passive-aggressive vengeance. Be polite, or your paperwork might "accidentally" end up in the shredder.

Exhibit 11- The Court Reporter: Human typewriter with dead eyes. Their job is to transcribe every lie, every fake apology, and every gavel slam into the record – as if it matters. They're not listening to your sob story. They're just trying not to fall asleep while you explain how it was all a misunderstanding. The real mystery? How they manage to keep a straight face through so much bullshit.

The Marshals: These are the courthouse bouncers with badges. Half law enforcement, half over-it security guards, all muscle. They move prisoners, babysit the court, and glare at everyone like they're waiting for a reason to throw you into a wall. They run the hallway like prison guards run the yard – with quiet menace and a clipboard full of names you don't want to be on.

Who Roams the Hallways: Faces of Fear and Regret

Now that you've survived the strip show at security, welcome to the real horror: *the people*. Not the judges, not the lawyers–*them*, the warm bodies clogging the hallways like extras in a courtroom snuff film. This is the human wreckage the system chews on. And it ain't pretty.

First, the defendants—you can spot them right away. Poor bastards who look like they just woke up from a coma, got slapped with a federal indictment, and teleported here with ten minutes to prepare. You'll spot them instantly standing outside the courtroom: suits two sizes too big, ties dangling like nooses, paperwork clutched in trembling hands like it's some kind of legal security blanket. Half of them look like they lost a bet, the other half look like they lost their soul. Either way, they're fucked, and everybody knows it—especially them.

Panic In A Polyester Suit—That's The Dress Code

Watch their eyes. That's where the real story's written. Wide, darting, shell-shocked stares that scream, "How the hell did I end up here?" Spoiler alert: they already know. They just don't know how deep the knife's going yet. Every step toward that courtroom is like walking the Green Mile—except there's no final meal, no curtain call, just the cold gavel drop of institutional indifference.

The Bleachers of Despair

Now pan over to the gallery—the wooden benches where hope goes to die. **That's where the family members sit,** twisted into awkward poses of prayer, rage, and complete psychological detachment. Mothers, wives, girlfriends, uncles—none of them ready for what's coming. Some are crying. Some are staring at the wall like they've just been told Earth is canceling tomorrow. All of them are bargaining with a god who doesn't return calls from this ZIP code.

You'll see tissues clutched like crucifixes, trembling hands rubbing away invisible sins, and blank stares so vacant you could lease them as commercial real estate. Nobody talks. Nobody moves. Just this thick, slow suffocation hanging in the air. These people came hoping for justice—maybe even mercy. But the courthouse has other plans. It's not here to save them.

Of course, there are the lawyers, too—those high-priced shysters who strut around the place like they own it. They're wearing expensive suits, their briefcases swinging like weapons of mass destruction. They glide through the courthouse with an air of confidence, talking in low, measured tones to their clients, reassuring them that everything's going to be fine. But you can see right through it.

This is just another day for them—another case, another paycheck, another life ruined. They'll do their job, collect their fee, and be back at it tomorrow. To them, it's a business. To you? It's life or death.

The Smells: Stale Air and Cold Sweat

You walk a little further into this den of despair, and the smells hit you like a freight train. It's a strange mix of stale air-conditioning, industrial cleaner, and cold sweat. The kind of smell that sticks in your throat and won't go away. The air is thick with it, heavy, almost metallic, like it's been recycled so many times that it's more machine than air. It clings to you, seeps into your skin, into your clothes, and you can't shake the feeling that this building is alive—alive with the fear and desperation of everyone who's ever stepped inside.

There's the faint scent of cheap cologne, the kind you spray on in a futile attempt to mask the stink of fear. Defendants wear it like armor, hoping it'll make them feel a little more human as they march toward their doom. But it doesn't work. Underneath it all, you can still smell the raw panic, the sweat of people who know their lives are about to be torn apart. It's a sterile smell, like a hospital, but with a dark, desperate undercurrent that makes you feel like you're standing on the edge of a cliff, waiting to fall.

The Hallways: A Mausoleum of Bureaucracy

The hallways stretch out before you like a sick joke. They're painted that awful shade of beige—the kind of color that makes you feel like you're already losing. It's the color of defeat, of resignation, of knowing that no matter how hard you try, the system is going to grind your ass down. These hallways aren't designed for comfort. They're designed to remind you that you're fucked and insignificant.

Every few feet, you're greeted by more flags. American flags, state flags, courthouse flags—they're everywhere, draped limply like symbols of a failed promise. The government seals are stamped on every door, every wall, every surface, reminding you that you're walking through the belly of the beast. The eagle stares down at you from every angle, its talons ready to strike, its eyes gleaming with a cold, cruel light.

The fluorescent lights overhead cast a sickly glow on everything, making the place feel even more lifeless than it already is. The floors are polished to a mirror-like sheen, reflecting the dead-eyed stares of everyone around you. It's a mausoleum, a tomb for the living, where souls come to be judged and sentenced to whatever fate the government has in store for them.

The Courthouse Conspiracy and the Myths That Keep It Alive

Every courthouse runs on myths. The myth of order, the myth of fairness, the myth that marble can make men honest. They call it justice, but it's theater–an old ritual that survives because no one questions the script. The real power hides behind the paperwork, watching the myths do their work. You don't need to understand the conspiracy to feel it; you just walk in, and the walls start lying for them.

1. The Courthouse Is Intimidating, But It's Just a Building

The Myth: Oh, don't worry about the federal courthouse. It's just a fancy building–no need to feel intimidated. It's all marble floors, shiny elevators, and a nice view of justice being done. Nothing scary here.

Reality Check: Yeah, just a building–one where they're deciding whether you get to go home or spend the next few years in a concrete cell. The courthouse isn't just intimidating; it's designed to make you feel small, powerless, and utterly screwed the minute you walk through those doors. Fancy as hell, sure, but it's basically where dreams go to die.

2. The Judge Is Impartial–You've Got a Fair Chance

The Myth: Don't worry; the judge is completely unbiased. They'll listen to both sides and weigh the evidence fairly. It's a level playing field in that courtroom.

Reality Check: Fair? Yeah, right. That judge has seen a thousand cases just like yours and already has a pretty good idea of how this is going to play out. Fair and impartial goes out the window when they're fed up with hearing the same excuses day in and day out. You're about as "even" as a one-legged man in a butt-kicking contest.

3. It's Just Another Day in Court

The Myth: Oh, it's no big deal. It's just another day at the courthouse, nothing to get worked up about. This is routine for them, so you should totally relax.

Reality Check: Routine? For the lawyers and judges, maybe. But for you, it's the most anxiety-ridden day of your life. It's not just "another day" for you–it's the day you find out if your life gets thrown into chaos. So, yeah, maybe don't "relax" just yet.

4. Federal Prosecutors Play By The Rules

The Myth: Prosecutors are professionals; they always follow the law. They're just here to see justice done, so don't expect any dirty tricks or underhanded tactics in the courthouse.

Reality Check: Ha! Federal prosecutors are pros, all right–professionals at getting a conviction by any means necessary. Sure, they play by the rules–*their* rules. If you think you're walking into an ethical debate, think again. It's more like a well-organized ambush.

5. You'll Be In And Out In No Time

The Myth: Don't worry, your hearing will be quick. It's just a small matter, so you'll be in and out of the courthouse in no time. Easy-peasy.

Reality Check: Quick? In and out? The federal courthouse runs on government time, which means a "quick" hearing can last hours, and "in and out" can stretch into half a day. There's nothing fast about the federal system except for how quickly your patience runs out.

6. The Jury Will Understand Everything

The Myth: Oh, don't worry about the jury. They'll follow along with all the legal jargon and complex arguments just fine. They're smart, and totally get your side of the story.

Reality Check: Sure, the jury will totally understand everything–like how bored and confused they are after hearing three days of mind-numbing legalese. You're banking on a group of random idiots to grasp the intricacies of your case, when half of them are just thinking about what's for lunch. Good luck with that.

7. If You Dress Nicely, The Judge Will Be Impressed

The Myth: Just make sure you wear a suit and tie, and the judge will be impressed. Looking sharp goes a long way in the federal courthouse. It's all about appearances.

Reality Check: Oh sure, because the judge is totally going to throw out your case because you're rocking a killer tie. Dressing well is the bare minimum. The only thing that really impresses the judge is airtight legal arguments–not how much starch is in your collar.

8. It Won't Feel Like a Movie Courtroom Drama

The Myth: Federal courtrooms aren't like what you see in the movies. It's all calm, collected, and professional. There's no drama here–just boring legal proceedings.

Reality Check: It's every bit as dramatic as the movies, except you're not a spectator—you're the one on trial. The tension in the air is real, and every word spoken could determine your future. And unlike the movies, there's no dramatic last-minute evidence swooping in to save your ass.

9. The Security Is Just a Formality

The Myth: Oh, the security at the courthouse is nothing to worry about. It's just metal detectors and a quick bag check—pure formality. It's not like you're entering a fortress.

Reality Check: You'll feel like you're walking into a maximum-security prison. Those guards aren't smiling, and the metal detectors beep if you even think about metal. It's less "quick bag check" and more "Welcome to Fort Knox."

10. You Can Always Appeal If It Doesn't Go Your Way

The Myth: Don't stress too much. If things don't go your way, there's always the option to appeal. You'll have another shot if this trial doesn't work out.

Reality Check: Appeals are about as easy to win as the lottery. Sure, you can appeal, but the odds of getting a second chance are slimmer than you think. An appeal is a long, expensive process that rarely works out in your favor—so don't bank on that "do-over" too much.

Exhibit One: The Bottom Line

> *So here it is—the ugly truth, stripped of marble, flags, and fake smiles. The courthouse isn't a monument to justice; it's a factory for misery. Every hallway, every courtroom, every judge's smirk exists to feed the same machine that's been grinding people down for generations. You walk in thinking you'll get fairness, but what you're really getting is processed—run through a bureaucratic blender that doesn't care if you're guilty, innocent, or just breathing wrong.*

Justice isn't blind here; it's deaf, dumb, and on a government salary. The courthouse doesn't serve the people–it consumes them. The lawyers? They're sales reps for the despair industry, hawking false hope by the billable hour. The judge and prosecutor aren't enemies–they're actors in the same tired play, and you're the unpaid extra.

The real verdict was written before you even walked through the metal detectors. By the time you hit security, the game was over–you just didn't know it yet.

Next Up – Exhibit Two: Grand Juries

If the courthouse is the slaughterhouse, this is where they pick which pigs get sent to the line. Welcome to the secret room where your fate's decided before you even know you're on the menu.

U.S. KANGAROO COURT
THE COURTROOM CONSPIRACY
OFFICIALLY SCREWED

EXHIBIT TWO

Grand Jury Conspiracy

"Twelve Good Men and a Bullshit Story"

Let's kill the bedtime story right now: the grand jury didn't come from some noble dream about protecting the innocent. It came from **one lazy, paranoid bastard in a crown – King Henry II** – who wanted control without the hassle. In **1166**, this royal prick didn't have the time or the balls to investigate crime properly. His kingdom was a mess: thieves, rebels, political headaches, and pissed-off peasants everywhere.

Where Justice Goes to Die and Bureaucrats Play God

Rather than get his hands dirty, Henry decided to **outsource the blame**. His genius idea? **Create a snitch squad.** Wrap it in fake legitimacy. Call it justice. Hand the pitchforks to the people, whisper names in their ears, and step back while they did the dirty work. It was royal efficiency: blame by proxy. No trial. No defense. Just **accusation equals execution**, and the king gets to keep his robe clean. This wasn't about justice. It was about **clearing the streets and covering the throne's ass**. Grand juries were born to move bodies fast, not sort out facts. If your name came up, that was it. You weren't going to court–you were going to the chopping block.

Knights, Landowners, and Snitches

Who made up the first grand juries? **Not your peers. Not your neighbors. Not a jury of fairness.** Henry recruited **landowners, knights, lords, and lackeys**–guys who had everything to gain by pointing fingers and nothing to lose if they were wrong. Think of it like a medieval version of "fuck around and find out," only the ones doing the fucking around were **your local rich assholes**, and you were the one finding out–with a noose.

These weren't impartial observers. These were power players in the local drama. They owed favors, held grudges, and knew damn well that **accusing you got them in good with the crown**. You banged someone's wife? Took too much grain? Laughed at the wrong joke? Boom–you're a "threat to the realm."

And don't get it twisted: **they weren't looking for evidence.** They were **delivering suspects.** Henry didn't ask them to prove shit. Just bring him names. Guilty? Innocent? Who cares? If your name got whispered in that room, your ass was headed for a dungeon or a beheading.

This wasn't some early form of democracy. It was **mob rule with a royal seal**. And the mob was led by the same men who already owned the land, the titles, and the power. You didn't stand a chance–and you weren't meant to.

Why the Crown Needed a Middleman for Injustice

Here's the real reason the grand jury was born: **plausible deniability**. Henry wanted people dead or jailed–but he didn't want the backlash of being the executioner. So he rigged a system that **outsourced the bloodshed**. Blame the process, not the monarch. Brilliant in its evil simplicity.

By creating the illusion that "the people" were making decisions, he could **distance himself from the outcome**. "Oh, you were falsely accused? Tough luck, the jury said so." Meanwhile, the whole system was built on whispered rumors, half-truths, and political games.

It was never about finding the truth. It was about **controlling the chaos**—and **silencing anyone who threatened the status quo**. And that hasn't changed. The same structure, the same psychology, the same goal: **get the accused to shut the fuck up, disappear, and let the machine keep rolling.** The grand jury was the **perfect weapon** for the ruling class. Disguised as justice. Wrapped in ceremony. And always aimed at the throat of the powerless. Next time your lawyer tells you the grand jury is a "constitutional safeguard," tell him to choke on a history book.

How We Took the Crown's Scam & Pretended It Was Freedom

So here's where the bullshit gets patriotic. The colonists fled England swearing they'd never bow to another king. "No more tyranny!" they screamed. "No more crowns, no more axes!" Yeah, real rebels— until you check their luggage. Because tucked between their Bibles and muskets was the same goddamn legal system Henry II cooked up centuries earlier. They didn't ditch the grand jury; they imported it like fine china.

England's favorite tool for control, polished up and wrapped in parchment. They just slapped a "freedom" label on it and called it justice. What a joke. The grand jury was never a shield for the people —it was a leash for the mob. It kept order, just like Henry wanted, only now the guys holding the whip wore powdered wigs instead of crowns.

The colonists loved pretending the people had a say, so they kept the structure and renamed the scam. "Community oversight," they called it, as they used it to crush dissent exactly like their royal predecessors. Different uniforms, same oppression. Instead of branding you a traitor to the king, they branded you a traitor to the colonies.

They traded swords for quills, tyranny for "procedure," and called it progress. The end result was identical—whoever had the power got to weaponize the law. The poor, the loud, the inconvenient—they all got lined up and steamrolled under the banner of "justice." Checks and balances? Please. Checked by the same rich bastards, balanced squarely on your neck.

From Chains to "Checks and Balances"

The grand jury in the colonies wasn't about fairness; it was about obedience. It was a way for the new boss class—merchants, judges, plantation owners—to act like they were benevolent while they gutted anyone who threatened their grip. They hid behind process, pointed to paperwork, and smiled while the gallows creaked. "Justice by peers," they said, except your peers were never the ones with power. You got a handful of terrified locals nodding along with whatever the prosecutor fed them, because nobody wanted to be the one who said no and wound up on the other side of the table. That's "democracy" for you—fear distributed equally.

Then the Founding Fathers swaggered in with their feather pens and started writing love letters to liberty. The crowd swooned while these powdered hypocrites—slave-owning lawyers and paranoid land barons—sold the biggest rebrand in history. They didn't kill the old English systems; they just gave them a paint job. "Due process." "Consent of the governed." "Fair trial." Buzzwords for the masses. None of it meant a damn thing while the grand jury stayed right where it was—rigged, sealed, and serving the same ruling class. They didn't fix it. They just made the cage look patriotic.

The Founders Didn't Fix It – They Just Made It Sound Nice

Fast-forward a century and these same men are scribbling the Constitution like it's the Bible of freedom. Every line drips with virtue and irony. And buried right there in the fine print is the infection that never got cured—the grand jury clause. They could've ripped it out. They didn't. Because they *needed* it. They knew the power of secret control wrapped in public approval. You don't kill a beast that works—you feed it. So instead of burying the grand jury, they dressed it up in red, white, and blue and called it a safeguard. Execution committee turned "citizen shield." Same sword, just polished.

The Founders weren't idiots—they were brilliant manipulators. They understood that if you can't trust the people, you give them a process that *feels* like power but actually takes it away. That's the American grand jury: democracy on the outside, dictatorship under the hood. The same crowd that screamed "no taxation without representation" handed you "indictment without defense." Hell of a deal, huh?

The Fifth Amendment Scam

Then came the masterstroke–the Fifth Amendment. "No person shall be held to answer for a capital crime unless on indictment by a grand jury." Sounds noble as hell, doesn't it? Sounds like protection. But that line right there–that's the poison pill. They sold it as a safeguard against government abuse, but the government's the one running the goddamn show.

The prosecutor picks the witnesses, picks the evidence, spins the story, and you don't even get a chair in the room. Your "peers" never hear your side. They just nod along to whatever version of you the state wants them to believe. It's a one-man puppet show starring the guy trying to bury you.

And the Founders knew it. They weren't blind, they were strategic. The Fifth Amendment wasn't about justice–it was about optics. It let them pretend they'd built something fair while secretly preserving their control system from England. It's the oldest hustle in politics: keep the people calm with the illusion of safety while you sharpen the blade behind the curtain.

And it worked. Two and a half centuries later, that same relic still gets waved like a patriotic badge while prosecutors use it as a **pretrial slaughterhouse**. The innocent aren't protected–they're processed. The guilty aren't punished–they're convenient examples. The Fifth Amendment wasn't written to keep you safe. It was written to keep you *quiet*.

The Aftermath Chaos

So here we are, still worshipping a broken relic from a time when powdered wigs were fashion and oppression was policy. America didn't overthrow the Crown; it just learned to impersonate it. The grand jury was never a firewall against tyranny–it *was* the tyranny, wearing a powdered grin and quoting scripture. The Founders didn't save us from the king. They *became* him. And they did it so damn well that we still thank them for it.

The Modern Prosecutor's Playground

So here we are, centuries later, and the grand jury's still kicking like a drunk old man who won't leave the bar. The powdered wigs are gone, but the bullshit stayed. What used to be the king's tool for silencing rebels is now the prosecutor's favorite toy. The robes got darker, the vocabulary got fancier, and the scam got smoother. This isn't justice anymore–it's **performance art with paperwork.** The grand jury room is where prosecutors get to act like gods, controlling who lives, who gets ruined, and who gets offered up as the daily sacrifice to the system. You walk in accused, and they already know how the movie ends. Spoiler alert: you're the villain.

The Secret Courtroom with No Referee

You ever wonder what a courtroom would look like if they took out the judge, the defense, and the truth? That's the grand jury room. It's the government's private sandbox, a locked chamber where prosecutors can say whatever the hell they want without anyone calling bullshit. No objections. No cross-exams. No "wait, that's not what really happened." Just a one-man show performed for twelve confused civilians who probably thought they were showing up for jury duty on a traffic ticket.

Inside that sterile little box, the prosecutor runs the table. They handpick the evidence, cherry-pick the witnesses, and frame every sentence to make you look like the second coming of Satan. They control the script, the stage, and the lighting. You? You're not even in the room. Hell, you don't even get a lawyer in there to whisper, "This is bullshit." It's the legal equivalent of shadowboxing against a guy who tied your hands behind your back and called it a fair fight.

And the best part? Everything that happens in there is sealed tighter than a mob informant's coffin. Nobody ever gets to see the transcripts unless the court suddenly grows a conscience–which never happens. It's justice in the dark, with the prosecutor holding the flashlight and deciding who gets illuminated and who disappears.

The Myth of Impartial Review

They tell the public the grand jury is this noble buffer between citizens and government power. Yeah, and fast food is health food if you put enough lettuce on it. The truth is the grand jury isn't a shield–it's a shield *for the prosecutor*, not the people. It gives them cover. "Hey, don't look at me," they say, "the citizens agreed." Sure, they agreed after you fed them one side of the story like a bunch of toddlers eating from a spoon. That's not deliberation–that's indoctrination.

The jurors themselves? They mean well, but they don't know shit. Most of them couldn't tell a subpoena from a sandwich. They walk in thinking they're part of something sacred, then get buried under legalese until they're too embarrassed to ask questions. They nod because everyone else nods. They agree because it's easier than looking stupid. And the prosecutor—oh, that slick bastard—makes sure they feel like heroes for indicting somebody. "You're upholding justice," he tells them, right before he hands them the indictment he wrote himself.

By the time it's over, everyone walks out smiling. The prosecutor gets his scalp, the jurors feel righteous, and the defendant gets a one-way ticket to federal court. Nobody checks the evidence. Nobody questions the process. It's not impartial—it's industrial. Crank out the indictments, keep the machine fed, move on to the next poor bastard.

The Ham Sandwich Massacre

There's a saying that's been around forever: "A grand jury would indict a ham sandwich." That's not a joke—it's a confession. You could walk in there with a pile of cold cuts and a prosecutor could convince those jurors that the mustard conspired with the mayonnaise. That's how easy it is. Because when there's no defense, no scrutiny, and no accountability, you can make *anyone* look guilty.

And prosecutors love that power. They treat indictments like trophies. Each one goes up on their mental wall—another notch for the résumé. Doesn't matter if the case collapses later. By then, they've already cashed the political credit and moved on to their next victim. The system rewards them not for being right, but for **getting the indictment.** Accuracy doesn't matter. Optics do.

Meanwhile, the defendant's life burns down. They lose their job, their reputation, their freedom—sometimes all three—over an accusation built on half-truths and hearsay. But hey, the prosecutor gets to stand at a podium and say "Justice was served." Served cold, rotten, and wrapped in a flag.

The grand jury isn't a filter for truth. It's a **factory for guilt.** It mass-produces indictments the way fast food joints crank out fries—cheap, fast, and designed for public consumption. You don't have to be guilty to end up in its grinder; you just have to be convenient.

The Aftermath

And that's the ugly reality: the modern grand jury isn't about fairness—it's about efficiency. It keeps the machine humming. It lets prosecutors play God while pretending to be civil servants. It's the safest room in America for lies to become law. You'll never see it, never challenge it, and never stop it. Because it doesn't need to be fair—it only needs to look official.

So yeah, congratulations, America. You took the king's secret tribunal, upgraded the lighting, added some flags, and called it progress. The grand jury's not broken. It's working *exactly* as designed.

Who the Fuck Are These People?

They file in, clutching their jury summons like a golden ticket, expecting to serve truth and patriotism. What they actually get is a script they don't understand, a coffee that tastes like rust, and a prosecutor feeding them the story line. They're not your peers—they're the audience in a bad courtroom sitcom. Most have never even been inside a courthouse before. They'll treat this like a field trip until the prosecutor starts tossing around legal jargon, and then the fear sets in. They'll cling to every word coming from the man in the suit, because he sounds confident—and in rooms like that, confidence *is* truth.

TV Law Experts with Real Power

You ever wonder who's sitting behind that locked door deciding if your life gets flushed down the toilet? You think it's some elite panel of educated citizens cross-examining evidence like a Supreme Court highlight reel? Hell no. It's your damn neighbor who once served on a PTA committee and thinks that makes them a public servant. It's the retired guy who spends his mornings screaming at the news. It's the woman who's convinced that watching a few seasons of *Law & Order* makes her a part-time legal analyst. These people aren't justice-minded; they're drama-minded. They're chasing that "important civic duty" buzz like it's their one shot at meaning.

And here's the kicker: these folks think they're doing God's work. They're sitting in judgment over lives they don't know, signing papers that might as well be death warrants, and they feel patriotic doing it. They'll go home and tell their families they "helped put away the bad guys." They won't mention they never met those bad guys, never saw a defense, never questioned a thing. But hey, they got free coffee and a story to tell at Thanksgiving.

Confused, Overwhelmed, and Easily Led

The grand jury room is the perfect trap for the well-intentioned idiot. The prosecutor walks in with the calm authority of a surgeon and starts slicing reality apart with words half the jurors can't even spell. "Probable cause," "superseding indictment," "predicate acts"—it's a foreign language to them. They nod because nodding hides ignorance. They take notes that'll never make sense later. Half the time, they don't even know what crime's being discussed. They just hear, "This guy did bad things," and think, "Well, someone's gotta pay."

The prosecutor knows the psychology cold. Keep the jargon thick enough to sound impressive, sprinkle in a few emotional beats, and watch the jurors melt into compliance. He plays them like a preacher plays a Sunday crowd: loud enough to sound righteous, vague enough to sound deep. They'll believe every damn word because they're scared to admit they don't understand. The minute confusion hits, authority wins. It's not about logic—it's about tone. The prosecutor controls the rhythm, the pace, the mood. Every sigh, every pause, every smirk is designed to herd them toward one conclusion: indict.

And let's not forget—these jurors aren't trained investigators. They're civilians pulled from their jobs, their routines, their small lives, and dropped into a legal meat grinder. They don't have the bandwidth to fight the narrative. They want to go home. They want to feel smart. They want to feel safe. And the easiest way to feel all three is to agree. Indict the guy. Nod. Move on. Justice served in under an hour.

Herd Mentality Behind Closed Doors

Once the prosecutor leaves and that door shuts, the real rot sets in. Individual thought dies faster than truth. You've got twelve strangers in a box, sweating under fluorescent lights, all desperate not to be the "difficult one." So they pick a leader—the loudest, most self-righteous person in the room—and follow them like ducks in a parking lot. One says, "Seems guilty to me," and the others nod just to avoid looking like idiots. It's not justice–it's peer pressure with paperwork.

There's always one person who hesitates, someone who feels the weight of what they're about to do. But hesitation gets eaten alive in that room. The group moves like a tide–one push of collective certainty, one flash of authority, and doubt drowns quietly. The foreperson wants to be efficient. The others want to be liked. Nobody wants to slow things down or look soft. So they sign. They stamp. They destroy lives before lunch break.

And the worst part? They walk out feeling noble. They think they served democracy, that they protected society. They don't realize they were just tools–cheap, replaceable, well-meaning tools in a machine built to indict anything that breathes. No one leaves that room questioning the process. They leave believing they did their part. It's delusion disguised as duty.

The Aftermath

So who are these people? They're not evil masterminds. They're civilians fed a script and told they're heroes. They go home thinking they upheld justice when all they really did was check a box and keep the gears turning. The prosecutor doesn't need villains–he just needs volunteers. Average people with average morals and just enough ignorance to mistake obedience for righteousness.

That's the grand jury's secret weapon–it doesn't run on corruption; it runs on conformity. It takes ordinary citizens, strips away their doubt, fills them with borrowed authority, and sends them out thinking they saved the world. But peel back the pride and what you'll see is twelve confused souls who never realized they were the executioners.

Sterile Room, Bloody Purpose

You ever step into a place that smells like bureaucracy and fear had a baby? That's the grand jury room. It's clean but not *comfortable.* Sterile but still somehow filthy. The kind of room where the air's too thin and the silence has weight. You can feel it pressing down on you–the hum of the fluorescent lights, the clink of bad coffee cups, the shuffle of nervous shoes. This isn't a courtroom. It's a morgue for innocence. Nobody's dying in here physically, but careers, reputations, and futures are bleeding out quietly while the system pretends it's just "procedure."

The table's long, the walls are bare, and the vibe's all wrong. It's not justice—it's anticipation. The prosecutor stands at the head of the table like a preacher at a funeral, rehearsing your eulogy before you even know you're dead. There's no judge to balance the scales, no defense to throw a punch, no witnesses on your side. It's one man with a microphone and a story, and everyone else playing their assigned part. The grand jurors don't even know they're extras in a setup scene. The prosecutor's already written the script, and spoiler alert: you're the villain, the monster, the reason America needs another conviction to feel safe.

Everything in that room is psychological. The lighting, the posture, the tone—it's all theater. The prosecutor controls the temperature, the rhythm, the speed. He talks low when he wants sympathy, fast when he wants fear. He pauses like he's giving them time to "reflect," when really, he's just letting the guilt sink in. The jurors don't know it, but they're not being informed—they're being directed. This is not a hearing. It's conditioning. It's persuasion in a government-issued suit.

No Lawyer, No Defense, No Mercy = Screwed

Here's the fun part—you're not even allowed in the damn room. The grand jury gets to decide whether you should stand trial, but you? You don't get to stand anywhere. The prosecutor is the only voice that gets to speak. He gets to shape your story, twist your words, and throw you under a metaphorical bus while you sit outside hoping your lawyer's doing something useful. Spoiler: they're not. Because they can't. Defense attorneys aren't invited to this party.

The entire process is built on silence—yours. They don't want your rebuttal, your context, or your version of what happened. The prosecutor tells his story, fills in the blanks with dramatic pauses, and paints you as a walking headline. "Danger to the community." "Flight risk." "Pattern of deception." He builds an entire character around you, one that fits the narrative he's selling. And the jurors? They eat it up. They've got no reason not to believe him. He's the only one in the room who sounds like he's sure.

You could have proof you were on another planet when the crime went down, and it wouldn't matter. The prosecutor decides what gets shown, what gets said, and what gets buried. You're a ghost in your own trial. A rumor with a pulse. They'll discuss your future like you're a math problem—just numbers on a chart, percentages on a board. And by the time you find out what they decided, it's already too late. Your name's on an indictment, your face is on a screen, and your freedom's in a file folder labeled *DONE*.

Prosecutorial Theater Behind a Locked Door

Let's not pretend this is about justice. The grand jury room is a goddamn stage. Every inch of it is designed for performance. The prosecutor doesn't present evidence—he delivers a monologue. He doesn't build a case—he tells a story. And he's not talking to equals; he's working a crowd. He's got body language down to an art form. The way he leans on the table when he wants to look sincere. The way he points subtly toward your photo when he wants to plant disgust. The way he raises his voice just enough to make them feel like they're part of something righteous.

Behind that locked door, justice isn't blind—it's scripted. Every "presentation" is an act. Every "exhibit" is a prop. The jurors think they're participating, but they're just reacting to cues. The prosecutor reads them the right lines, waits for the gasps or nods, and keeps them hooked like an audience at a cheap magic show. By the time it's over, they're convinced they made a moral choice, when really, they just followed a plot written to make them feel heroic.

There's no oversight, no accountability, and no fucking referee. Just a man in a suit holding court over a dozen people too polite to interrupt. The door locks for "confidentiality," but really, it's to make sure no one ever sees how flimsy the performance is. The entire thing's a power trip—a secret ritual where the government pats itself on the back for another life wrecked "by the book." And the punchline? Everyone inside thinks they're doing the right thing.

The Aftermath

That's the setup. A quiet, controlled slaughterhouse with paperwork and coffee stains. They call it procedure; I call it premeditated guilt. You'll never see it. You'll never hear it. You'll just feel it when your life starts collapsing. The prosecutor will walk out calm and proud, another "victory" for justice, while you're still outside wondering when the fair part begins. Spoiler–it doesn't. The grand jury room isn't about fairness. It's about finishing the job before the fight even starts

Dodging The Hellfire and Flipping the Script

Legal warfare. Ten real ways to weaponize the grand jury's flaws. Not quaint hypotheticals – dirty, brutal moves you use when the state wants to turn rumor into a warrant. Unpolished. Mean. Practical.

When Secrecy Becomes Your Leverage

The whole grand-jury thing runs on one power: secrecy. They lock the door, hush the room, and call that "integrity." Bullshit. That secrecy is a rotten plank you can pry up and beat them with. The prosecutor thinks hiding stuff protects him. It doesn't – it exposes him. Your job (and your lawyer's job) is to make that secret stink in public.

Start by demanding what they don't want you to see. File every motion available to force disclosure: witness statements, exhibits, agent notes, transcripts – everything they slipped into the room while you weren't allowed in. If the prosecutor refuses, scream about prosecutorial misconduct. Not politely. Loud enough to make the judge squirm. You don't need to prove malice; you need to prove the omission matters. Withhold exculpatory evidence? That's a brick you toss through the prosecutor's window.

Use the absence of evidence like a weapon. The grand jury heard one script – theirs. So show the court the parts of the story that never got read. Who didn't testify? What files didn't appear? If they're building their house of cards with missing pieces, you don't have to topple it – you just have to expose the gaps and let gravity do the rest.

Loopholes, Landmines, and Legal Ambush

They fish wildly; you set traps. Grand juries are sloppy and greedy – they'll indict on anything that tugs. That sloppiness leaves prints. A good lawyer punches those prints into the courtroom record until the indictment looks like a joke.

Attack vagueness like it's a felony. Indictments that read like a bad checklist are vulnerable. Make them spell it out. Demand a bill of particulars. If their charges are fuzzy, file motions to dismiss for lack of specificity. Judges hate looking at vague garbage when a defense lawyer makes them stare at it.

Hearsay is their secret sauce. Grand juries eat it for breakfast. So subpoena the raw stuff: original statements, recordings, logs, the underlying documents. If the prosecution's pyramid rests on someone else's memory, pull the base out. If a witness can't produce the original notes or changes their story when confronted with the raw record, you've got a smoking hole to drive a truck through.

Forensics? Don't let the lab man wave a report and walk. Demand lab notebooks, chain-of-custody, analyst's emails, instrument printouts – the whole boring mess. If the chain's frayed or the analyst can't explain steps, you turn their "science" into theater. That kills credibility faster than any closing argument.

Don't forget procedure. Warrantless searches, agents testifying outside their scope, evidence presented without authentication – those are bureaucratic landmines. Step on one at the right time and watch the prosecutor scream.

Turning The Asshole's Swords Against Them

Make the grand jury indict itself. Turn every overreach into a liability they must defend.

Overcharging is their play. They throw in everything and hope something sticks. Use it against them. File motions about multiplicity, prejudice, and dismiss counts that are clearly padding. Force them to justify each charge before a judge. Put them on the record: why is this count here? If they can't answer without hand-waving, you win the argument and they lose momentum.

Pressure the timeline. Their tactic is "indict now, figure it out later." So deny them the luxury. Demand discovery, file early motions, push for speedy hearings. If they're scrambling, they make mistakes. Those mistakes can be exploited – missing witnesses, forgotten reports, sloppy affidavits. Speed eats sloppy prosecutors alive.

Dig into the jurors. Yes, grand jurors are secret, but you can pry. Look for conflicts, vendettas, prior statements, social media crap. If one juror had a beef with your client, or was bought by a local cop's story, bang that drum. One revealed conflict can topple the whole indictment like a cheap prop.

Make them bleed in public. If a prosecutor's methods are gross – withholding, coercion, misdirection – you leak the right details, file for partial unsealing, and let the press do the rest. Judges hate being embarrassed. Public pressure turns stubborn prosecutors into deal-makers. Use shame as leverage. It works.

Ten Dirty, Practical Moves – Street-Legal and Effective

1. **Demand disclosure loud and early.** Motion to disclose grand jury exhibits and witness statements. Don't whisper–file and litigate. Force them to show their hand.

2. **Brady/Rosario sweeps.** Insist on every bit of exculpatory material and impeachment evidence. If it's hidden, move for dismissal or a remedy that guts their case.

3. **Bill of particulars.** Make them identify the exact conduct they allege. Vague charges are your bread and butter. Tighten or toss.

4. **Chain-of-custody and lab dive.** Subpoena lab notebooks, raw data, analyst notes. If they can't explain the process, their "evidence" is theater.

5. **Attack hearsay foundations.** Demand original statements and recordings. If the building blocks are hearsay-piled-on-hearsay, show the judge the house of cards.

6. **File motions to unseal selectively.** Don't ask for everything–ask for the parts that expose omission or misconduct. Judges will begrudgingly open when the pages stink.

7. **Juror vetting and bias strikes.** Investigate jurors. Social media, local ties, prior convictions, vendettas–anything to raise a red flag and demand inquiry. One exposed bias can kill the indictment.

8. **Motion to dismiss for prosecutorial overreach.** Show the court the political theater: overcharging, selective prosecution, piling on for optics. Judges hate being used as props.

9. **Push timing and deadlines.** Faster is better for you. Force the state to hurry; hurried prosecutors screw up. Demand early hearings and short discovery windows.

10. **Strategic leaks & public pressure.** If the prosecutor's posture relies on secrecy and optics, make the case public in controlled ways. Judges respond to embarrassment; prosecutors make deals under heat.

This list isn't theoretical. It's the blueprint for getting a sloppy indictment turned into an administrative headache for the state. It's how you convert secrecy into exposure, how you take a thing built to intimidate and make it stumble.

The grand jury is a crude instrument – fast, secretive, and loud. But it's not bulletproof. It survives on assumptions and sunk costs. If you force the state to account for what it did, to publish what it hid, to explain what it skipped, you take their weapon and make it a liability.

If your lawyer gets cute and polite, you die in paperwork. If your lawyer fights, files, and embarrasses, you stand a chance. This is not about being noble; it's about being vicious in court, by the book, and without mercy. Dodge the hellfire by making the fire burn the people who lit it.

Fairy Tales That Can Get You Indicted

Lawyers love to lie – not because they're evil geniuses, but because they're lazy, scared, and desperate to sound in control. You walk into their office shaking, broke, and hoping for hope. They give you bedtime stories. "Don't worry, this is all routine." "The grand jury is just a formality." "You're not the target." Sure, and that burning smell in your kitchen is just "aromatic feedback." These people will tell you *anything* to keep you calm long enough to sign the retainer check.

Every word out of their mouth is designed to keep you paying, not to keep you free. They'll call the grand jury "a safeguard." They'll call your silence "strategy." They'll call your panic "overreacting." What they won't call it is what it really is – a slaughter. They know once that prosecutor walks into the grand jury room, you're done. They can't stop it. They can't even see it. But they'll sure as hell pretend they've got a plan. It's theater for desperate defendants.

Here's the thing: lawyers need you hopeful. Hopeful clients write bigger checks. Hopeful clients don't ask why nothing's filed. Hopeful clients don't notice they're being prepped for a plea, not a fight. The grand jury is where they feed you fairy tales while the government sharpens the knife.

When Your Lawyer Sells You Out and Becomes Their Messenger

Ever notice how your lawyer suddenly starts talking like the prosecutor? The tone changes. The optimism fades. The phrases get weird: "We just need to cooperate." "It'll look good if we're transparent." "The prosecutor said…" – hold up. The prosecutor said? When the hell did you start working for them?

That's the moment your lawyer switches sides – not legally, but spiritually. They become an interpreter for your enemy. They tell you what "the government" wants, what "the office" thinks, what "the agent" hinted at. Translation: they've been invited into the club. The prosecutor pats them on the head, calls them "reasonable," and boom – your lawyer's hooked on approval like it's crack. Now they want to be liked, not feared. They're not fighting for you anymore; they're managing you.

You'll know it's happened when your lawyer starts pitching surrender like it's strategy. "If we just cooperate, they'll go easy." Sure. And if you pet a rattlesnake, it won't bite. Cooperation isn't mercy – it's bait. You're the catch. The prosecutor doesn't respect your lawyer's civility; he counts on it. He knows your lawyer will bring you in line because fear makes people obedient. And every time you ask, "Can we fight this?" your lawyer sighs like a parent whose kid won't nap. That's how you know you're screwed – when your own counsel's more tired than the system trying to kill you.

Legal Myths that Sound Like Comfort but Smell Like Prison

These are the lullabies lawyers whisper when they need you calm enough to walk into your own slaughter. They sound soothing – "The judge is fair," "We'll work something out," "It's just a formality," "You'll be home soon" – but every word drips with the stink of surrender. It's the legal version of a bedtime story told by a hitman – soft tone, steady smile, knife behind the back. These lies aren't meant to protect you; they're meant to protect them – from extra work, from confrontation, from having to actually fight. The comfort's a sales pitch, and the ending's always the same: you in cuffs, them in court, pretending it was fate instead of fraud.

1. "The Grand Jury Protects the Innocent."

The Myth: Your lawyer smiles that fake calm smile and tells you, *"Relax – the grand jury is there to protect citizens like you from wrongful charges."* Oh really? Like a guard dog protects the steak. That's the bedtime story they tell nervous defendants to keep them from hyperventilating in the waiting room. They want you to picture twelve noble patriots sitting around a polished table, sifting through facts, protecting truth, and shielding the innocent. It's a Norman Rockwell painting – all flags, wisdom, and balance.

But the real scene looks more like a hostage meeting run by the government's PR department. Nobody's protecting shit. The jurors are civilians who were tricked into thinking they're part of democracy, when they're really just props in a rigged play.

Reality Check: The grand jury protects *the system,* not you. It's the prosecutor's invisible force field – a rubber stamp with a halo. They don't check evidence; they echo it. They don't question power; they obey it. The prosecutor feeds them a script and they nod like bobbleheads. You could show up with a halo and a baptism certificate, and they'd still indict you if the government needed a win that week. Innocence doesn't even get invited to the room. The only thing being "protected" is the illusion that justice still means something.

2. "You're Not the Target – You're Just a Witness."

The Myth: "You're not in trouble – they just want your help." You hear that and your lawyer looks proud of himself, like he just negotiated peace in the Middle East. It's the legal version of "I swear I just want to talk." They'll tell you it's no big deal, that your name just *came up.* You're a *witness,* not a suspect. You're just there to *clarify a few things.* Sure. Because the government always invites people over for tea and honesty.

Reality Check: If they want you to talk, you're already on the list. You're just too naive to know it. "Witness" is code for *"soon-to-be co-conspirator."* The prosecutor's goal isn't to learn – it's to *lock in.* They're testing you for weak spots, seeing how easily you lie, panic, or fold. Every word out of your mouth becomes evidence – not for justice, but for convenience. You're not there to clear anything up; you're there to hand them rope. Keep talking and you'll tie the noose yourself.

3. "If You Testify, You Can Clear This Up."

The Myth: Here comes the "heroic transparency" speech. Your lawyer says, "Just go in there and tell your side. They'll see you have nothing to hide." Right. And if you swim with sharks, they'll see you're not food. This is the dumbest advice a lawyer can give – and yet it's the most popular. It sounds brave, responsible, grown-up. You think, *"I'll just tell the truth."* But truth doesn't matter in a room where lies wear badges.

Reality Check: Testifying in a grand jury is volunteering for a firing squad and asking to hold the target. You walk in alone, no lawyer, no rules, no way to stop the bleeding when they twist your words. The prosecutor can ask anything, show anything, and spin every answer into something that sounds criminal. You say "I don't remember" – they call it "evasiveness." You say too much – they call it "inconsistency." You tell the truth – they call it "strategy." There's no winning, only degrees of getting fucked.

4. "They'll Respect You for Cooperating."

The Myth: Ah, the "play nice" illusion. Your lawyer says, "Cooperation shows good faith. It'll make them see you're reasonable." Yeah – and smiling at a mugger makes him forget he has a knife. The government doesn't "respect" cooperation. They expect it. It's how they keep their conviction rates high and their paperwork short.

Reality Check: Cooperation doesn't buy mercy; it buys them convenience. Once you start talking, they own you. They'll take your information, twist it, and use it to bury you or someone you love. And when it's time for sentencing, that same "cooperation" becomes the excuse for why you're still getting time – just "less" time. It's the oldest scam in the book: pretend to reward obedience while punishing it quietly. Respect? The only thing they respect is silence and leverage – and you just gave up both.

5. "If You're Indicted, We'll Fight It at Trial."

The Myth: That one's a crowd-pleaser. "Don't panic. If you're indicted, we'll fight it later." It sounds noble – like your lawyer's strapping on armor, ready to charge the gates. It's cinematic bullshit. Nobody's fighting.

What they're doing is *stalling*. They know that once the grand jury hits you, the government's already spent months building the case. You're showing up to a war that started before you knew it existed.

Reality Check: Fighting at trial after a grand jury is like trying to glue the Titanic back together mid-sink. You're already underwater. The indictment isn't a starting point – it's the finish line. The prosecutor's already got the narrative, the witnesses, the discovery, the leverage. Your "trial" is just the postgame interview. Most lawyers know it. They talk about trial because it keeps you hopeful while they quietly negotiate your surrender. They're not warriors – they're funeral directors with law degrees.

6. "The Grand Jury Is Fair."

The Myth: "The process works," your lawyer says. "The grand jury is about balance and oversight." That's like saying the casino is about fairness and math. The house always wins. They talk about "checks and balances" like it's not just a polite way of saying "pre-approved execution."

Reality Check: Fair? The only thing "fair" about a grand jury is the lighting. It's one-sided theater – no defense, no cross-exam, no rebuttal. The prosecutor tells the story, and twelve random citizens pretend to be judges. They hear one voice, one version, one narrative – yours isn't even allowed in the room. It's not a proceeding; it's a performance. The outcome's decided before the curtain even rises.

7. "We Can Appeal the Grand Jury Decision."

The Myth: This one's for the hopeless optimists. "Don't worry, we can always appeal." It sounds comforting, adult, like there's still some higher power that gives a damn. Spoiler: there isn't. You can't appeal what never belonged to you in the first place. The grand jury is God in that room, and God doesn't explain himself.

Reality Check: You don't "appeal" a secret vote. You can't unring a bell that was never supposed to make noise. Once you're indicted, the machine moves on without you. Lawyers toss around "appeal" to keep clients from having panic attacks, not because it's real. The only appeal that matters is the one you make before the indictment – to the court of public humiliation, strategic leaks, and procedural chaos. After that? You're cargo on the train.

8. "If You Take a Plea, It'll Go Away."

The Myth: The classic con: "Take the deal and move on." It's the legal equivalent of "just close your eyes, it won't hurt." They tell you a plea brings peace, closure, stability. What it really brings is a criminal record and a lifetime subscription to regret.

Reality Check: A plea deal doesn't end it – it just locks it in. You're not buying peace; you're buying silence. You waive your rights, your appeal, your dignity, and then the system pats you on the head for being "cooperative." The prosecutor gets his win, your lawyer gets his fee, and you get a permanent scar. Everyone wins except the guy signing the deal.

9. "The Prosecutor Seems Fair."

The Myth: Your lawyer says, "He's not that bad. He seems reasonable." Sure – so did Ted Bundy when he wore a suit. Prosecutors are professional charmers. They know how to look human while building coffins. They call you "sir," "ma'am," and "defendant" all in the same breath.

Reality Check: Prosecutors don't do "fair." They do "finished." They want closure, conviction, and clean paperwork. They get bonuses for wins, not forgiveness. The only thing they balance is the press release with your mugshot. If you think one's fair because he smiles, you've already lost.

10. "This Is How Justice Works."

The Myth: "This is the process," they say. "This is how justice is done." That line should come with a laugh track. They want you to believe the system is a self-correcting machine – grind up the bad guys, spit out the truth. It's a bedtime story for adults too tired to think.

Reality Check: This isn't justice – it's paperwork. It's the bureaucratic version of execution, where everything looks official so nobody feels guilty. The grand jury isn't about truth; it's about throughput. The faster they move, the more they can brag about "efficiency." The process works, alright – just not for you.

The System That Pretends to Give a Shit

Let's quit pretending this thing was ever noble. The grand jury ain't justice—it's camouflage. A goddamn mask for government power. They call it "citizen oversight" so you'll sleep better while they decide who gets buried. The system loves this setup because it looks democratic. Twelve ordinary folks in a room, solemn faces, the flag in the corner—what could go wrong? Everything.

The prosecutor controls every syllable that comes out of that room. The jurors don't deliberate—they absorb. They don't question—they obey. The system pretends to care, but only long enough to say, *"See? You were involved."* That's the joke. They hand you a fake steering wheel, let you pretend to drive, then run you over with the real one.

The grand jury is how the government keeps its hands clean while breaking your spine. They've been running this same illusion since Henry II—only now the crowns are in federal offices, and the robes got taxpayer funding. The whole machine is built to *look* like accountability while guaranteeing conviction. You think you're being reviewed by your peers, but you're being processed by the state's private conviction factory.

Smoke, Secrecy, and the Rubber Stamp

They love secrecy because secrets kill questions. Every time you ask "why," they say "it's sealed." Every time you demand proof, they say "classified." Every time someone gets railroaded, the judge shrugs and says, "The grand jury decided." The grand jury decided jack shit. They just nodded along.

The prosecutor drafts the script, reads it out loud, and calls it a vote. Twelve strangers sign the dotted line like they're approving a grocery list. Boom—indictment granted.

"Probable cause" is supposed to mean evidence, not suspicion—but in that room, it means *whatever the prosecutor says it means.* You can indict a priest, a sandwich, a ghost, it doesn't matter. Nobody checks. Nobody cares. They could show the jurors a stick figure and say, "This is the suspect," and they'd ask, "Where do I sign?"

The secrecy protects one thing: *them.* It hides mistakes, erases bias, and sterilizes abuse. It's the government's get-out-of-blame-free card. If the grand jury screws up, the prosecutor shrugs. If the prosecutor lies, nobody knows. If an innocent person's life gets obliterated–well, that's "procedure." The courts don't call it corruption–they call it efficiency.

If You're in the Room, You're Already Screwed

The truth nobody says out loud? The minute your name touches a grand jury file, your life's already on fire. You're not getting "reviewed." You're getting measured for chains. If your lawyer says "it's just a formality," that's code for *"You're fucked, and I'm billing you for optimism."* The whole room is built on assumption–if you're being investigated, you must be guilty. And if you're guilty, who needs a trial?

You'll never get your shot to defend yourself in there. You'll never see the evidence, never question the witnesses, never explain a goddamn thing. You're the ghost they're convicting in absentia. It's medieval justice with Wi-Fi. The jury doesn't see your face, doesn't hear your voice, doesn't know you exist as anything more than the villain in a story they were handed.

That's the bottom line, right there: the grand jury was never about finding truth. It's about manufacturing certainty. It's not oversight–it's overkill. It's the government's shadow court, where the rules don't apply and the outcome's already written.

Exhibit Two: The Bottom Line

> *The grand jury was never justice – it was a cover story. Born in a castle, baptized in blood, and reborn in a courtroom with fluorescent lights, it still serves the same master: power. What started as a king's excuse to kill his enemies became a prosecutor's playground to destroy lives behind closed doors. The only thing that's changed is the accent of the people giving orders.*

> *You can dress it up in flags, carve it into amendments, and call it due process – it's still the same medieval scam wearing a badge. The jurors aren't heroes; they're props. The prosecutor isn't truth's servant; he's the executioner with a smile. The grand jury's not about finding guilt – it's about manufacturing it. It's not oversight – it's overkill.*
>
> *So if you ever hear the phrase "The grand jury decided," remember: they didn't decide a goddamn thing. They just nodded when the government told them to. The verdict was written before the door even locked.*

Next Up – Exhibit Three: Indictments

If the grand jury is where they write the script, the indictment is the opening scene – the paperwork bullet that kills your freedom before the trial ever begins.

EXHIBIT THREE

Federal Indictment Conspiracy

"Justice isn't blind — It's Just Scripted"

An indictment ain't just paper. It's a goddamn weapon — a federal blade wrapped in legal jargon and dipped in your blood before they even swing it. They call it "a formal charge," like it's some civilized handshake between justice and procedure. Bullshit. It's an ambush. A declaration of guilt signed before you even open your mouth. Once your name hits that page, your life stops belonging to you.

Weaponized Fiction at its Best

Once your name hits that page, your life stops belonging to you. You become property of the system – a headline, a docket number, a punchline in a game you never agreed to play. The second that thing drops, you don't have rights; you have rituals. Fake ones. They'll say you're "presumed innocent," but that's the biggest joke in the courthouse. Innocence doesn't trend. Guilt sells. The indictment is the government's way of saying, *We don't need proof – we've got paper.* And that's all it takes. They'll build the illusion of justice around a stack of PDFs and call it due process while they carve your reputation up in public.

The Illusion of Due Process

The system sells "fairness" like a luxury brand. You walk in thinking you're part of a legal process – wrong. You're part of a production. Everyone in that courtroom's got a script: the judge plays God, the prosecutor plays executioner, your lawyer plays therapist, and you're just the poor bastard they feed to the machine to keep it running. You're not there for justice. You're there for *closure.* For them. Not you.

The indictment gives them the green light to treat you like you already confessed. The paperwork's written to sound official, but it's propaganda in black ink. Each word is a preloaded bullet, carefully aimed to make sure you never crawl out clean. That's why the Feds write like poets – because they know nobody reads poetry anymore. You skim it, you get scared, you surrender. And that's how they win before the fight even starts.

Prewritten Guilt

By the time you see your indictment, your fate's already been storyboarded. The media's got the headline queued. Your lawyer's already thinking about the plea deal. The judge hasn't read your case, but he's read your name – that's enough. Every paragraph in that document is a setup. It's not "charges," it's choreography. They build the rhythm of fear right into the layout. "Count One: Wire Fraud." "Count Two: Conspiracy." "Count Three: You're Fucked." Each count adds another pound of pressure until you crack.

Here's the part they don't tell you – the indictment doesn't need to be true. It just needs to sound *possible*. The system runs on imagination, not evidence. They toss your name in a blender with a few phrases like "knowingly," "willfully," and "with intent," and suddenly you're Al Capone with a laptop.

They say it's about "probable cause," but what it really means is they *probably* decided to ruin you. Probable cause is the legal system's way of saying "we're guessing, but we're confident." They'll call it justice, but it's really just theater with better costumes and worse morals.

The Language of Accusation

Let's get something straight – indictments aren't written to inform. They're written to *intimidate*. The government doesn't talk like humans. It talks like it's reciting scripture from a crooked bible – full of "knowinglys," "willfullys," and "intents to defraud," like some bureaucratic priest performing a ritual sacrifice over your life. That's what this shit is – a ritual. And you're the offering.

They call it "charging language," but it's not language at all. It's hypnosis. They use words as weapons, mixing half-truths with legal jargon to build a story that sounds airtight – because they know most people are too scared or too broke to fight it. It's psychological warfare in paragraph form. You read the first page and already feel doomed, and that's the point.

"Scheme to defraud." "Material misrepresentation." "With intent." You see those lines and your stomach drops. You start asking yourself questions they already answered for you. Did I mean that? Was it fraud? Did I *intend* anything? That's the setup. They plant doubt so deep in your head that you start doing their work for them. It's not about justice – it's about *narrative control*. They're not proving guilt; they're *authoring* it.

By the time the ink dries, your life story has been rewritten in third person, starring you as the criminal mastermind. The indictment doesn't reflect reality – it replaces it. It's an official government hallucination, notarized and sealed, where the truth is optional and the drama is mandatory. You're not being "charged." You're being *fictionalized*.

Frankenstein Charges

An indictment isn't crafted – it's *assembled*. Like a monster. You've got a federal prosecutor sitting in some overpriced chair at the U.S. Attorney's Office, slapping together a story using whatever scraps they can scavenge: a half-heard conversation, a missing receipt, an email that reads weird out of context. Stitch it all together, zap it with a few lines from the criminal code, and boom – you're the villain in their horror movie.

They don't build cases anymore. They build *composites*. That's why every indictment reads like the same recycled bullshit: mail fraud, wire fraud, conspiracy, money laundering, obstruction. The greatest hits. They don't even pretend these overlap – they just multiply them. The goal is quantity, not quality. Ten counts sound scarier than one, so they throw everything at the wall and let the media decide what sticks.

And they *love* the dollar figures. "Millions stolen." "Investors defrauded." "Complex financial scheme." Yeah, sure – maybe you screwed up a business deal, or maybe you moved money around in a way they didn't like. But to them? That's intent. That's fraud. That's a headline. They don't care if it's true. Truth doesn't pay their mortgage or get them promoted. Convictions do. Every inflated accusation is another notch on their résumé.

So they keep sewing pieces together until they've got their monster – part rumor, part assumption, part pure invention. You look at the indictment and think, "Who the hell is this guy?" That's the Frankenstein effect. They took fragments of your life and reanimated them into something unrecognizable, then called it evidence. And when the monster starts moving, they'll swear you built it yourself.

The Grand Jury Indictment Circus

Now let's revert back to **"Exhibit 2"** talk about the grand jury again – the system's favorite magic trick. They sell it like democracy in action: "The people have spoken." No, the people have nodded along to a slideshow they didn't understand while the prosecutor narrated the script. You weren't there. Your lawyer wasn't there. The only version of you they met was the one the prosecutor invented – the "defendant" they could point at from a PowerPoint slide.

The grand jury is supposed to be the gatekeeper between freedom and prosecution. Instead, it's a rubber stamp with a coffee break. They'll tell you it's "probable cause." Translation: it's *probably bullshit, but we're rolling with it.* It's the easiest part of the process for the government – no cross-examination, no defense, no context. Just a one-man show where the audience claps on cue and the curtain falls when the foreperson signs the dotted line.

And the best part? The jurors think they're heroes. They get their little civic-duty high while they unknowingly destroy lives. They don't see the aftermath – the headlines, the family that breaks, the bank accounts frozen, the lawyers circling like vultures. They just drive home thinking they did their part for justice, not realizing they just greenlit another slow-motion execution.

The prosecutor leaves that room smiling, knowing they could've indicted a ham sandwich, a parking meter, or a ghost – and the jury would've said "amen." That's not law. That's theater. And the punchline is, everyone in the system knows it. They just pretend not to notice because pretending pays better.

So yeah – "the system works." It works for them. It works for the machine. But if you're on the wrong side of the indictment, the system doesn't "work." It feeds. It feeds on your confusion, your fear, your silence. That's how the setup runs. They don't need to prove anything – they just need you to start doubting yourself while they tighten the paper noose. That's how they win. Not with facts. With fear printed in Helvetica.

Indictment Counterattack Tactics

Every charge is a formula, and formulas can be broken. Don't get hypnotized by the code numbers – **18 U.S.C. this, 21 U.S.C. that.** It's all theater. Every crime they throw at you comes with specific elements they have to prove beyond a reasonable doubt. And guess what? Most of the time, they can't. They rely on intimidation, not precision. Wire fraud? They've gotta show a *scheme to defraud*, *material misrepresentation*, and *interstate wires*. If they miss one, that whole shiny charge collapses like a wet paper bag.

You want to fuck with their heads? Force them to define *everything*. What's the "scheme"? What's "material"? What the hell does "defraud" even mean in *your* case? They hate that shit because the more you pick at it, the less airtight it looks. They want you confused – not curious. So learn the code like they do. Every paragraph in that indictment is a spell, and every spell has a flaw. You just have to find the crack and jam a crowbar in it.

Counterattack #1 – The Timeline Trap

Here's the thing about the feds – they love a good calendar. They'll claim your "criminal conspiracy" ran from 2019 to 2023, like you were running a cartel out of a Starbucks. Why? Because wide timelines give them breathing room to bullshit. It's lazy lawyering – the kind that sounds powerful but collapses under specifics.

Your move? *Hammer the clock.* If they say you committed wire fraud in March, where were you in March? What were you actually doing? Were you even in the damn state? Every timeline they build has holes – vacations, business trips, meetings that don't line up. You show one date that doesn't match the narrative, and suddenly their "scheme" looks like a government daydream. The jury starts wondering, *"If they got this part wrong, what else did they invent?"*

Time is your weapon. Use it like a sniper, not a shotgun.

Counterattack #2 – The Jurisdiction Judo

Federal prosecutors are territorial. They want *their* district because they've got *their* judges, *their* clerks, and *their* reputation. So they stretch geography like taffy to make sure your case lands where they want it. You might live in Arizona, do business in Texas, but somehow you're charged in the Southern District of New York. Magic, right?

Nah – manipulation. Challenge that shit. Jurisdiction isn't invincible. If the core of your alleged "crime" didn't happen there, they've overstepped. File the motion. Force them to prove why this case belongs in their playground. You might not win the transfer, but you'll make them sweat – and every motion drains their time, their focus, and their confidence. You're not just defending yourself; you're forcing them to play by their own damn rules for once.

Counterattack #3– The Vague Allegations Trap

Indictments are written like bad horror scripts – all tension, no substance. "The defendant engaged in a scheme to defraud." Okay, great – *what scheme?* "The defendant knowingly misrepresented material facts." Which ones? When? To whom? Silence. They love the fog because fog hides weak evidence.

Your job is to burn it down. File motions demanding clarity. Force them to specify the "who, what, when, where, and how." Every vague sentence they have to explain out loud makes them sound dumber. They built their indictment on smoke; make them prove there's fire. If they can't, you've just gutted half their case before the trial even starts.

The system thrives on generalities. You survive on precision.

Counterattack #4 – The Inflated Dollar Game

Prosecutors don't sell truth – they sell numbers. The higher the dollar figure, the scarier you look. "$10 million in losses." Yeah, maybe in a parallel universe. In reality, it's more like $75k and a broken dream. They don't care. Big numbers sound sexy in the press release. It justifies their paychecks and gets them TV interviews.

So here's your play: *Follow the money.* Every dollar, every cent. Track what came in, what went out, what was real versus "intended." You expose one phantom dollar in their total, and suddenly the rest of the figure smells like bullshit. Prosecutors can't handle math in the sunlight – it melts their narrative. You want to scare them? Say these words in court: "Prove the loss amount." Watch their faces twist.

Inflated numbers are like fake muscles – they look impressive until someone pokes them.

Counterattack #5 – The Multi-Count Overkill

Ever seen a scared prosecutor? It's the one who throws twenty counts at you for one act. That's not confidence – that's desperation in a suit. They think stacking charges will break your will and make you take a plea. It's legal terrorism, plain and simple.

You dismantle it by treating each count like its own fight. Don't let them blur the lines. "Wire fraud," "mail fraud," "conspiracy," "obstruction" – all the same bullshit painted different colors. Force them to prove *every single one* separately. The moment you show overlap, you plant doubt. And doubt spreads faster than their press leaks.

They use volume to fake strength. You use precision to expose weakness.

Counterattack #6 – The Paper Trail Puzzle

White-collar cases live and die on paper. Bank records, emails, receipts – all the shit that makes you look guilty in black and white. The trick? They rarely read what they have. They skim and assume. If your name shows up on a wire, they call you "the mastermind." If your signature's on a document, you're "the architect." But did you *authorize* it? Did you even know? Doesn't matter – they've got ink, and they've got narrative.

Your counterattack is forensic. Tear through the documents like you're doing surgery. Find the gaps – the missing initials, the third-party signoffs, the digital timestamps that don't match. Paper trails are like fingerprints: there's always smudges. Find one and make it a spotlight. Prosecutors depend on lazy assumptions. Don't give them the satisfaction.

Paper doesn't lie – people do. Especially people with badges.

Counterattack #7 – The Conspiracy Cop-Out

When all else fails, they yell "conspiracy." It's their comfort zone. It means, "We can't prove shit, but you talked to someone who did." That's it. You don't even have to *do* anything illegal. Just being in the same zip code as the real suspect is enough for them to rope you in. It's guilt by association, wrapped in Latin.

So how do you fight that? You expose how thin their connections really are. Who did you "conspire" with? What did you "agree" to? Where's the evidence of coordination? Force them to produce the smoking gun they don't have. Half the time, their conspiracy case is built on snitches and speculation – people who traded lies for leniency.

Don't let them lump you in with crooks you barely knew. Force separation. Rip the "joint venture" lie to shreds until their case looks like what it really is – a social network gone wrong.

Counterattack #8 – The Prosecutorial Overreach

The feds are drunk on power. They'll charge you with everything short of treason just to look tough. It's performance art – throw in every statute they can find, then hope something sticks. They call it "comprehensive charging." I call it overcompensation.

You beat this by stripping their case naked. File to dismiss redundant counts. Demand proof that each charge is distinct and necessary. Make them explain why they need ten versions of the same crime. You'll hear them stutter. Because it's not about justice – it's about negotiation leverage. Every extra count is another hammer they can hold over your head at the plea table.

They call it "strategy." You call it what it is – extortion with stationery.

Counterattack #9 – The Intent Gambit

Here's the crown jewel of prosecution bullshit: *intent*. They can't read your mind, but they'll swear they can. "Knowingly and willfully" – two words that ruin lives every day. Intent is the catch-all. It's what they use when the evidence sucks. If they can convince a jury that you "must have known," congratulations – you're guilty.

Your move? Show that you were dumb, distracted, or misled – anything but deliberate. They hate ambiguity because juries understand human error. Everyone screws up. But malice? That's harder to sell. Make them chase intent like a ghost. Force them to build motive out of fog. When they can't, the whole charge collapses under its own ego.

Intent is the hill they die on. Hand them the shovel.

Final Counterattack – The Aftermath

You don't beat the system clean – you survive it dirty. Every motion you file, every line you challenge, every inch of paper you bleed on is a message: *you picked the wrong target*. The goal isn't to walk out spotless – it's to walk out standing. The feds want surrender; you give them exhaustion. They expect you to beg; you make them chase.

That's the real counterattack – endurance. They've got unlimited money, time, and ego. You've got desperation, rage, and truth, which are way more combustible. You don't play their game – you drag them into yours, where every delay costs them, every lie gets exposed, and every victory feels pyrrhic.

When it's over, they'll still call you "defendant," and you'll still have scars – but you'll also have the one thing they can't indict: *proof you didn't break*.

Delusional Indictments Lies And Myths

Let's kill the fantasy right now: your lawyer isn't defending you. He's **managing your surrender**–cleaning up the wreckage while pretending to fight the fire. You think he's there to protect you, but he's really there to keep the process moving. His loyalty isn't to justice or truth; it's to the machine that signs his paycheck. The courtroom is his office, not your battlefield. You're not his client–you're a problem to minimize, a file to close, and a future testimonial about how "sometimes justice just doesn't work out." Every time he tells you to "stay calm" or "trust the process," he's soothing your panic while the system tightens the noose.

1. "It's Just A Piece Of Paper – We Can Fight This."

The Myth: You hear that line and almost feel hope. "Just a piece of paper." Like the government accidentally filed your name on the wrong form. No, it's not *just paper*. It's a declaration of war. It's the government telling you they've already mapped your life, your bank accounts, your habits, and your weaknesses. They're not guessing – they're **ready**.

Reality Check: That "piece of paper" isn't the beginning of a fight; it's the middle of your funeral. You've already been tried in secret. The grand jury was the rehearsal, the prosecutor the playwright, and you're the tragic ending they've already scripted. By the time your lawyer says, "We can fight this," he's already planning how to **negotiate your loss**. The system doesn't care about evidence; it cares about efficiency. The indictment's not paperwork–it's paperwork with teeth. And your lawyer's already reaching for the leash.

2. "They Don't Have All The Evidence Yet – Discovery Will Save Us."

The Myth: Bullshit. Discovery isn't your rescue; it's the autopsy. It's when your lawyer opens the folder and realizes the government's been living inside your life rent-free for a year. They've got your emails, your texts, your voice messages, your browser history, your credit card charges. They know where you've eaten, who you've called, who you've cheated, and how many times you googled "federal sentencing guidelines."

Reality Check: Discovery doesn't expose holes–it shows you the size of the crater. You're not "building a defense." You're counting bodies. The feds never indict without a full file ready to bury you. Your lawyer might act shocked, but he's not. He just needs you to keep believing he's the guy who can pull a rabbit out of the evidence pile. But there's no rabbit–just a paper trail that ends in your cell block.

3. "The Indictment's Vague – They Don't Know The Full Story Yet."

The Myth: Wrong. They know the story–they wrote the damn script. Vague doesn't mean weak. It means **flexible.** They use soft language so they can twist it later. "Scheme to defraud," "knowingly," "with intent"–those aren't gaps. They're *open doors* for the prosecution to walk through later and rewrite your reality as needed.

Reality Check: A vague indictment is a loaded gun. It's built to move. Every time you think you've nailed down a detail, they'll shift it just enough to keep you chasing ghosts. That's how they control the game. They don't need to prove specifics–they just need to **make you defend fog.** Your lawyer will call it "strategic ambiguity." Translation: you're screwed in multiple directions, and he doesn't know which one to face first.

4. "We'll Clear This Up Before Trial."

The Myth: That's lawyer code for *"We're begging for a plea."* There's no clearing it up. Once the indictment hits, the train's already left the station and you're tied to the tracks. Prosecutors don't backpedal–they double down.

Reality Check: "Clearing it up" means your lawyer is looking for a soft landing, not a fight. It's not about truth–it's about **damage control.** They'll smile while explaining your "options," but every option ends in you losing something. Plead out and you lose years. Go to trial and you lose decades. That's not strategy–that's a hostage negotiation. Your lawyer just happens to be working for both sides.

5. "You're Not The Main Target – You're Just Collateral."

The Myth: Cute story, but no. Once your name's on that indictment, you're the **main event**. They don't indict extras; they indict examples. You're the example. The government doesn't waste ink on bit players–it's all about body count.

Reality Check: The prosecutor will pretend you're small potatoes because it helps them flip you. Your lawyer repeats it to keep you calm. But every "small player" ends up the same way–standing in front of a judge while the real sharks cut deals behind the scenes. If you're indicted, you're not a witness, you're not a pawn–you're prey. And the system's hungry.

6. *"It's Just Leverage – They Want A Plea."*

The Myth: Sure they do. That's the scam. The indictment isn't about guilt–it's about **leverage.** They charge big, overreach, inflate the case, and then act generous when they offer you ten years instead of twenty.

Reality Check: A plea isn't mercy–it's math. The prosecutor's calculating wins. The lawyer's calculating billable hours. You're the only one calculating what ten years feels like in real time. They make you believe it's a choice. It's not. The system doesn't "offer" deals–it **forces** them. And your lawyer will call it a "good outcome" while you trade your freedom for their convenience.

7. The Myth: *"We Can Get The Charges Reduced."*

The Myth: Reduced? You think they wrote those charges in pencil? No, those were carved in stone by some career-fed who gets off on stacking felonies like trophies.

Reality Check: "Reduced" means they'll drop the bullshit charges they never intended to prove–after you plead to the one that sticks forever. It's theater. You'll feel like you won something, but the only thing reduced is your freedom. The government builds the case like a Jenga tower, then lets your lawyer pull a few pieces so it looks like victory before it collapses on you anyway.

8. *"The Charges Sound Worse Than They Are."*

The Myth: You wish. The language in that indictment is nuclear-grade PR. "Conspiracy," "scheme," "defraud"–words designed to melt your reputation before the verdict. It's not exaggeration; it's branding. They're turning you into a headline.

Reality Check: The indictment is the story that sticks. The trial, if it even happens, is the fine print nobody reads. Every phrase they use was engineered to rot your name in public. By the time your lawyer explains what it "really means," your neighbors, your boss, and your family already believe you're a criminal genius. The case doesn't have to be real—it just has to **sound good on CNN.**

9. *"Most Cases Never Go To Trial."*

The Myth: Yeah, because the process breaks people before the jury ever sits down. The feds don't need verdicts—they need **compliance.** They grind you financially, emotionally, physically until you beg to end it.

Reality Check: The plea system isn't about guilt—it's about **survival math.** You take the deal or they drown you in counts, enhancements, and "relevant conduct." Trials are for TV; real defendants fold under pressure because the system was built to make you. And your lawyer will call it "a wise choice" because it keeps his win rate high and his weekends free.

10. *"We Can Drag This Out – Time's On Our Side."*

The Myth: That's a delusion wrapped in optimism. Time doesn't heal in federal court—it decays. Evidence gets stale, witnesses disappear, your bank account bleeds, and your mind goes soft from the waiting.

Reality Check: The government has endless stamina. You don't. They'll file continuances until you're too broke or too broken to fight. Your lawyer calls it "strategy." The prosecutor calls it "pressure." You'll call it hell. Every delay buys them more time to fortify while your life crumbles in slow motion. Drag it out long enough, and you'll forget what freedom even felt like.

Closing Hammer That's the defense delusion – the bedtime stories lawyers tell to keep the panic down while the walls close in. They don't defend you; they *negotiate your destruction*. You walk in thinking you've hired a fighter, but what you really bought was a translator for your own execution. When the judge asks if you "understand the charges," your lawyer will smile, nod, and whisper, "Just say yes."

You want to know what justice looks like? It's a handshake across the aisle while you're led out in cuffs.

The Paper Was the First Bullet

You thought the indictment was the start of the fight. Wrong. It was the **first shot**–the moment the system declared war and didn't bother to tell you until you were already bleeding. That paper wasn't a "charge," it was a goddamn **execution order with your name typed neatly at the top.** You open it, you read the words, and the air changes. Everyone around you looks at you different. Your lawyer talks slower. Your friends talk less. The government talks louder.

That's the trick–make it look like due process while they quietly strip your life for parts. You're not a person anymore; you're a **case number** with a pulse. They'll call it justice, but it's really asset forfeiture for your existence. Everything you've built gets repurposed as evidence.

The System Isn't Broken–It's Working Perfectly

Don't fall for that "the system's broken" crap. It's not broken–it's **custom-built to crush you.** Every person in that courtroom has one job: to keep the machine fed. The judge gets his calendar cleared, the prosecutor gets his conviction stat, and your lawyer gets your last dollar. You? You get processed.

The indictment wasn't paperwork–it was permission. Permission for them to snoop, seize, and sell your story. You'll see it when your house gets raided, when your accounts freeze, when your so-called friends start ghosting because they "don't want to get involved." You'll swear you can still fight, but the conspiracy's already in full swing. The government doesn't need to frame you when it can just **bury you in forms.**

Everyone's in on the Game

You want to believe someone in that courtroom gives a shit. They don't. The prosecutor wants a scalp, the judge wants silence, and your lawyer wants closure. You're the only one dumb enough to still want truth. Every conversation from here on out is transactional–**freedom has a price tag now.**

And the conspiracy? It's not some secret handshake in a smoke-filled room–it's a shared understanding. A rhythm. A wink across the aisle. They all know their roles, and they play them perfectly. Your lawyer says "justice," the prosecutor says "accountability," and the judge says "final ruling." All three mean the same thing: **you lose.**

The Fight Isn't Over–It's Just Mutated

Here's where it gets real. You're gonna be tempted to fold. To plead. To "get it over with." That's exactly what they want. The system doesn't need your conviction–it needs your **submission.** The moment you say "guilty," they win on every level. You become the proof that the process works, even when it's a goddamn lie.

So yeah, the fight's still on, but it's changed shape. You're not fighting for acquittal anymore–you're fighting to survive the slow bleed. To keep your sanity when they drag you through hearings, delays, and headlines that read like obituaries. You learn to weaponize patience, to play dead when it suits you, to speak only when silence would hurt more.

This is where you stop playing defendant and start playing insurgent. They've got paper and power; you've got **rage and time.** Use both.

The Paper Noose Tightens

When it's all over–after the plea, after the sentence, after the bullshit "justice served" statement–you'll look back and realize the indictment wasn't a beginning. It was the **blueprint of your dismantling.** Every motion, every delay, every whisper from your lawyer about "strategy" was just another loop in the noose.

But here's the twist: it's not over. Not for you.

The paperwork's done, but the conspiracy doesn't end–it just moves underground. The system feeds on your silence. So don't give it that satisfaction. You document. You expose. You stay loud. Because the next person to get that envelope in the mail needs to know what's really coming.

Final Hammer – Survival Is the Only Verdict

This isn't the end of your story–it's the start of your rebellion. You don't fight an indictment with law. You fight it with endurance, defiance, and scars. You survive every petty hearing, every crooked ruling, every fake smile from the defense table, because that's how you win–by refusing to vanish.

They wanted you broken. They wanted you quiet. Instead, you walked through their paper firestorm and came out meaner, sharper, louder. The indictment didn't end your freedom.

It proved who really owns this system—and it sure as hell ain't justice. Once the paper hits the seal, the rest of your life becomes Exhibit A. But if they wanted silence, they picked the wrong defendant.

Exhibit Three: The Bottom Line

An indictment isn't justice – it's theater. The government doesn't need facts; it needs headlines. They write your guilt in advance, wrap it in Latin, and call it law. Every page is a trap, every word is a setup. The prosecutor smiles, the judge yawns, and your lawyer sells hope by the hour while pretending this isn't all choreographed.

You're not being charged – you're being scripted. They build a story, cast you as the villain, and sell your downfall like prime-time news. The indictment isn't a mistake; it's a business model. Your fear keeps the system running, your silence keeps it clean. They don't want truth. They want closure – and you're the product that gets processed to provide it.

But here's the twist – the paper only wins if you let it. They expect you to fold, to beg, to disappear. Don't. Survive louder. Every motion you file, every lie you expose, every breath you take after the verdict is proof the script failed. The system doesn't fear guilt – it fears defiance. Be the defendant who refuses to die quietly.

Next Up – Exhibit Four: Arraignments

If the indictment is the bullet, the arraignment is the show trial that makes it look legal. This is where they read your fate out loud, pretend it's a choice, and call it justice with a straight face.

EXHIBIT FOUR

Federal Arraignment Conspiracy

Where Justice Takes A Break & Freedom Gets Processed

Rise and shine dumbass. It's arraignment day where you'll make your initial court appearance, and the system's all lubed up, ready to bend you over, and take you from behind. See right now they're in a rush cause the clocks ticking and according to law, they only have 48 hours to bring you in front of the court to hear the charges against you and make your initial plea.

Welcome to the Chain Gang Parade

If you weren't lucky enough to stroll in through the Courthouse doors in and through the security check – you probably woke up in a 6 x 8 concrete shoebox next to a steel toilet to the smell of piss, regret, and dead hope.

By now you've been jarred awake by the lovely melody of clanging metal doors and the ever-cheerful guard, who is probably on their fourth energy drink and hating their lives only slightly less than you hate yours. Before you even have a chance to fully comprehend the nightmare you're in, they're at your cell door, barking at you to get up and get ready. Ready for what? Oh yeah, the big show–your arraignment!

The day you finally get to wear those fancy accessories the government has been saving just for you: handcuffs and leg shackles. Forget about room service. Today's house special is a dirty cold, steel toilet about two feet from your head and the sound of some asshole down the cellblock puking his guts out. There is nothing like the ambiance of a sterile detention center to really make you feel alive.

Cuffed and Shackled

Nothing screams "life goals" like the cold *clink-clank* of government-issued bracelets snapping onto your wrists while they slap shackles on your ankles. Forget the tux, forget the limo – this ain't prom night. This is the U.S. Marshals' version of glamour: a chain so short between your feet that walking turns into an elite test of coordination. You're not "walking" so much as performing an awkward zombie shuffle through fluorescent-lit purgatory. Only difference is, the zombies had better posture and more dignity.

Basement of Broken Dreams

And then comes the cherry on the shit sundae – the grand tour through backdoor hallways, stairwells, and concrete corridors until you land in the courthouse's best-kept secret: the basement holding tank. Welcome to the U.S. Marshals' private dungeon – a gray-on-gray bunker that smells like armpits, bleach, and the slow death of hope. This is where they stash all the unlucky souls like you, lined up like a chain gang in some low-budget prison flick. The only thing missing is a harmonica solo and a tearful monologue about redemption.

Congrats, You're the Star, But This Ain't a Movie

Now you're sitting in holding with a dozen other morons – wrists cuffed, ankles hobbled, eyes scanning the floor like maybe you'll find your last shred of pride under the bench. You ain't going anywhere, except up the stairs to your courtroom debut. You ever seen a hog paraded at a county fair? Yeah, it's like that. Except the hog has more room to move and probably better representation.

Your dignity? That's back in the tank with your rolled-up jumpsuit and the stainless steel shit throne. Your freedom? That's a fairy tale at this point. What you've got now is a front-row seat to your own humiliation, dressed up in shackles and a booking number.

And there you are–fully shackled, fully screwed, waiting for the stagehands (or, you know, the U.S. Marshals) to escort you to your grand entrance in the courtroom. Enjoy the ride, champ.

Entering the Courtroom

With a Marshal at your side, your shuffled into the courtroom – wrists cuffed, belly-chained, ankles shackled like you're Hannibal fucking Lecter. A bored Marshal guides you to a hard-ass wooden bench that feels more like a pew at your own execution than a seat in a court of law. The vibe? Picture a funeral procession with fluorescent lighting. And the only thing being lowered into the ground is your shot at freedom.

If you looked around you'd see the courtroom is built to scare the shit out of people. That raised judge's bench isn't for show – but to remind defendants who their God was gonna be today. Wood-paneled walls try to give off some kind of old-school respectability, but the whole place reeks of manufactured authority and thinly veiled threat. It's a theater of punishment, where the lead players of the show usually end up in the big house.

When the Clerk Calls Your Case: The Legal Roll Call of Doom

Now comes the part where the court clerk–bureaucracy's very own Grim Reaper–gets to play ringmaster in this government-sponsored humiliation parade. Their job? To deadpan your name like it's just another coffee order at a DMV-run Starbucks. But instead of a venti latte, you're getting served a hot, steaming plate of bullshit federal charges.

It always starts the same way: the clerk stares down at that master list of doom, barely blinking, voice flat as roadkill, calling "United States versus [Your Name]." That's the cue you're to pick your ass up and take the walk of shame to center stage.

People in the courtroom eye fuck you like you're a big titty teen stripper about to dance for spare change in a strip club full of truckers. You can feel it—judgment, pity, curiosity, all swirling together in a disgusting cocktail of shame. And don't think for a second that you can disappear into the crowd. No, this is your moment in the spotlight. One misstep, one tear, one sign of weakness, and they'll eat you alive. So go ahead and shuffle forward.

Your Courtroom Debut

Now that you've got to make the journey to the defendant's table, the show's about to begin. Whether you're sporting a cheap suit that still smells like freedom or clanking around in chains and an orange jumpsuit, this is your moment in the spotlight. Every step feels like you're marching toward a firing squad, and the only thing missing is the fucking blindfold.

Just to formalize shit, a Marshal drops a legal document in your lap showing you've been indicted by a federal grand jury and now you know you're officially fucked.

The Lawyer Roll Call—"I Hope You Brought Help"

What happens next is a real treat. The clerk mumbles something like, "Counsel, state your appearance," and that's when your government appointed "defense lawyer", a guy in an old suit who looks like he's been slamming cheap booze all night waddles up to stand beside you. If it's a public pretender, don't expect a damn speech.

They'll sleepily grunt out their name like they're ordering lunch at a drive-thru, and maybe toss yours in for good measure if they care to remember who you even are, and then slump back down like defending you already wore them out. You're maybe one of twenty new broke-ass cases they're dragging through the system today, and guess what? You ain't special at all.

Now, if you somehow scraped together enough money to hire a real lawyer–maybe sold a kidney or pawned grandma's teeth–congrats. He'll pop up like he owns the room, hit the judge with some fake-smile bullshit, and act like your case is beneath him. You're not his client. You're his invoice.

Either way, you're standing there hoping they don't call you by the wrong name or mix your file up with the guy who actually *did* rob that liquor store. 'Cause at this point, all you got going for you is the hope that your own damn lawyer knows who the fuck you are. So let me tell you about the PD game and how it works

Meeting Your Public Defender: The Unveiling of Reality

Don't expect a TV dream-team legal fantasy where a lawyer in a slick suit saves your ass with a dramatic closing argument and a surprise witness. This is budget justice assembly-line lawyering, with just enough duct tape to keep the whole system from collapsing into the gutter where it belongs.

Let's not sugarcoat shit: you're not special. You're just a line item on someone's roster. A number. One more sad bastard with their balls locked in the federal meat grinder. And your defender? They're a glorified firefighter trying to put out twenty brushfires at once with a leaky garden hose and no goddamn sleep.

Now don't get me wrong–these people aren't stupid. They know the system inside and out, mostly because they've been swallowed by it. They've memorized every fucked-up nuance of the guidelines, every crooked prosecutor's move, and every judge's favorite brand of bullshit. But they've also got a hundred other defendants crawling up their ass all at once looking to avoid a stretch in the big house.

Courtroom Triage

Think of your lawyer like this: an overworked doctor at a charity hospital ER flying by the seat of their pants with a line out the door. Well that's your Public Defender, except they're running   Damage control, who's bleeding the worst? Who needs a plea jammed through before trial? Who's about to get railroaded with a "management role" sentencing enhancement, just because they were the poor bastard who decided what toppings were going on a pizza with during a drug conspiracy? It's whack-a-mole law, and you better hope you're not the mole they skip.

Now maybe you're sitting there thinking, *"Well, at least they care, right?"* Yeah. They care. Somewhere deep in the tired, caffeine-soaked core of their soul, they give a damn. But the system isn't built for caring. It's built for efficiency, docket-clearing, and plea-churning. You'll get your motions filed, your ten minutes of face time, maybe even a well-argued objection–but don't hold your breath for some long, tear-filled conversation about your childhood trauma and misunderstood innocence.

You are not the priority. The system is. And your public defender? They're just trying to survive it with their sanity intact and their inbox under 1,000 unread emails.

The Charges Get Read–Welcome to Your New Nightmare

You made it through the small talk–the judge pretending to care, your lawyer pretending to be awake, and the evil grin on the prosecutor's face as he scribbles meaningless notes on a legal pad. Now comes the part where Uncle Sam officially tells you how badly you're fucked.

The court clerk stands up, looking about as excited as a DMV worker at the end of a double shift, and starts droning on through the charges like they're reading the ingredients on a cereal box. "Count One: Conspiracy to defraud the United States", "Count Two: Wire fraud." Yeah, that one's a crowd favorite. Then come the rest–racketeering, obstruction, money laundering–like a fucked-up Spotify playlist called *Federal Hits to Ruin Your Life*.

The courtroom might as well have a scoreboard in the back that says **Government: 10, You: 0**.

When You Truly Know You're Fucked

And here's the real kick in the teeth–they don't just hit you with one or two. Oh no, the Feds like covering their bases. They love stacking charges like they're building a damn Jenga tower of misery. Bank fraud, tax fraud, wire fraud, mail fraud–hell, if they could find a way to charge you with *breathing too suspiciously*, they'd do it. Every extra count makes them look tougher, and makes you look more like public enemy number one. It's like a "buy one, get twenty free" deal on criminal charges and whatever they can throw at you, they will.

And you're expected to sit there and take it like this is all totally normal. No big deal, right? I mean, it's only your entire life hanging in the balance. You'll try to keep up at first, nodding like you understand, until your brain taps out around Count Seven. After that, it's just noise–legal gibberish echoing off the walls while you stare at the floor wondering how the hell your name ended up in the same sentence as "United States versus."

By the end, you're not even human anymore–you're paperwork. A case number. A defendant in the machine. You'll glance over at your lawyer for some sign of life wondering" What the hell just happened?" But hey, welcome to the system! You're officially in it now, and there's no turning back.

The Judge's Steps In to Keep the Circus Going

Now it's the judge's turn to earn their government paycheck as the grand overseer of chaos, as the circus ringmaster in a black robe who's been running the same routine since dial-up internet was a thing. The clerk finishes droning through your list of sins, and here comes His or Her Honor, all puffed up with self-importance, ready to pretend this is justice instead of theater.

They fix you with that ice-cold "I've seen a thousand of you" stare and drop the same robotic line they've said ten thousand times before: **"Do you understand the charges against you?"**

Let's not kid ourselves – they don't give a fuck if you do. They just want the record to show you nodded like a trained seal so the transcript looks clean when this gets appealed in three years. So you nod and say "**Yes Your Honor**" Not because you understand a damn thing – hell, half those charges sound like they were written in another language – but because that's what's expected. It's the federal version of "smile for the camera."

And let's be real–**nobody cares if you actually understand a damn thing.** The judge doesn't. The prosecutor definitely doesn't. Your lawyer might–but they're three clients behind and checking their phone under the table.

The Machine Must Run

The judge doesn't slow down for you. They don't repeat shit. They don't translate. You could be standing there bleeding out, holding a legal dictionary upside down, and they'd still be plowing through the script like they've got a dinner reservation in twenty minutes.

This isn't about truth or understanding. It's about *momentum*. The courtroom is a goddamn conveyor belt, and the judge's job is to keep it moving – guilty, not guilty, next case, rinse, repeat. You're not in court to be heard; you're in court to be processed.

So you sit there, nodding like a bobblehead doll in a cheap suit, pretending this all makes sense while the system keeps grinding forward – a smooth, bureaucratic death march set to the rhythm of a gavel.

Not Guilty The Lie The Buys You Time

This is it, showtime. The judge turns to you like he's ordering fried chicken at a take out and asks how you plead–like you're in a reality show where your fate hangs on whether you say spicy or crispy. You'll stand there shackled like a criminal mastermind out of a bad crime thriller, and declare with all the conviction you can, muster the magic words: **Not Guilty.**

That's right; *Not Guilty*. And sure, it might feel like the biggest lie you've ever told, but hey, this isn't about the truth. It's all part of the game. The entire system is based on lies starting with the agents who busted you, the prosecutor who drafted your slanderous indictment, to your public pretender who acts like he gives a shit in defending you. And the Judge buys into all of it because he's part of the **Courtroom Conspiracy** too!

Looking about as engaged as a Zombie, the clerk scribbles some shit down in the official records, like they're checking off a to-do list. And just like that, the beast lumbers forward.

It doesn't matter what evidence they think they've got against you. It doesn't matter if the Feds have your fingerprints, DNA, and a videotape of you smiling for the camera mid-crime. Who cares if they've got a signed confession from your childhood teddy bear at this point? *Not Guilty* is your golden ticket to keeping this farce going for just a little while longer. This isn't the time to break down and confess all your sins like you're auditioning for the role of a guilty martyr.

Hell no. You're not in a confessional, and the judge sure as fuck isn't your priest. So, you stand up tall—well, as tall as you can in shackles or after the mental beat down you've been living through—and you say it. *Not Guilty*. With all the conviction of a kid denying they broke the lamp, even though they're standing in a pile of shattered glass.

Temporary Reprieve

Congratulations! You've just bought yourself some time—time to let your defense team scramble and find some crack in the prosecution's armor, time to enjoy your fleeting freedom or come to terms with the metal bars that might soon be your new best friends.

The prosecutor across the room will smirk, knowing full well that this is just a formality, but it's a formality that buys you time. And time, in the federal system, is one of the few things that can work in your favor. A *Not Guilty* plea is the first defense against a machine designed to grind you into dust. It doesn't mean you're walking out scot-free, but it keeps the wheels turning and gives you room to breathe. You're putting off the inevitable—for now.

The Referral to Pretrial Services

Without glancing up half the time, the judge **refers you to Pretrial Services** for a bail recommendation. It's their job to assess whether you're too dangerous or too much of a flight risk to be out in the real world. Spoiler alert: they will probably recommend something wildly inconvenient for you. But the judge won't be fazed; they're used to making these snap decisions all day. Conversely, you will feel your stomach tighten as you're sent off to be evaluated like a stray dog at the pound. And that's it. The clerk moves on to the next poor soul in line, the judge shuffles some papers, and you slink back to your seat, knowing that this was just the beginning of a long, painful ride.

Lies Lawyers Tell About Arraignments

They'll tell you the arrangement's "no big deal," just a quick formality to enter a plea and move on. Bullshit. The arraignment is where the government puts your neck on the chopping block and your lawyer pretends it's a meet-and-greet. They'll act like nothing important happens, but that's when the stage gets set – bail, charges, narrative, all locked in while you're still trying to remember how to breathe. Your lawyer's calm because they're not the one getting cuffed again. They'll tell you to "just say not guilty" like it's a magic spell, but the system already decided your guilt when they stapled your name to that indictment. The arraignment ain't harmless – it's the opening scene of your conviction.

1. The Arraignment Is Just a Formality

The Lie: Your lawyer will smile and assure you that the arraignment is no big deal—just a procedural formality. You'll be in and out, no sweat. They make it sound like a casual meet-and-greet with the federal court system, where everyone shakes hands, and nothing really happens.

The Truth: The arraignment is the moment when reality hits you square in the face. It's when the government officially lays out the charges and sets the stage for the fight of your life. While your lawyer might downplay it, this is when the Feds make it clear they mean business. The charges are read, and the judge asks how you plead. Suddenly, you're no longer a free person strolling through life—you're a defendant facing serious federal crimes.

2. The Judge Is Just There to Keep Things Moving

The Lie: They'll tell you the judge at your arraignment isn't really involved in your case yet, just there to make sure things stay on schedule. It's like the judge is just a glorified timekeeper making sure the docket doesn't get too backed up.

The Truth: The judge at your arraignment may not be diving deep into your case right then, but they're far from just a timekeeper. This person will be setting your bail, determining the conditions of your release, and making key decisions that can affect the entire trajectory of your case. You better believe they're paying attention to every detail, especially how you present yourself.

3. The Charges Are Probably Overblown—Don't Worry

The Lie: Your lawyer might suggest that the charges are exaggerated, and once they dig into the case, things will calm down. They'll make it seem like the government has just thrown everything at the wall to see what sticks.

The Truth: The charges might be overblown, but don't think the Feds aren't serious about them for a second. Every count on that indictment is a tool they'll use to pressure you into a plea deal or crush you at trial. The government doesn't throw around words like "fraud" or "conspiracy" lightly. Each charge is a weapon aimed right at your life.

4. We Can Get Bail, No Problem

The Lie: Your lawyer will confidently say that getting you out on bail won't be an issue, like it's just a matter of filling out a few forms and waiting for the judge to rubber-stamp your release.

The Truth: Bail in federal court is a whole different beast. The Feds aren't just looking for cash; they want guarantees that you won't skip town. This means property bonds, restrictions, and possibly even home confinement. Bail could be denied outright if you're deemed a flight risk or a danger to the community. Getting out on bail is far from a given–it's a high-stakes negotiation.

5. The Pretrial Services Interview Is Just Routine

Lie: Your lawyer might brush off the Pretrial Services interview as a minor formality where they gather some basic info about your background. They'll tell you not to worry because it won't really impact your case.

The Truth: That Pretrial Services interview is actually critical. The report they generate is what the judge uses to determine whether you'll be released on bail and under what conditions. How you present yourself, the information you give (or withhold), and how you explain your ties to the community can make or break your chances of walking out of that courtroom. It's far from routine–it's the prelude to your freedom or continued detention.

6. The Prosecutor Will Be Fair in the Bail Request

The Lie: Your lawyer might tell you the prosecutor will be reasonable when asking for bail. After all, this isn't some Hollywood drama–these are serious professionals who play by the rules.

The Truth: The prosecutor isn't interested in being fair–they want you locked up or tied down with so many conditions that you can barely breathe. They'll argue that you're a flight risk, a danger to society, or that your financial assets make it easy for you to disappear. Their job is to make sure you're either sitting in jail or sweating bullets trying to make bail.

7. If Bail Is Too High, We Can Always Appeal

The Lie: Lawyers might reassure you that if the judge sets an unreasonably high bail, there are plenty of options to appeal and get it reduced. It's not a big deal, they'll say–just a little paperwork and another hearing.

The Truth: Appealing a bail decision is not as easy as your lawyer might make it sound. It's a long shot, requiring more hearings and more arguments in front of judges who rarely overturn their colleagues' decisions. If you think you'll just waltz in and get the bail lowered because it's "unfair," you're in for a rude awakening. The courts are stacked against you, and appeals often fall flat.

8. You'll Be Out in Time for Dinner

The Lie: They'll tell you that you'll likely be released on bail by the end of the day, just in time to catch up on Netflix and relax with your family.

The Truth: Federal arraignments and bail hearings don't move at lightning speed. Even if the judge grants bail, there's paperwork to process, bonds to be signed, and sometimes delays in getting property approved for bond purposes. You'll be out in a couple of days if you're lucky. If not, you might be sitting in a cell much longer than you expected.

9. Pleading 'Not Guilty' Buys You Plenty of Time

The Lie: Lawyers will tell you that entering a not guilty plea at the arraignment is just the first step in a long, drawn-out process that will give you time to prepare your defense. They'll paint a picture of months of investigation and strategy before you need to worry.

The Truth: While a not-guilty plea does kick the can down the road, the federal system moves faster than you think. Deadlines for filing motions, discovery, and trial dates will come up quicker than expected. The clock starts ticking the moment you say "Not Guilty," and the government is already preparing to nail you. Time is never really on your side.

10. Once We Get Bail, Things Will Settle Down

The Lie: They'll try to calm your nerves by saying once you're out on bail, the dust will settle, and you'll have some breathing room. It's just a matter of getting past the first hurdle.

The Truth: Getting bail is just the beginning of the rollercoaster. The conditions attached to your release can be suffocating–ankle monitors, home confinement, constant check-ins with Pretrial Services. Every move you make is scrutinized; one misstep could land you back in a cell. Things won't settle down–they'll shift into a new level of tension and surveillance.

Exhibit Four: The Bottom Line

The arraignment isn't a "formality." It's the system's way of breaking you in – the first psychological chokehold that tells you exactly who runs the show. You show up chained like livestock, paraded in front of strangers, and forced to play your part in a legal ritual that's already scripted. They call it "due process," but it's really just the first act of your public execution – sanitized, bureaucratic, and wrapped in flags. You stand there nodding, pleading, pretending you understand, but the truth is simple: this is your indoctrination into the federal meat grinder. You're not a person anymore. You're a case number with a pulse.

By the time you shuffle back to your seat, the message is loud and clear: You belong to us now. Your lawyer's pep talk, the judge's polite monotone, the prosecutor's smirk – they're all part of the same production. You're watching justice theater performed for an audience of ghosts. The arraignment isn't about guilt or innocence; it's about submission. They don't need your confession – they've already got your compliance. That's the real win for them. Every click of the cuffs, every word you're forced to say on command, every nod of obedience – that's the sound of your freedom being auctioned off one syllable at a time.

Next Up-Exhibit Five – Pre Trial Services & Bail Scam

Where "Pretrial Services" means government babysitters with badges, and "bail hearings" are the new stock market for human desperation.

EXHIBIT FIVE

Pre Trial Services Bail Conspiracy

Tell Us About Yourself So We Can Fuck You With It Later

Congrats, you survived the arraignment circus, and now it's time for the next act: meeting with the backstabbers at Pretrial Services. If you thought your judge had an air of detached indifference, wait till you meet these folks. Pretrial is the arm of the court that pretends to give a shit whether you should be allowed to roam free while awaiting your dance with Lady Justice, and your first meeting with them is basically an interrogation dressed up as an interview.

The Interview That Isn't Your Friend

It's like a job interview, except instead of seeing if you're qualified to work, they're sizing you up to decide if you're going to bolt for the border the moment they turn their backs. They'll ask about your job (or lack thereof), your family (or lack thereof), your ties to the community, and your criminal history (which, let's be honest, is why you're here in the first place).

We're Here to Help: They love saying that line, like they're social workers on some crusade to save your soul. "We're here to help." Help who, exactly? Because it sure as hell isn't you. Pretrial's job isn't to hold your hand–it's to hand the judge a report that decides whether you walk out the door or get sent back to your cage. Think of it as a smiling middleman in the business of controlled freedom.

They'll ask about your job, your family, your roots–like they actually give a damn. They don't. Every answer is a checkbox on a form that'll either buy you daylight or lock you in fluorescent hell. Stability? That's code for "how easy will it be to find you when you screw up." Community ties? That's "how fast can you bolt to Mexico." Court history? "Do we need to call the marshals now or later?"

"You Seem Like an Upstanding Citizen... For Now"

By the time that little "interview" wraps up, Pretrial's already got your fate typed, stamped, and filed. They've got enough ammo to build you up or bury you. Maybe you came off calm and dependable, so they let you out with a smile and a leash–weekly check-ins, random piss tests, maybe even a shiny ankle monitor to remind you who's boss. That's the *win*. That's "freedom" in quotation marks.

But if you blink wrong or say something that smells like risk? Enjoy your complimentary stay at the nearest federal dungeon. No refund, no appeal, no sympathy. Pretrial doesn't hate you–they just don't care. You're data on a screen. A name on a docket. Their job is to make sure the system doesn't lose track of its prey before trial day. So they smile, nod, and write your obituary in bureaucratic language while pretending it's "just procedure."

Don't let the fake friendliness fool you. This isn't about fairness. It's about control. You're not being evaluated–you're being measured for the right length of leash.

The Babysitters of Justice

You're probably thinking, "Well, at least they're there to help, right?" Sure. If by "help" you mean tracking your every move like a parole officer who never made it to the big leagues. They call themselves "Pretrial Services Officers," but let's be real–they're just glorified babysitters with a badge and a court mandate to stick their noses into every facet of your life. Think you're free while you're out on bail? Think again, because the Pretrial Services Officer is here to remind you that freedom is a very flexible concept.

The Personality of a DMV Employee on a Power Trip

You know the type, you've seen them at DMV and the Unemployment Office – the kind of person who gets drunk on a whiff of authority. Well that's your Pretrial Services officer. A former hall monitor turned professional snitch-wrangler, armed with a clipboard and a God complex. They're what happens when you give a DMV worker the power to wreck someone's week.

They strut around like they're the last line of defense between civilization and chaos, but really, they're just bureaucrats with delusions of grandeur. They'll smile like they care, nod at your sad little story, and then – without missing a beat – deny your request because "rules are rules." Translation: they get off on saying no. You're not a human being to them; you're paperwork with a pulse.

Pretrial isn't freedom – it's probation with better branding. You're out, but only on their terms. You can breathe, but only when they say you can. You're stuck in a legal purgatory where they call it "supervision" but it feels a hell of a lot like punishment. So next time somebody tells you being out on bail means you're free, remember this: Pretrial's not letting you live. They're just letting you dangle. And the one holding the leash? Some clipboard warrior who's been waiting their whole life for someone to call them "sir."

The All-Seeing Eye of Pretrial Surveillance

Let's start with their favorite toy: the ankle bracelet. You know, that little piece of fashion tech that makes you feel like a high-tech prisoner in your own home. Welcome to the age of *surveillance on steroids.* Oh sure, you're not behind bars, but don't for a second think that you're off the hook. You get to walk around, sure, but only within the tight little leash that Pretrial Services so generously gives you. Want to go somewhere outside your designated zone? Better call your Pretrial Officer and beg for permission like a teenager asking for the car keys. Spoiler alert: the answer will probably be "no."

And even if you're one of the "lucky" ones who doesn't get the ankle bracelet, don't think you've escaped the ever-watchful eye of Big Brother's junior varsity team. Random check-ins, mandatory office visits, home inspections—it's all part of the package. They'll pop up at the most inconvenient times, like a low-rent version of the FBI, asking you to account for every second of your day. Did you go to work? How many hours? Did you make that court-ordered AA meeting? Pretrial Services is on it, and they've got the paperwork to prove it.

Drug Tests: The Ritual of Humiliation

Of course, we can't forget about the drug tests. It's like some twisted form of ritualistic humiliation they get off on. Doesn't matter if you've never touched a drug in your life—they're going to test you anyway, because that's what they do. You'll get to know your local testing facility better than your own bathroom. You'll be peeing in cups so often you'll wonder if this whole pretrial thing is just a massive pharmaceutical experiment. Maybe it is—who knows? After all, *you* don't get a say in it.

And forget about privacy. These tests aren't about trust; they're about power. It's all very theatrical. You shuffle in like a good little defendant, do your business while they stand just close enough to make it awkward, and then hand over your bodily fluids like some kind of criminal sacrament. The whole time, they're watching, waiting for you to screw up so they can tighten the noose. **For good measure piss on their shoe and they'll back off!**

Curfews and Social Life Annihilation

Pretrial Services also delights in controlling your social calendar. Curfew violations? That's their bread and butter. If you thought maybe you could sneak out for a late-night drink with friends or catch a midnight movie, think again. Your Pretrial Services Officer has mapped out your every move and isn't about to let you have even the slightest bit of fun. Miss curfew by five minutes? Congrats you just earned yourself a "stern talking to" and maybe even a trip back to court. And let's be honest, the only thing worse than court is another meeting with Pretrial!

Oh, and don't even think about leaving town. You might as well have shackles around your ankles with the level of freedom they allow. Want to visit a sick relative out of state? Need to take a last-minute business trip? Ha! The answer is usually a resounding "hell no," unless you can somehow produce a notarized letter from God himself, delivered in triplicate. The hoops you'll have to jump through to get any kind of travel approved would make Cirque du Soleil performers jealous

The Judge's Final Act: Freedom or Federal Housing?

After Pretrial's done crawling up your ass with a flashlight and a clipboard, the judge strolls in like the grand finale of your personal circus. This is the moment of truth – freedom or a taxpayer-funded stay in a jail. The judge pretends to "weigh" the Pretrial report, but let's be honest: these assholes have already made up their fucking mind before you even walked in.

If you're lucky, you get bail. Great. Pop the champagne – just don't spill it, because your "freedom" comes with an instruction manual thicker than the Bible. Curfew, ankle bracelet, drug tests, phone check-ins, and a warning that sounds a lot like, "Step out of line once and I'll personally send your ass back."

But if the judge decides you're too risky or just rubs them the wrong way? Boom – instant eviction from society. You're going back to your concrete suite with all the other "public safety threats." No appeal, no pity, just a guard with handcuffs and a bad attitude waiting to escort you out. Either way, you're stuck in the same machine – whether you're breathing fresh air or recycled jail ventilation. The judge just decides which version of the cage you get to call home.

A White-Collar Gamble in the Federal Courtroom

Here you are–still reeking of federal custody–sitting under flickering lights while the judge decides whether you walk out the front door or ride the bus back to lockup. This isn't salvation; it's roulette with your life on the line. The only question on the table isn't *did you do it*, it's *how fast could you disappear if we let you out?*

The federal court doesn't care about justice at this stage. It's not mercy, it's math–risk factors, community ties, bank balances, all turned into numbers that decide how tight the leash gets. You think "white collar" buys you slack? Cute. To them, you're not a criminal with a conscience–you're a spreadsheet with legs.

Fraud, embezzlement, Ponzi, whatever your flavor–none of it matters. You're dangerous in a different way. The junkie's threat comes with a knife; yours comes with a plane ticket and an offshore account. And the judge doesn't see a misunderstood professional–he sees a polished flight risk with enough brains to disappear before lunch.

The Price Tag on Freedom: How Bail is Determined

Bail isn't about letting you walk free – it's about putting a number on your ass and seeing if you can afford it. The judge slaps a price tag on your freedom like you're a used car, and if you can scrape together the cash, congratulations – you get to go home *temporarily.* Screw up once, though, and they'll drag you back faster than you can say "non-extradition country."

The whole thing's a leash. The court just wants to know they can yank it anytime you twitch. They call it a "release," but it's really just a rental agreement for your life. You're not free; you're on loan until they're done dismantling you.

And don't think for one second this is about fairness – it's about risk. The judge doesn't give a damn if you're innocent or guilty. They care about whether you're gonna run, hide, or embarrass them. They've got your whole life printed out in front of them: arrests, jobs, failed marriages, unpaid bills, your cousin's mugshot – all of it. Too many red flags, and you're not walking out that door.

White-collar? That doesn't help you. The system looks at you and sees a passport, a plane ticket, and a balance sheet that says "runner." You could have a spotless record and a golden smile, but if they think you've got offshore money or friends in warm countries, forget it. You're done. Bail's not justice – it's business. You're not buying your freedom; you're renting it from the same machine that plans to crush you later. And the interest rate? Let's just say it's paid in humiliation.

Two Defendants, Two Fates: Bail or No Bail?

Let's break it down with two examples of white-collar defendants: **Chuck** and **Megan**.

Chuck: a mid-level executive accused of insider trading, sits at one end of the spectrum. He's got no criminal history, a nice family in the suburbs, a steady job–everything that screams stability. His lawyer talks him up, emphasizing his community ties, his low risk of flight. The prosecutor mumbles something about the seriousness of the offense, but there's not much meat on that bone. The judge takes a glance at the Pretrial Services report–John's lived in the same town for years, no signs he's about to run off to a tropical island. Bail is set at a manageable $100,000, with conditions like home confinement and weekly check-ins. John scrambles the cash together and walks out a free man–for now.

For **Chuck**, the report paints a picture of a stable, low-risk defendant. Married, steady job, no criminal history, deep ties to the community. He's involved in local charities, coaches his kid's soccer team, and has lived in the same town for years. Pretrial Services recommends a low bail–maybe even a surety bond or house arrest. The prosecutor grumbles, but they can't argue with the facts. The judge follows the report's recommendation, and John's free to go, albeit under strict conditions.

But then there's Megan, the financial advisor accused of orchestrating a Ponzi scheme that drained millions from her clients. She's got the Feds breathing down her neck, accusing her of moving money offshore. The prosecutor leaps at the chance to paint her as a flight risk–a defendant with international ties and the resources to disappear at the drop of a hat. The Pretrial Services report isn't doing her any favors either: no family ties, lots of international travel, and too many rumors about missing funds. The judge listens, nods, and denies her bail outright. Jane's not going anywhere except back to her cell, where she'll sit for months, maybe years, waiting for her trial.

But for **Megan**, the Pretrial Services report is a nightmare. Offshore accounts, frequent international travel, no family, and millions of dollars unaccounted for? **The report paints her as a flight risk waiting to happen**. The recommendation is clear: no bail. The prosecutor seizes on this, hammering home the point that she could be on the next flight out of the country if they let her go. The judge nods and slams the door on any hope of release. Megan's not walking free anytime soon.

The Hell of Life Without Bail

For Megan, the nightmare didn't start with a verdict – it started the second the judge said *no fucking bail*. One gavel hit, and boom she was gone, swallowed by the system. Now she's sitting in freezing her ass off in a concrete box with no windows, no peace, and no sense of when the waiting ends. And in the feds, "waiting" doesn't mean days or weeks – it means months, sometimes years, before they even bother to call your name again.

She's thrown into the mix with violent offenders, petty criminals, predatory lesbians and everyone in between. White-collar crime means nothing in here–you're just another asshole in a sea of orange jumpsuits. Every day's the same damn loop. Wake up to the sound of metal and misery. Choke down whatever slop they call breakfast – something that tastes like it was scraped off the floor and reheated out of spite. Stare at the walls till your brain starts chewing on itself. Try not to think too hard, 'cause that's when the panic creeps in.

Once in a while, Megan's lawyer shows up looking like he'd rather be anywhere else and gives her a fake sympathetic smile, the one that says he's already moved on to his next client. Drops the same tired lines – *"We're working on it."* *"Be patient."* Yeah, sure. Easy to say when you're not rotting in a concrete box counting the minutes till someone remembers you exist.

The "Freedom" of Bail: A Different Kind of Prison

And for those who get bail–**Chuck**–freedom is a relative term. Sure, he's walking out the courthouse doors, but he's not free. Not really. They got him by the balls under **house arrest**, wearing an ankle monitor like a neon sign that says "flight risk," with his every move monitored. He's reporting to a probation officer weekly, checking in like a parolee, and one false move will send him right back to the can!

He can't leave the state, travel, or do much of anything without the court's permission. His life is in limbo, hanging by a thread as he waits for his trial date to roll around. And the financial cost of bail? It's crippling. Liquidating assets, borrowing from family, scraping together every fucking penny just to stay out of a cell–it's a different kind of punishment.

The Feds Want Your Property: The Hidden Cost of Bail

Welcome to the twisted world of federal bail – where freedom ain't just about cash, it's about collateral. The Feds don't just want your money; they want your damn life on paper. Mom's house, your sister's condo, that one piece of property your family's been holding onto since the Reagan years – yeah, that's what they're after. They don't just want a guarantee you'll show up; they want leverage. Something that bleeds when you lose it.

See, they figured out a long time ago that money's replaceable. Property? That's a pain. It's rooted, it's personal, and it makes sure you're not going anywhere. The Feds love that kind of control – the kind that turns your whole family into unpaid probation officers. You screw up, they lose the roof over their heads. It's not justice; it's hostage-taking in a suit and tie.

They call it "assurance." You'll call it emotional blackmail. Because nothing keeps you on a leash like knowing Mom's house is hanging by a thread tied to your ankle monitor. One missed call, one late check-in, and it's not just your freedom they're taking – it's everything your family owns. And when that happens, the Feds won't lose a minute of sleep. They'll just smile, file the paperwork, and move on to the next poor bastard dumb enough to think bail means freedom.

The Emotional Shakedown

Let's not forget the real kicker: you now get to guilt-trip your family into putting their home on the line. Imagine sitting them down to have that fun little conversation. "Hey, Mom, mind signing away the house? Don't worry, I'm sure everything will be fine." Yeah, right. Property bonds don't just tie you down; they drag your whole family into your mess. Now, every time you step out the door, they'll be waiting for the other shoe–or, in this case, the foreclosure notice–to drop. It's the ultimate mind game, and the Feds are playing to win.

How to Play the Game - Hacks and Loopholes - Before Bail

Welcome to the world of federal court, where the rules are rigged against you from the start. But that doesn't mean you're completely powerless. If you play your cards right, there are ways to work the system to your advantage–at least as much as the system allows. Here are some hacks to help you survive (and maybe even exploit) the arraignment and bail process.

Bail Hack #1: Master the Art of the "Sickly Saint"

When you walk into court, looking like you just rolled out of bed after a long night of crime won't help your case. Instead, play the part of the unfortunate soul unjustly dragged into this nightmare. Dress conservatively–think Sunday church-goer, not nightclub regular–and adopt a look of sorrowful innocence. Judges are human, and as much as they pretend to be neutral, they're influenced by appearances. Looking like the underdog who's been wrongfully accused can subtly sway their judgment.

How to Exploit It: If you come across as pitiful enough, the judge might be slightly more lenient when setting bail. Play up your health problems, family obligations, or community ties to make yourself appear less like a flight risk. Don't oversell it, but a well-placed mention of your sick relative or volunteer work never hurts.

Bail Hack #2: Weaponize Pretrial Services

You'd think Pretrial Services are just there to gather facts, but they're also heavily relied upon by judges to make bail decisions. So why not use this to your advantage? Pretrial Services officers will ask all sorts of questions about your employment, family, community ties, and history. This is your chance to feed them information that paints you as the most dependable person on the planet.

How to Exploit It: Prepare in advance. Get letters from employers, community leaders, or religious figures praising your character. Have documentation ready that shows you've got stable roots–a job, a house, kids in school–whatever makes you seem less likely to skip town. Your goal is to make the Pretrial officer your ally so they recommend lower bail or even release on your own recognizance.

Bail Hack #3: The "Paperwork Barrage"

Federal courtrooms run on paperwork, and if you know how to use it, you can slow the process down to a crawl or make the judge think twice. The government loves charging you with everything under the sun, so why not return the favor by filing every legitimate motion possible? Each motion adds a layer of complexity that makes the prosecutor's job harder and might make the judge more willing to consider a reasonable bail.

How to Exploit It: File motions for discovery, to suppress evidence, for additional discovery–whatever keeps the court buried in paper. Not only does this show you're fighting back, but it gives your lawyer time to poke holes in the prosecutor's case. If you bury them in enough motions, the judge might start seeing you as more of a legal hassle than a flight risk, which could tip the scales in your favor for bail.

Bail Hack #4: Make the Prosecutor Sweat

Prosecutors are used to having all the power, but they hate being embarrassed. If you (or, more likely, your lawyer) can spot any misconduct or shady practices, use it. Pointing out a prosecutor's overreach or mistakes in front of the judge can put them on the defensive, making them less likely to push for sky-high bail.

How to Exploit It: Go on the offense. If the prosecutor overcharges you or exaggerates your threat level, have your lawyer call them out. File motions to challenge the charges or to get the judge to force them to show their cards. If they're acting like you're a flight risk without objective evidence, put them in a corner where they have to back down or look bad in front of the court. This could pressure the judge to set a more reasonable bail amount.

Bail Hack #5: Leverage the "Broke but Honest" Defense

Let's face it: the federal system loves to crush people under financial burdens. If they think you've got the resources to flee, they'll jack up the bail to insane levels. So, what do you do? Play the broke card, and do it well. Show that you don't have two pennies to rub together—let alone the cash to escape to a non-extradition country.

How to Exploit It: Get your finances in order, and by that, I mean prove that they're in shambles. Have your lawyer present bank statements, debt records, and anything else that shows you couldn't flee even if you wanted to. If the judge sees that you're barely scraping by, they might lower bail just because they know there's no point in setting it high.

Bail Hack #6: Family Ties Are Your Golden Ticket

Federal courts are more likely to grant bail if they believe you're grounded by family. Kids, spouses, elderly parents—they all make it harder for you to disappear without a trace. This can be one of your strongest arguments for reasonable bail or even release on your own recognizance.

How to Exploit It: Bring the family into it—literally. Have your lawyer show the court that you've got deep ties to the community. Highlight any responsibility you have as a caretaker. When the judge knows that skipping bail would destroy your family life, they're more likely to give you a break.

Bail Hack #7: Public Perception—A Media Strategy

Sometimes, the court of public opinion is just as powerful as the courtroom. If you've got a case that could gain sympathy or shine a light on prosecutorial overreach, don't be afraid to court the media. Prosecutors hate bad press because it forces them to play nice.

How to Exploit It: Leak your side of the story to a sympathetic journalist or make some noise on social media. Highlight any injustices or missteps in the case, and watch as public pressure pushes the prosecutor and judge toward a more lenient bail decision. Just be careful—this can backfire if not handled correctly.

Bail Hack #8: Force the Court to Show Its Cards

Judges and prosecutors like to think they're playing chess while you're stuck playing checkers. But what if you could flip the board? Force them to show their cards early by filing motions that demand specifics. Make them prove why you're a flight risk or dangerous.

How to Exploit It: Demand evidence from the prosecutor—real evidence, not just speculation. Have your lawyer file a motion for the government to prove why bail should be denied or set outrageously high. If they can't back up their claims, you've got a better shot at getting out on reasonable terms.

Bail Hack #9: Play the Long Game

The arraignment and bail hearing are just the opening moves in a long, drawn-out battle. Sometimes, the best strategy is to keep the game going, buying yourself more time. The longer the case drags on, the more chances you have to exploit mistakes or weakened resolve from the prosecution.

How to Exploit It: Delay, delay, delay. File for continuances, request more time to gather evidence, and request extensions on every possible deadline. This keeps you out of trial longer and gives you more opportunities to work out a favorable bail deal as the prosecution starts to tire out.

Bail Hack #10: Bring the Community to Court

Judges and prosecutors love to act like they're impartial, but they're just as influenced by the people around them as anyone else. Pack the courtroom with supportive friends, family, and community members who can vouch for your character and ties to the area.

How to Exploit It: At your bail hearing, make sure your lawyer brings up your community involvement and have supporters in the courtroom to back it up. When a judge sees a dozen people sitting there for you, it puts pressure on them to give you the benefit of the doubt. The judge doesn't want to look like the heartless bureaucrat who ignores your deep community roots.

Loopholes for Dealing with Pretrial Services - After Bail

Dodging the Babysitters of the Legal World

When you're stuck under the watchful eye of a Pretrial Services Officer, it feels like every move you make is scrutinized by someone who enjoys their job a little too much. But don't worry—there are loopholes lurking in the shadows of this bureaucratic nightmare. Here's how to slip through a few cracks and get some relief from the iron grip of Pretrial Services.

1. The "Too Much Compliance" Trick: Weaponize Your Own Good Behavior

Pretrial officers want you to blow it. It's almost their hobby. So flip the script: be annoyingly, painfully perfect. Show up ten minutes early for every check-in, pee on command for every drug test, answer the phone like you're auditioning for sainthood. Call them with pointless updates until they start praying for silence. Make being your caseworker a full-time nuisance—because nothing gets a bureaucrat to loosen the leash faster than the thought of managing one more nailed-down saint.

Levine Tactic: This is not accidental virtue—it's tactical martyrdom. Flood them with confirmations, paperwork, receipts for every tiny thing. Be the person who RSVP's to their own curfew. The goal is to make your compliance more trouble than you'd ever be if they ignored you. When the officer realizes you're less drama and more administrative workload, they'll quietly stop sweating the small stuff. They'll cut you slack just to reclaim their sanity.

2. The "Family Emergency" Card: Tugging at the Heartstrings

Pretrial officers eat up a good sob story – it's the one thing that makes them feel human for five minutes. So play the game. Got a sick grandma? A dying dog? Hell, make it a cousin with "complications." Lean in just enough to make it believable. They love feeling like they're doing something noble, and nothing screams "noble" like letting you out early to "take care of family."

Levine Tactic: You don't beg, you *perform*. Drop little nuggets of sympathy bait – "She's not doing well," "Doctor says it could be any day now," "I just want to be there." Say it with the right mix of pain and guilt. Make it sound like denying you makes *them* the villain. Works like a charm if they've got a shred of empathy left. But don't overplay your hand. You pull too many funerals out of thin air, and they'll start asking for death certificates. Keep it subtle, keep it tragic, and for God's sake, keep track of which relative you killed off last.

3. The "I've Got a Job" Loophole: Stay Busy, Stay Free

Pretrial officers glow when you say you've got a job – nothing makes them feel more useful than helping a "productive citizen." So weaponize that. Stack your calendar with extra shifts, slap on "mandatory" business trips, and suddenly you're a busy professional instead of a liability. If your job can plausibly involve travel or weird hours, milk it. The more you look like someone the economy can't afford to lose, the more likely they are to bend the rules.

Levine Tactic: Sell the bullshit like it's patriotic duty. Frame every scheduling request as a critical business necessity – "I can't miss this call; the whole project falls apart." Drop words like "overtime," "client," and "deadline" until they start picturing you as essential. Ask your lawyer to phrase it in legal-sounding terms so it reads like urgency, not excuse. Make being hard-to-reach sound like public service. It's hard to leash someone when their job makes them "irreplaceable."

4 The "Good Lawyer Request" Play: Make Your Lawyer Do the Dirty Work

Hit a wall with Pretrial Services? Good. That's when you send in the hammer – your lawyer. Pretrial officers will blow off a defendant's plea like it's background noise, but you get a lawyer involved and suddenly they perk up. Have your attorney draft the request, slap on some legal-looking language, and watch the paperwork make them sweat. Bureaucrats hate hassle more than anything. If they sniff the smell of motions and hearings, they'll fold just to avoid the paperwork avalanche.

Levine Tactic: This is pure delegation. Your lawyer knows how to write the kind of officious-sounding letter that makes clerks tremble. Have them frame your request in formal legalese, cite rules, ask for specific relief, and threaten the tiny administrative apocalypse that comes with pushback. Pretrial officers don't want extra hearings, extra deadlines, or the judge asking awkward questions – so they'll often give you the nod just to shut it down. Let the lawyer be the angry referee; you stay clean and play it like you knew the score all along.

.5. The "Medical Necessity" Escape Route: Play the Health Card

Got a legit condition? Jackpot. Don't? Still useful – a little drama plus a doctor's note goes a long way. Medical appointments are the slickest excuse in the Pretrial playbook. Need to skip a piss test? Miss curfew for a "procedure"? Claim a sudden crisis and watch them squirm. Pretrial officers get nervous around anything that smells like liability, and a medical file is a liability grenade they'd rather not pull the pin on.

Levine Tactic: Make the illness sound complicated and expensive – the kind of thing that requires specialists, multiple visits, and a paper trail thick enough to make them quit reading. Doctors' notes, discharge papers, appointment confirmations – stack the paperwork so high they give up trying to second-guess you. You don't need to fool a doctor; you just need paperwork that looks official enough to make a clipboard warrior prefer shutting up to signing another form. Keep it believable, don't overdo the theatrics, and use the health card sparingly – it's golden, but it loses shine if you cry wolf every other week.

6. The "Volunteer Work" Facade: Play the Saint

Want to look like a reformed, upstanding citizen? Pretrial Officers eat up anything that makes you seem like you're turning your life around. Regular volunteer work is the golden ticket to making you look untouchable. Food banks, homeless shelters, whatever shit you can find. Not only does it look great in their reports, but you can also use it to tweak your schedule or bend curfew rules. After all, who's going to argue with a saint helping the less fortunate?

Levine Tactic: This is where you channel your inner Mother Teresa. Volunteer work is untouchable in the eyes of Pretrial Services–if you're feeding the homeless or saving stray kittens, they're going to look bad if they say no to a schedule tweak. Plus, it gives you extra moral high ground when you're asking for a little freedom. Make sure your "good deeds" are high profile enough to make them look like a jerk for questioning your commitment to charity. Volunteer on weekends, during curfew hours, or even at far-flung locations so you've got an ironclad excuse to be wherever you need to be.

7. The "Paper Trail Blitz" Strategy: Drown Them in Documents

Pretrial lives on paper. So become a fucking paper monster. Don't make them chase you – bury them. Flood their inbox, voicemail, and mailbox until the stack tips over and they give up. Every receipt, schedule change, friend's note, work log – document it, scan it, email it, text it. Make compliance such a full-time job for them that they can't be arsed to nitpick every single damn misstep.

Levine Tactic: This isn't neat record-keeping – it's warfare. Create so many status reports, confirmation emails, and appointment proofs that their system chokes. Send daily check-ins, weekly summaries, weird little updates about nothing – "Just confirming I shut the garage at 8:03 AM" – force them to file it or ignore it. When administrators are drowning, they stop policing. Small violations slide. Deadlines get missed in the inbox abyss. You want them busy playing paper Tetris while you live in the gaps. Keep it relentless, petty, and boring – the kind of busywork that breaks a bureaucracy's spine.

8. The "Technicality Trap": Out-Smart the System

Pretrial officers treat their rulebook like scripture – which is great, because scripture is riddled with loopholes. Every line of your conditions has wiggle room if you're willing to read the fine print and think like a bureaucrat. "Within the state"? Figure out how far "within" actually goes. "Evening hours"? Define what "evening" means on paper and you've bought yourself time. The system craves certainty; you exploit ambiguity.

Levine Tactic: Become obsessive. Read every clause until the wording bleeds. Flag vague phrases, file clarifying requests that sound like compliance but expand your options, and force them to either tighten the language (which buys you time) or leave it fuzzy and hope you behave. Push on the gray areas – not by breaking rules, but by stretching their literal meaning – and let the procedure junkies argue over punctuation while you live in the margins.

9. The "One Step Ahead" Plan: Preempt Their Surveillance

Pretrial officers love a good ambush. Random visits, surprise calls, pop-up piss tests–it's their version of fun. So screw that. Beat them to it. Check in before they can. Call early, send updates, act like you've got your shit so together it's almost suspicious. Be the guy who calls *them* to confirm you're following the rules. It'll drive them nuts, but it'll also make them lazy. No one wastes time chasing the golden child.

Levine Tactic: Flip the script. Make their job redundant. Every time they think about calling you, they already have three voicemails and two emails waiting. Drop casual little updates–"Just got home," "Heading to work," "Checking in per schedule." They'll start assuming you're always compliant because you *sound* like you are. You're not just following orders–you're writing them. Stay two steps ahead, and every "random" check becomes another moment where you already won the game.

10. The "Endearing Act" Ploy: Play the Human Card

Even Pretrial Officers have soft spots. Maybe it's their kids, their pets, or a particular sob story that hits home. Find out what they care about and casually weave it into conversation. If they start seeing you as a person, not just a file number, they might relax the reins a little.

Levine Tactic: It's time to humanize yourself. Pretrial Officers aren't robots (though they act like it), and if you can get them to relate to you as a person, you might earn some extra trust. Start with small talk–ask about their kids, their weekend plans, whatever gets them to drop their guard. Slowly weave in how your life parallels theirs. Once they start seeing you as someone with a "real life," the scrutiny might ease up a little. You're turning their professional detachment into personal empathy, and that's where the leash loosens.

Conclusion: The Art of Subtle Rule Bending

Dealing with Pretrial Services Officers is like playing a game where the rules are rigged against you–but that doesn't mean you can't find a way to win. It's all about subtlety, creativity, and knowing how to play the system without getting caught. Loopholes aren't just for lawyers–they're for anyone smart enough to see the gaps in the bureaucratic wall and slip through unnoticed.

Bullshit Lawyers Tell About Pretrial and Bail

1. We Can Get Bail, No Problem

Your Lawyer's Bullshit: Your lawyer will confidently say that getting you out on bail won't be an issue, like it's just a matter of filling out a few forms and waiting for the judge to rubber-stamp your release.

The Fucking Truth: Bail in federal court is a whole different beast. The Feds aren't just looking for cash; they want guarantees that you won't skip town. This means property bonds, restrictions, and possibly even home confinement. Bail could be denied outright if you're deemed a flight risk or a danger to the community. Getting out on bail is far from a given–it's a high-stakes negotiation.

2. The Prosecutor Will Be Fair in the Bail Request

Your Lawyer's Bullshit: Your lawyer might tell you the prosecutor will be reasonable when asking for bail. After all, this isn't some Hollywood drama–these are serious professionals who play by the rules.

The Fucking Truth: The prosecutor isn't interested in being fair–they want you locked up or tied down with so many conditions that you can barely breathe. They'll argue that you're a flight risk, a danger to society, or that your financial assets make it easy for you to disappear. Their job is to make sure you're either sitting in jail or sweating bullets trying to make bail.

3. If Bail Is Too High, We Can Always Appeal

Your Lawyer's Bullshit: Lawyers might reassure you that if the judge sets an unreasonably high bail, there are plenty of options to appeal and get it reduced. It's not a big deal, they'll say–just a little paperwork and another hearing.

The Fucking Truth: Appealing a bail decision is not as easy as your lawyer might make it sound. It's a long shot, requiring more hearings and more arguments in front of judges who rarely overturn their colleagues' decisions. If you think you'll just waltz in and get the bail lowered because it's "unfair," you're in for a rude awakening. The courts are stacked against you, and appeals often fall flat.

4. You'll Be Out in Time for Dinner

Your Lawyer's Bullshit: They'll tell you that you'll likely be released on bail by the end of the day, just in time to catch up on Netflix and relax with your family.

The Fucking Truth: Federal arraignments and bail hearings don't move at lightning speed. Even if the judge grants bail, there's paperwork to process, bonds to be signed, and sometimes delays in getting property approved for bond purposes. You'll be out in a couple of days if you're lucky. If not, you might be sitting in a cell much longer than you expected.

5. Once We Get Bail, Things Will Settle Down

Your Lawyer's Bullshit: They'll try to calm your nerves by saying that once you're out on bail, the dust will settle, and you'll have some breathing room. It's just a matter of getting past the first hurdle.

The Fucking Truth: Getting bail is just the beginning of the rollercoaster. The conditions attached to your release can be suffocating–ankle monitors, home confinement, constant check-ins with Pretrial Services. Every move you make is scrutinized; one misstep could land you back in a cell. Things won't settle down–they'll shift into a new level of tension and surveillance.

6. They're Just Here to Help!

Your Lawyer's Bullshit: Oh, of course, they're here to *help*. Help you feel like a grounded teenager under house arrest, that is. My lawyer tried to sell me the story that Pretrial Services Officers are basically legal life coaches, making sure everything runs smoothly. What a crock. These people are babysitters with a badge, watching your every move and just waiting for you to slip up. One toe out of line and their idea of "help" becomes "let me tattle to the court about every minor violation like you're a delinquent child."

The Fucking Truth: They're not helping. They're *monitoring*. Every single thing you do is being observed, and they're practically waiting for you to step out of line so they can document it with a smile. They're the hall monitors of the legal world, but instead of giving you a detention slip, they'll make sure the court knows if you dared to blink without permission. Their version of help is making sure you stay in the box they've put you in, and God forbid you even think about stepping outside it.

7. "They Want to See You Succeed."

Your Lawyer's Bullshit: Of course they are because they're your personal cheerleading squad, rooting for your redemption arc. My lawyer spun this beautiful tale about how Pretrial Services is just *so* *invested* in seeing me turn my life around. Reality check: they don't give a damn. Their job is to make sure you don't make *them* look bad. If you mess up, they're going to be the first ones to kick you under the bus to save their own skin. You're not their success story–you're a liability they need to keep on a tight leash.

The Fucking Truth: Let's be real–your success is about as important to them as the expiration date on their yogurt. Their only concern is making sure you don't embarrass them by screwing up. And if you do? They'll drop you like a bad habit. The idea that they're sitting there, hoping you'll "turn your life around," is laughable. They're more interested in crossing their T's and dotting their I's so they can move on to the next sorry case they have to babysit.

8. "They're Flexible if You Have a Good Reason."

Your Lawyer's Bullshit: Flexibility? Oh, sure. They're just brimming with understanding, right? My lawyer made it sound like Pretrial Officers are human beings who understand life happens. Ha! You could have the best excuse in the world–emergency surgery, alien invasion, whatever–and they'll still treat you like you're trying to game the system. Flexibility? The only thing flexible is how quickly they can tighten the leash around your neck.

The Fucking Truth: "Flexible" is a word they don't even understand. You could be walking out of the ER with a cast on your leg and an IV in your arm, and they'll still ask you why you didn't call them immediately. Forget about any leniency. Their only job is to make sure you stick to the rules–*their* rules– and they couldn't care less about your personal emergencies. Their version of "flexible" is giving you a five-minute grace period before slamming you with a violation report.

9. "They'll Respect Your Privacy."

Your Lawyer's Bullshit: Oh, sure, just like a TSA agent respects your privacy when they're rifling through your underwear at airport security. My lawyer swore that Pretrial Officers wouldn't dig into my personal life beyond the basics. What a load of crap. They want phone records, bank statements, work schedules–your life is an open book, and they're flipping through it like it's the latest trashy novel.

The Fucking Truth: Privacy? You might as well forget you ever had any. These people will dig so deep into your life, you'll feel like you're living in a fishbowl. They want *everything*–from where you're going, to who you're seeing, to what you're spending your money on. If they even *think* you're hiding something, they'll come down on you harder than a sledgehammer. So yeah, privacy? That's a luxury you lost the second they got involved.

10. "You'll Be Treated Like an Individual."

Your Lawyer's Bullshit: Right, because Pretrial Officers definitely see you as a unique snowflake, not just another case number. My lawyer promised I'd be treated with respect and empathy, that my personal situation would be taken into account. Guess what? You're about as unique to them as a fast-food burger–processed, packaged, and indistinguishable from the next guy. You're just another name in the stack of files they need to babysit.

The Fucking Truth: Forget individual treatment. You're just another cog in the system, a faceless case number in the bureaucratic machine. They don't care about your personal struggles, your background, or your circumstances. You're just a problem to be managed, and they'll do it with as little effort and empathy as possible. You're not getting the VIP treatment here; you're getting the "next!" treatment.

11. "They Won't Hold Every Little Thing Against You."

Your Lawyer's Bullshit: Sure, because Pretrial Officers are famously chill, right? My lawyer assured me that as long as I followed the *big* rules, they wouldn't sweat the small stuff. Reality check: they *love* sweating the small stuff. Miss a call by three minutes? That's going in the report. Forget to mention a tiny change in your schedule? Get ready for a "talk." They hold onto every little thing like it's some kind of sacred text.

The Fucking Truth: If you think they're not keeping track of every tiny misstep, you're dreaming. These people are like elephants–they never forget. Miss a phone check-in by five minutes? That's a "concern." Didn't report a slight change in your work schedule? That's a "violation." Every minor mistake gets documented and filed away for future use, and if you think they won't whip it out at the worst possible moment, you're in for a rude awakening.

The System's Rigged, So Rig It Back

Federal court isn't fair. It's a machine designed to steamroll defendants into submission. But if you're smart, savvy, and willing to fight back, there are ways to slow that machine down and maybe even turn it to your advantage. The arraignment and bail hearing are your first big tests, and with these hacks, you might just be able to tip the scales—if only for a little while.

Bail isn't about justice – it's about leverage. It's the system's way of testing how much pain you can take before you break. You're not buying freedom; you're renting it, month to month, from the same people who plan to take it away. The courtroom calls it "risk management," but it's really *fear management* – their fear of losing control, and your fear of losing everything. They slap a price tag on your existence and call it due process, knowing damn well most defendants can't afford the down payment on dignity.

What the judge calls "conditions," you'll come to know as invisible shackles – curfews, ankle bracelets, check-ins, restrictions, rules written by people who've never spent a night in a cell but love pretending they know what's best for you. And the kicker? Even when you win bail, you don't win freedom. You're just paying rent on a cage with better lighting. The Feds don't need to keep you behind bars when they can make you build your own.

Exhibit Five: The Bottom Line

> *Pretrial Services isn't freedom – it's freedom for sale. Bail is the down payment on your own supervision, and the Feds make damn sure you never stop paying. They'll slap a price tag on your existence, call it "reasonable," and then hand your leash to some clipboard warden who smiles while tightening it. You didn't buy freedom – you rented it, at interest, from the same system that plans to take it back.*

They call it "release," but it's really probation with paperwork. You might not be in a cell, but the walls just got invisible – made of curfews, ankle bracelets, check-ins, and fear. Every text, every mile, every missed call becomes a new form of evidence. They don't need bars when they've got compliance. They don't need guards when you've learned to police yourself.

The fucking truth? You're not out. You're managed. Bail bought you breathing room, not liberty. Pretrial bought them time to finish the job. You're still property of the machine – just repackaged for public consumption. The system didn't free you; it franchised your captivity.

Next Up – Exhibit Six: Pre Trial Motions

Think arraignment was the first round? Nah, that was just the intro. Now comes the paperwork war – a legal knife fight fought with motions, delays, and bullshit strategy. This is where they bury you before the trial even begins.

EXHIBIT SIX

Pre Trial Motions

The Courtroom Conspiracy - Illusions of Justice

The courtroom door hasn't even closed behind you yet, and already the battle lines are being drawn. The federal prosecutor, with their badge of justice gleaming, is a shark in the water, circling, waiting for the right moment to lunge. Across the aisle, your defense attorney is scrambling—reviewing documents, filing motions, looking for any loophole that could derail this train before it gains full steam. This, my friend, is where the real fight begins: Pretrial Motions and Strategy. In federal court, the trial itself is almost an afterthought.

Pretrial Motions and Strategy

The real bloodletting happens in the pretrial phase. Here, where the government unveils its supposedly airtight case, both sides start to throw legal grenades. Each motion is a carefully calculated maneuver to gain the upper hand, slow down the other side, or eliminate their most damaging evidence. You think the trial is going to be a circus? Pretrial motions are where the clowns take off their makeup and start throwing knives.

Pretrial motions are, in essence, weapons. And strategy? Strategy is everything. Without it, you're a sitting duck, waiting for the feds to turn you into another statistic on their victory sheet.

The Defense Gambit: Motion Mayhem

For the defense, pretrial motions are like loading up a slingshot and hoping to take down a giant. Your attorney, if they have any sense, knows that this is where the battle can be won or lost. Federal prosecutors come armed with a staggering amount of resources, evidence, and legal clout, but the right motion, at the right time, could strike a blow so deep that the prosecution will never recover.

Defense lawyers have a toolbox full of motions to file at this stage, each one designed to chip away at the government's case, and each filed with the hope of walking you out the door before a single juror ever lays eyes on you. Think of it as guerrilla warfare in the courtroom.

Here are the heavy hitters:

1. **Motion to Suppress**
   This is the defense's biggest gun. The argument here is simple: the evidence that the prosecution is planning to use against you was obtained illegally. It could be a wiretap that wasn't authorized, or maybe the feds stormed your office without a proper warrant, grabbing files like kids at a candy store. If the judge grants this motion, that juicy evidence they were going to parade in front of the jury? Gone. It evaporates into thin air, and the prosecutor is left holding an empty bag.

2. **Motion to Dismiss**

It's rare, but it's bold—a request for the judge to throw the entire case out before it even starts. Your lawyer argues that the charges are either legally insufficient, baseless, or that the government has overstepped its bounds. This motion almost never works, but when it does, it's like hitting a grand slam in the bottom of the ninth. You're walking out, not because you're innocent, but because the prosecution couldn't even make it to the starting line.

3. **Motion for Discovery**

Think of this as the poker player's motion. Your lawyer wants to see every single card the government is holding. From surveillance footage to witness statements, financial records, and even emails you thought were long deleted—this motion demands the entire deck be put on the table. The more they get, the more chances they have to poke holes in the government's case or find evidence that exonerates you.

4. **Motion in Limine**

This motion is a preemptive strike, asking the judge to rule certain evidence out of bounds before the trial even starts. It could be that your prior criminal record is irrelevant to the current charges, or that a particular piece of evidence is too inflammatory and would prejudice the jury. A successful motion in limine can keep damaging evidence from ever seeing the light of day.

5. **Motion to Change Venue**

Your lawyer might file this one if they believe the trial location will result in a biased jury. Maybe you're a local celebrity in town for the wrong reasons, or maybe the media has turned your case into a spectacle. If the judge agrees, you'll find yourself on the road, heading to a new courthouse far away from the frenzy.

6. **Motion for Continuance**

Also known as the delay tactic. Your attorney might need more time to prepare, to gather evidence, or to sort through the mountain of discovery. The prosecution wants to move fast, but your lawyer wants to buy time. The longer the trial is delayed, the more chances there are for something unexpected to happen—witnesses forget details, evidence weakens, or a new strategy is born.

Tactic #1: The Kitchen Sink

Some defense attorneys will file every possible motion they can think of, hoping that something sticks. This is the "throw everything at the wall" approach, designed to overwhelm the prosecution and, ideally, distract them long enough for them to make a mistake. It's chaotic, it's messy, but when the stakes are high, chaos can sometimes be your best weapon.

Tactic #2: The Surgical Strike

Other defense attorneys take a more calculated approach, waiting for the right moment to file the right motion. They'll hold back their best shot until the prosecution has laid out its case, then drop a motion so precise and devastating that it leaves the government reeling. It's like waiting to play your ace in the hole—and when it works, it's a thing of beauty.

Prosecution's Power Play: The Government's Response

Of course, the prosecution isn't just going to sit around and let the defense tear their case apart. The government comes loaded with its own arsenal of pretrial motions, designed to block the defense at every turn. Federal prosecutors are like prizefighters, trained to anticipate every punch and counterpunch with brutal efficiency.

Here's the government's playbook:

1. **Motion to Admit Evidence**
   The government wants everything on the table. If they've got wiretaps, surveillance footage, or financial records, they're filing a motion to make sure it's all admissible. The prosecutor will argue that this evidence is critical, and if the defense tries to keep it out, the government will fight tooth and nail to make sure it's heard by the jury.

2. **Motion to Exclude Defense Evidence**
   The prosecution loves a double standard. While they want every shred of evidence against you admitted, they'll do their best to block anything that could help you. If your lawyer has evidence of police misconduct or testimony that shows you weren't even in the same state

when the crime happened, expect the prosecutor to file a motion to exclude it. They'll argue it's irrelevant, prejudicial, or improperly obtained.

3. **Motion to Strike**

This is the prosecutor's cleanup crew. If something slips into the record that shouldn't be there —a damning accusation of misconduct, a stray comment about their tactics–they'll file a motion to strike it from the record. It's as if it never happened, and the jury will be instructed to forget they ever heard it.

4. **Motion for Protective Order**

The government might file this if they're trying to keep certain evidence out of the hands of the defense–at least until the right time. They could claim that releasing it too soon would jeopardize an ongoing investigation or compromise witness safety. It's a way for the prosecution to control the flow of information and keep the defense in the dark as long as possible.

Prosecutor's Strategy: Overwhelm and Conquer

The prosecution's goal in this phase is simple: overwhelm the defense with a mountain of evidence and motions, keep their own evidence rock solid, and block the defense at every turn. They don't just want to win–they want to crush any hope of the defense even mounting a real challenge.

The Mind Game: Strategy in Motion

Legal battles are fought with paper, but they're won in the mind. Pretrial motions aren't just about legal arguments; they're about *strategy*. When to file, what to file, and how to frame your argument can make all the difference. Timing is everything. Drop a motion too soon, and the government has time to adjust. File it too late, and the judge might get irritated and brush it aside. The best defense attorneys know this is more like a game of chess than checkers.

1. Delay Tactics

The defense can buy time with a barrage of motions. Every motion delays the trial, giving the defense more time to build their case or wear down the government. Prosecutors thrive on quick resolutions–dragging things out makes them nervous.

2. Smokescreen Motion

This is where a defense attorney files a motion with no real expectation of winning, purely to distract the prosecution. While they're busy fighting this phantom issue, the real attack is being prepared from another angle. It's like lighting a fire in the distance so the enemy runs towards it, leaving their base undefended.

3. Leverage Building

Sometimes motions are filed not for immediate victory, but to gain leverage. Maybe the motion to suppress won't succeed, but it weakens the government's confidence, forcing them to come to the negotiating table. The defense can use this uncertainty to extract a better plea deal or dismissal of charges.

Final Thought: Survival of the Bold

Pretrial motions are the calm before the storm—the place where sharp lawyers earn their keep. Every motion filed, every argument made is a chance to change the course of the case. It's not about truth or justice; it's about survival. Only the bold, the cunning, and the relentless make it through this phase unscathed. If your lawyer knows how to work the system, you might just find yourself walking

What the Defendant Can and Should Do: Surviving the Legal Crossfire

Now, as the defendant, you're not just some passive observer watching your fate unfold like a bad TV drama. No, this is your life on the line, and you better get your head in the game. Federal court isn't a place for the meek. You might think all the legal mumbo-jumbo is above your pay grade, but during this pretrial blitzkrieg, your involvement is critical—whether it's in front of the judge or in that dingy backroom with your lawyer.

1.   **Educate Yourself**

     Don't just sit there nodding along like a damn bobblehead while your lawyer rambles off Latin phrases and obscure case law. You need to know what's happening. Ask questions. Force your attorney to explain every motion they're filing, why they're filing it, and what they hope to accomplish. If you don't understand, speak up. This isn't the time to be shy or polite. Your future is on the line, and blind trust is the fastest route to federal housing with barred windows.

2. **Stay Involved**

This isn't the time to mentally check out and let your lawyer steer the ship. You need to be as involved as possible. Review every document they send you. Show up to every meeting and court appearance ready to participate. Be proactive. Have your lawyer explain the motions and strategies they're using. Push back if something doesn't sound right. Your lawyer might be the expert, but no one knows your situation better than you.

3. **Maintain Your Cool**

This process is designed to wear you down. The government will throw every piece of incriminating evidence they have at you, and some of it might be flat-out lies or exaggerated nonsense. It's easy to panic. But don't. Freaking out in front of the judge or during a meeting with your lawyer is only going to make things worse. Keep your composure, even when the pressure builds. Trust me, they want you to crack, to get desperate, to plead out. Don't give them the satisfaction.

4. **Gather Your Own Evidence**

Your lawyer isn't Sherlock Holmes, and the truth is, they're probably juggling 20 other cases while half-heartedly working on yours. So help them out. If there's evidence that can prove your innocence, gather it. Find witnesses, documents, photos—whatever you've got. Feed it to your attorney. They won't thank you, but it could save your skin.

5. **Trust Your Gut**

If something feels off about the way your lawyer is handling the case, it probably is. Lawyers are supposed to defend you, but some will take the path of least resistance, meaning they'll push you into a plea deal to avoid the hard work of trial. If you feel like your lawyer's selling you out, say something. This is your life, not theirs. You've got the right to push back, to demand more, or even fire them if necessary. And don't be afraid to get a second opinion. Better safe than staring down 20 years in the clink.

In short, don't just sit there like a deer in the headlights while the legal system chews you up. Stay engaged, be vocal, and don't let these overpaid suits steer you into oblivion. It's your fight—start acting like it.

Lie #1 "We'll file a motion to dismiss–this whole thing could go away."

Oh, the sweet sound of false hope. Your lawyer will hype up the motion to dismiss like it's the legal equivalent of a get-out-of-jail-free card. Don't bet on it. The chances of a judge tossing the case before trial are about as likely as Elvis showing up in court to testify. The feds didn't spend months or years building a case against you just to have it thrown out because your lawyer wrote a cute little motion. That motion to dismiss? It's just a procedural blip on the radar–nothing more.

Lie #2 "We can suppress most of the evidence–they won't have a case."

Suppress the evidence? Good luck with that. Your lawyer will act like the evidence is hanging by a thread, just waiting to be knocked out with a well-placed motion. Wrong again. The feds are pros at covering their tracks. By the time you're in pre-trial, they've got all their ducks in a row. Sure, maybe a scrap of evidence gets tossed, but the real meat of their case? That's sticking around, and it's going to hit you like a freight train when trial day comes.

Lie #3 "We'll file motions that will drag this out–you've got plenty of time."

Your lawyer might tell you that pre-trial motions are a great way to delay the inevitable, buy you some time to figure things out. What a joke. All those motions do is slow down the car crash that's coming. You might get a few extra months of freedom, but the feds have all the time in the world. They're not in a rush, and every day that goes by, they're sharpening their knives. Pre-trial delays don't mean the case is getting better–it just means the noose is tightening.

Lie #4 "Don't worry, the prosecution's case is weak–they'll fold."

Here's another line they love to throw your way, but the truth is, the prosecution isn't playing poker. They didn't indict you because they have a 'weak case.' By the time you're staring down federal charges, they've got enough evidence to bury you. The feds don't bluff. Even if your lawyer says the case is shaky, remember, they've got stacks of evidence hidden away, waiting for just the right moment to drop the hammer. Thinking the government will fold is a fantasy–this isn't a game they're looking to lose.

Lie #5 "We can settle this quietly with a plea deal later."

Oh, how reassuring. Your lawyer might give you the impression that once all the motions are filed and things get rolling, the prosecutor will suddenly feel generous and offer you a sweet little deal. Don't hold your breath. By the time pre-trial motions are in play, the government is gunning for a win. They don't want a deal–they want a conviction. Sure, plea deals happen, but it's not because you've filed a few pre-trial motions. It's because they know they've already got you cornered, and the deal they offer will feel more like a chokehold than a handshake.

Lie #6 "We'll challenge their experts and win the case that way."

You might hear that your lawyer will rip apart the government's expert witnesses, making it sound like a slam dunk. Here's the reality: federal expert witnesses are professionals–hardened, credible, and often untouchable. They're brought in because they know their stuff, and the judge is likely to trust their testimony over anything your lawyer throws at them. Challenging experts is a shot in the dark–it's not the silver bullet your lawyer is promising.

Lie #7 "We're building a defense that will blow them away."

Ah, the grand finale–your lawyer says they've got a defense strategy that's going to shock the courtroom, leaving the prosecution scrambling. The only problem? It's not true. In reality, most defense strategies in federal court are variations of the same themes: poke holes in the prosecution's case, throw doubt on the evidence, and hope for the best. There's no magical defense that's going to flip the script in your favor. If you're banking on your lawyer to blow the prosecution away, you're in for a rude awakening.

Exhibit Six: The Bottom Line

> Pretrial motions ain't about justice – they're about paperwork warfare. Every motion is a bullet, every hearing a chess move, and every lawyer in that room's got their own agenda. You think this is where you prove innocence? Hell no. This is where they grind you down, one filing, one delay, one fake smile at a time, till you're too tired to fight back.

The prosecution ain't playing fair – they're building a coffin outta procedure and calling it due process. Your lawyer ain't your savior – they're just trying to look busy enough to justify the bill. And the judge? They're the referee who already picked the winning team before the game even started. Every word in that courtroom's a setup, every deadline's a trap, and every "motion denied" is just the system reminding you who runs the show.

So don't buy the bullshit about "strategy." This ain't chess – it's demolition. The government's tearing down your defense brick by brick while your own lawyer pretends it's part of the plan. The only "motion" that matters is the one where they move you from the holding cell to the courtroom, back to the van, and straight into the machine.

The fucking truth? You're not defending yourself – you're surviving a process built to prove you guilty before the trial even starts. Pretrial motions aren't justice in motion; they're bureaucracy on steroids. The system doesn't need a verdict when it's already broken you in the paperwork phase.

Next Up – Exhibit Seven: Public Defenders

You thought the system was your enemy? Wait till you meet your *defender*. Up next is the biggest con of all: the lie that your court-appointed lawyer is on your side. Spoiler alert – they're not. They're underpaid, overworked, and half the time, already halfway sold out. If you thought the prosecution was out to bury you, just wait 'til you realize your own lawyer brought the shovel.

EXHIBIT SEVEN

Public Defender Conspiracy

The System's Proof It Pretends to Case

You don't pick your public defender. They appear, like a half-baked magic trick, pulled from the depths of bureaucratic hell. One second you're standing alone in your shackles, the next – poof – some stranger strolls up with a wrinkled suit, a stained folder, and that classic dead-in-the-eyes look of a man who's lost every argument he's ever had, including with his own reflection.

Welcome To The Cheapest Defense Money Never Had To Buy.

This is your "counsel." This is the legal warrior assigned to "fight for your rights." And by fight, we mean shuffle paper, whisper some vague bullshit about "options," and then urge you to throw yourself on the mercy of a court that doesn't have any. They introduce themselves like you're supposed to feel safe: **"Hi, I'm your public defender." Translation: *You're fucked.***

You look at them and you can already tell – they haven't read your case. Hell, they probably got your file on the elevator ride up. And you're expected to trust this government-issued stranger with your future? Your freedom? Your entire goddamn life?

Lost in the Shuffle, Doomed by the Docket

These aren't lawyers. They're cattle herders. And you're just the next cow mooing its way through the slaughterhouse. They've got forty cases to "handle" today – which means four minutes for you, tops. Don't waste their time with questions like "What should I do?" or "Is this serious?" You'll get a generic answer that sounds like it was printed off a legal fortune cookie.

"Let's just wait and see what the prosecutor says."
 "Maybe we can negotiate something later."
 "Don't worry, you probably won't do much time."

They're not reading the playbook – they *are* the playbook. Prewritten. Prepackaged. Pre-defeated.

And while you're panicking, trying to piece together what the hell is going on, your "defender" is busy juggling twenty other clients at once, nodding at the judge like a goddamn bobblehead, and whispering to the Prosecutor like they're planning brunch, not your future incarceration.

Don't Worry, They're Just as Good as a Private Attorney

Yeah, sure they are. And a tricycle's just as good as a Harley if you squint hard enough.

You walk in thinking your public defender's gonna pull some fucking courtroom miracle—storm in with righteous fury, slam a briefcase full of justice on the table, and save your ass. Newsflash: that cape you're picturing? It's torn, coffee-stained, and dragging behind him like roadkill. This ain't Superman—it's a tired office temp in a rented suit who's been beaten down so many times he calls it "routine."

My so-called "lawyer" told me the Public Defender's Office was full of dedicated fighters. Said it like he was handing me a sword and shield. What I got instead was a burned-out paper pusher who couldn't find my file without checking three others. He called me "buddy" twice before remembering my name. And this was the man standing between me and federal prison. Fantastic.

They'll smile, shake your hand, and tell you they've "reviewed your case." Translation: they skimmed the first page while waiting for the elevator. Yeah, they went to law school. So did every half-drunk idiot on late-night infomercials pushing credit repair scams. Doesn't mean they're cut out to save you from the guillotine. When you've got a hundred defendants and one overworked brain cell, "justice" becomes a punchline. These people aren't strategizing—they're triaging. You're not a client; you're one of the casualties.

And when it's your turn, don't expect fireworks. Expect a shrug, a mumble, and maybe a pat on the shoulder if you're lucky. That's your defense: a sympathy tap and a plea deal. Because the whole point isn't to fight for you—it's to keep the conveyor belt moving. Fast, quiet, and efficient.

The Caseload from Hell

You think your public defender's got time for you? Get the fuck outta here. These poor bastards are buried. I'm talkin' avalanche-level caseloads. Stack on stack on stack. They ain't prepping for your trial—they're *surviving* the week. And here's the twisted part: these are the same people who are supposed to protect your constitutional rights. They're your so-called shield against the government's legal sledgehammer. But they're so overloaded they can't even remember your fucking name by Tuesday. That ain't because they're lazy—it's because they're drowning. Every day is a legal triage, and you're just another body bleeding on the floor.

Try reaching them between hearings. You'll get a 30-second voicemail or a rushed-ass email with some bullet points written like a grocery list. Need to talk about your sentencing exposure? A guideline issue? Some nuance in your case? Good luck. You think they're gonna break that down for you in detail? They don't have time to break down a sandwich.

So when people tell you the system's fair 'cause "at least you get a lawyer," remember this: sure, you *get* one–but you don't *have* one. Not really. You've got a body in a suit, doing their best to play catch-up while the courtroom clock eats your life.

They'll Take the Time to Understand Your Case

Yeah, and the Easter Bunny's my bail bondsman. That's the sales pitch they give you when they're trying to calm you down: *"Don't worry, your public defender will really take the time to understand your case."* The fuck they will. These people don't have time to understand their own lunch orders. They're drowning in files, running on fumes, and praying nobody asks them an actual question they can't Google in the hallway.

Your case is a name on a manila folder buried in a stack tall enough to block sunlight. They're not "digging into" anything–they're skimming, guessing, and winging it. The "prep" you get is five minutes in a hallway that smells like fear and old coffee. That's where they drop their legal wisdom: *"We're gonna try to work something out."* Translation: *"You're taking a plea whether you like it or not."*

You won't get strategy. You'll get survival. They'll nod like they're listening while secretly praying your case doesn't blow up in open court. They'll ask you a few surface questions, maybe jot a note or two if they're feeling ambitious. You'll try to bring up that one critical detail, that tiny inconsistency that could flip the whole case–watch how fast their eyes glaze over. They don't have room in their head for nuance. They're not building defenses; they're building excuses. You're expecting Perry Mason. What you get is a part-time social worker with a law degree and no sleep..

The "Plea Deal Conveyor Belt"

Alright, let's get real about plea deals—because in federal court, that's the main event. You ain't walking into a courtroom to fight shit. You're walking into a factory where the product is guilt, and your signature is just another part on the belt. Public defenders don't push you toward trial—they push you toward paperwork. They won't come out and *say* "take the deal," but they'll sure lean hard enough that you get the message. Fastest way to clear their schedule? Get you to plead out and move on.

It's not betrayal—it's burnout. They ain't got the time or firepower to fight tooth and nail for every single case. Trials take time. Trials take work. Trials take energy—and that's in damn short supply. The system ain't built for fights; it's built for fast closures. And fast means deals. Guilty pleas keep the wheels spinning, and if you catch a lighter sentence in the process, well, lucky you.

So if your lawyer is sliding a plea across the table like it's your only way out, it's because–let's be honest –it *is*. Not because you're guilty. Not because it's right. But because the system runs on deals, and you're just another fucking gear in the machine.

"You'll Get Personalized Attention"

Really. The idea that a Federal Public Defender's gonna hold your hand, walk you through the process, and treat your case like it's the center of their universe? Pure bullshit. My lawyer told me I'd be treated like a human being, like someone who *matters*. What I got was a rushed five-minute handjob in a hallway that smelled like mop water and regret.

"Personalized attention" in the public defender world means they remember your name long enough to not call you someone else in front of the judge. You might get a quick call, if you're lucky. Half the time, they're scanning your file while talking to three other people. You ask a question? You'll get a half-answer and a pat on the back like that somehow solves shit.

Even if they gave a damn–and some of them do–they're drowning. There's no room for deep dives, no time to actually *listen*. You're on a moving belt with a hundred others, and the goal is to get you through the system without jamming the machine. That's the job. Not justice. Not compassion. Just survival.

They Have the Same Resources as the Prosecution

Now *this* one had me damn near choking. My lawyer actually said–with a straight face–that the Federal Public Defender's Office had the same kind of resources as the prosecution. Yeah, and crackheads have the same dietitian as Olympic athletes. The Feds got the FBI, ATF, DEA,, and enough investigators to fill a football stadium. Your public defender? They got an exhausted paralegal and maybe–*maybe*–some burned-out alcoholic investigator workin' three counties and livin' out of their car.

Resources? Please. You'll be lucky if they can afford an expert witness that isn't some dude with a mail-order PhD and a Gmail address. The government rolls into court like it's goin' to war–heavy weapons, full intel, air support. Your side shows up with a butter knife and a folder someone half-read in the elevator.

And look, they'll *try*. They'll file the motions, beg the judge for money, scramble to find someone credible. But it's never a fair fight. You're outgunned before the bell even rings. The prosecution's building a case with a SWAT team—your defense is held together with duct tape and caffeine.

So yeah, when they tell you it's an "even playing field," just know—you're in a heavyweight fight with your hands tied behind your back, and they brought brass knuckles. Good luck with that.

The Reality Check: They're Trying, But the System Isn't Built for You

Let's get this straight: Federal Public Defenders aren't the villains here. They're some of the hardest-working, most burned-out people in the building. But the system? That's the bastard. It's not built for them to win – it's built to process human beings like factory meat. They're not knights; they're soldiers in a losing war, patching holes on a sinking ship while the courtroom orchestra plays on.

They're buried in cases, short on time, and running on caffeine and despair. You want miracles? Go to church. These people are just trying to keep the machine from chewing you up completely before lunch. So when someone tells you, *"Public defenders are just as good as private attorneys,"* go ahead and nod – then start bracing yourself. Because they'll fight for you, sure. But in a rigged game like this, "fighting" just means losing slower.

They're forced to work within constraints that make it nearly impossible to deliver the kind of defense they wish they could provide. So, while they'll throw out these little lies to keep you calm and keep things moving, it's not out of malice—it's out of necessity. They're doing their best to keep you from panicking while they desperately try to hold the whole mess together with duct tape and good intentions.

Biggest Lies Told by Public Defenders

You may have seen a version of them before in one of my other books because lies are lies and you can't make this shit up! If you have good for you, if you haven't burn these into your brain and remember them

1. We've Got This Under Control!"

The Lie: Oh, really? Nothing screams *"under control"* like a public defender buried under 150 active cases, 37 pending motions, and a stack of discovery that could choke a horse. They'll sit across from you with that professional calm – the kind that looks like confidence but smells like caffeine and panic – and tell you your case is "handled." Handled *how*? Like a dumpster fire someone's trying to stomp out in flip-flops.

Reality Check: The only thing your public defender's got under control is their *blood pressure meds.* These folks are triaging chaos. They're juggling so many cases that Rule 1.3 on "diligence" is now more of a suggestion than an obligation. Your Sixth Amendment right to effective counsel? That's theoretical at best – like Bigfoot or an honest prosecutor. When they say, *"We've got this,"* what they really mean is, *"We're praying the prosecutor's too lazy to show up and the judge forgets your name."*

They're not building a defense; they're managing a schedule. You're not a strategy – you're a time slot between arraignments and sentencing hearings. The legal term for that? **Judicial efficiency.** The human term? **You're fucked.**

2. The Prosecutor's Offer is Fair."

The Lie: Oh, sure, it's "fair", because the prosecutor's job is to make life easier for you, right? Public defenders love to sell this line when they want you to take the plea deal. They'll smile and tell you it's the best deal you're going to get, even if it means admitting to something you didn't do or getting slammed with penalties you barely understand.

Reality Check: That plea deal is about as "fair" as a rigged carnival game. The prosecution isn't interested in fairness–they want a quick conviction, and your public defender just wants to clear your case off their to-do list. If they can convince you to roll over and plead, it's one less headache for them. Fair? It's not about justice; it's about convenience. For them, not you.

3. A Trial Would Be Too Risky

The Lie: Oh, absolutely. Trials are terrifying, unpredictable, and only for the brave–or so your public defender will tell you. They'll list all the reasons why going to trial is a bad idea: juries are unreliable, judges are harsh, and the evidence might not sway in your favor. Translation? A trial means actual work, and they don't have the time or resources to prepare for it. Better to scare you into taking a plea deal than risk burning the midnight oil.

Reality Check: The real risk isn't the jury—it's whether your overworked public defender has the bandwidth to put together a proper defense. Trials take time and effort, and time isn't something they have. Their reluctance to go to trial has more to do with their caseload than with your chances of winning.

4. Don't Worry, We'll File That Motion

The Lie: Oh, sure. They'll file that motion to suppress evidence, request discovery, or dismiss charges. Just as soon as they finish filing the dozen other motions they've promised their other clients. Motions sound proactive, and public defenders love to promise them because it makes you think they're on top of things. But after they leave the room, that motion might sit on their desk, collecting dust, while they scramble to keep up with everything else.

Reality Check: Unless you're nagging them like a broken record, that motion might never see the light of day. Public defenders are spread too thin, and your motion isn't exactly a top priority. If it gets filed, it'll probably be rushed, generic, and maybe even half-baked. Sure, they'll file it—eventually—but don't hold your breath waiting for it to move mountains.

7. We'll Fight This All the Way

The Lie: Oh, absolutely. They're ready for war. It's going to be an epic legal battle, and they're prepared to fight for you until the bitter end. They'll go toe-to-toe with the prosecution, dismantle their case, and leave them begging for mercy.

Reality Check: "All the way" usually ends at the first plea offer. Public defenders are pressured to resolve cases quickly, and the system isn't built for drawn-out battles. They'll fight as much as they can within the time and resources they have, but don't expect a courtroom drama. The harsh truth is that "all the way" often means "just far enough to push you toward a plea".

8. The Judge Will Be Fair

The Lie: Of course, the judge will be fair. This is the justice system, and it's all about fairness and impartiality, right? Your public defender will assure you that the judge will carefully weigh the facts and give you a fair shake.

Reality Check: Judges are human, and fairness is sometimes more of a suggestion than a reality. Some judges are tougher on defendants with public defenders, seeing them as part of the "system" rather than advocates for justice. Your public defender knows this but won't tell you because, well, what are they supposed to say? "The judge is going to fry you"? That doesn't exactly inspire confidence.

9. You're Our Top Priority

The Lie: You are the center of their universe! Your public defender will make it sound like your case is the one they're dedicating all their time and energy to. You're their star client, and nothing else matters.

Reality Check: You're not the top priority. You're one of dozens of cases, and they're just trying to survive the day without losing their mind. They'll do their best, but you're a file in a pile, not a VIP. Their attention is divided, and while they'll try to give you what you need, the reality is you're just one more person in an endless sea of defendants.

10. "You're Better Off With Me Than a Private Lawyer

The Lie: Public defenders love to tell you they're just as good—if not better—than any expensive private lawyer. They'll say private lawyers are just in it for the money and don't have the courtroom experience that public defenders do. Why waste your hard-earned cash when you can have a dedicated, experienced attorney for free?

Reality Check: Dedicated? Sure, to surviving their caseload, not necessarily to you. Public defenders may be experienced, but they're also buried under a mountain of cases and barely have the time to glance at yours. Private lawyers, for all their faults, can at least give you the one-on-one attention your case deserves. While public defenders do their best with what they have, "better off" is a stretch when they're juggling a hundred clients and your case is just another file in the stack.

Loopholes for Dealing with Public Defenders

When you find yourself strapped for cash and stuck with a public defender, you're not entirely powerless. While the system may be stacked against you, there are a few loopholes and strategies you can use to get the most out of your overworked attorney. Here's how to slip through the cracks and make sure your public defender doesn't leave you hanging.

1. The "Proactive Client" Trick

Public defenders are juggling more cases than an over-caffeinated circus performer. So what do you do? Be the squeaky wheel. Public defenders tend to focus their limited time on clients who are proactive and constantly in touch. Make sure you stay on their radar by regularly following up–politely but persistently–on your case. Send them emails, ask for updates, and remind them of important details. If you're out of sight, you're out of mind. The more visible and vocal you are, the harder it'll be for them to accidentally overlook your case.

2. The "Documentation Avalanche"

One way to make your public defender's life easier (and to ensure they give your case the attention it deserves) is to do some of the grunt work yourself. Organize all the documents, records, and evidence related to your case. Hand over a neatly compiled file, complete with timelines, witness contact info, and any relevant legal research you can dig up. The more you do for them, the less they'll have to scramble at the last minute. And if you're doing their homework for them, they're less likely to screw it up. Plus, this shows you're serious and engaged with your own defense–something they'll appreciate amid their chaos.

3. The "Law Library Hustle"

Here's a loophole you might not have considered: educate yourself on your case. Public defenders won't have the time to explain every nuance of your legal situation, so head to the law library (or online legal resources) and dig into the statutes, case law, and legal defenses that apply to your case. When you meet with your public defender, you'll be armed with knowledge and specific questions. This not only saves time but also signals to your attorney that you're no ordinary passive client—you're invested in your defense, which might just motivate them to take your case more seriously.

4. The "Expert in Your Back Pocket" Gambit

If your case requires expert testimony or analysis, but your public defender claims they don't have the resources to hire anyone, don't give up just yet. Reach out to local universities, legal aid groups, or nonprofits. You might find a law student, professor, or pro bono expert willing to lend a hand. Once you've found someone willing to testify or provide a professional opinion, present this option to your public defender. They'll appreciate the legwork, and it can tip the scales in your favor, especially if you're offering up a credible expert that didn't come out of their meager budget.

5. The "Involve the Court" Play

If you suspect your public defender is stretched too thin and not giving your case the attention it deserves, you have a right to bring it up in court. You can file a motion for substitution of counsel if your public defender's performance is lacking. Judges know that public defenders are overburdened, and they're sometimes sympathetic to these motions—especially if you can make a reasonable case that your current attorney is unable to provide effective assistance. It's a risky move, but if done tactfully, it could land you a fresh attorney with more time to focus on your case.

6. The "Public Pressure" Angle

Public defenders don't operate in a vacuum—they've got bosses, supervisors, and higher-ups to answer to. If your case is particularly high-profile or carries significant public interest, use that to your advantage. Garner media attention if possible—whether it's through contacting local reporters, organizing community support, or utilizing social media. Public defenders and their offices are often more motivated when they know there's a spotlight on their performance. It's not exactly subtle, but public pressure can be a powerful motivator for them to step up their game.

7. The "Private Attorney for Specific Tasks" Loophole

Even if you're stuck with a public defender, that doesn't mean you can't hire a private attorney for specific tasks—if you can scrape together some funds. Maybe you can't afford a full defense, but you can pay a lawyer for a single consultation, a legal strategy session, or to assist with a particular motion. If you can get a private attorney to write up a strong motion or give advice on a key part of your case, you can hand that over to your public defender and make their job easier. Think of it as supplementing your defense with extra firepower.

8. The "Mitigation Package" Strategy

Public defenders are often too busy to focus on anything other than the core aspects of your defense, meaning they may not have time to prepare a mitigation package for sentencing. This package can include letters of support, evidence of rehabilitation, documentation of mental health treatment, and any other factors that could lead to a reduced sentence. Take matters into your own hands and prepare a mitigation package yourself. Present it to your public defender—they can use it in negotiations or during sentencing to potentially reduce your punishment. Judges love a well-documented redemption arc.

9. The "Conditional Plea" Maneuver

If your public defender is pushing you toward a plea deal, but you're hesitant to give up your rights entirely, consider negotiating a conditional plea. This allows you to plead guilty while reserving the right to appeal certain legal issues—like the admissibility of evidence or a particular ruling that you and your attorney disagree with. You'll avoid a drawn-out trial while still keeping some options open down the road. It's a middle ground that can sometimes satisfy both the public defender's need for efficiency and your desire to preserve your legal rights.

10. The "Humanize Yourself" Approach

Public defenders are human, too, and they've been worn down by endless hours of dealing with difficult, disinterested clients. Humanize yourself to your public defender—let them know your story, your background, and why this case matters so much to you. Establish a personal connection, and they may be more likely to put in a little extra effort on your behalf. You're not just a file number; you're someone with a future on the line. By making them care about you as a person, you can inspire them to dig deeper than they might have otherwise.

Exhibit Seven: The Bottom Line

Look, if you're stuck with a public defender, stop dreaming about some legal fairy tale where they swoop in and save your ass. That ain't happening. But that doesn't mean you just roll over and take whatever bullshit comes next. The system's rigged, yeah–but cracks still exist. You gotta find 'em and wedge yourself in. Ask questions. Read everything. Double-check the discovery. Be the biggest pain in the ass they've got–because if you don't fight for yourself, no one else will.

The public defender ain't your enemy–they're just in survival mode. So treat it like what it is: damage control. Don't sit around expecting strategy sessions and custom-tailored defenses. That's for the folks with money. You? You're playing chess with missing pieces.

If you're lucky, you'll get a defender who's got enough fuel left to read your file, show up on time, and not totally tank your case. If you're not lucky? Hope you're good at laundry, 'cause you'll be rollin' orange in no time. That's not shade on them–it's just Reality Check. The system ain't built for justice. It's built for throughput. Volume. Optics. Shit that looks like help but smells like neglect.

So here's the play: push. Ask. Demand. Don't be polite about your freedom. Be the motherfucker who won't shut up. And even then, don't expect magic. You're running uphill in the rain, and half your team's asleep on the bench. The courtroom ain't a place for hope–it's a place for hustle. Justice? She ain't blind. She's exhausted, overbooked, and reading your case summary with one eye open and a coffee stain on the page. That's what you're up against. Now act like it

Next Up – Exhibit Eight: My Lawyer Promised Probation

You ever been lied to with a straight face? Get ready. Next up is the fairy tale every defendant hears – "Don't worry, you'll get probation." Spoiler: you won't. And the worst part? Your own lawyer's the one selling the dream right before the system crushes you.

EXHIBIT EIGHT

My Lawyer Promised Probation

The Courtroom Conspiracy - Illusions of Justice

So you've been caught, red-handed, facing charges that could have you locked up for a decade or more. Your lawyer looks you dead in the eye and tells you, "Don't worry, we'll push for probation. You're not going to prison." Ah, the sweet symphony of false hope, designed to keep you calm, cooperative, and most importantly, paying their outrageous fees while they prepare you for the slaughter. Let me break it to you–probation isn't just handed out like candy, especially not for serious crimes. That "probation deal" they're promising? It's about as real as Bigfoot riding a unicorn.

Probation Mirage: The Big Lie Your Lawyer Sells You

One of the first lies lawyers will trot out is the myth of leniency for first-time offenders. "You've never been in trouble before, you'll get probation!" they tell you, with the confidence of someone selling beachfront property in the middle of the desert. Sure, it sounds comforting. The reality? The law doesn't care if you've never been caught before. If you're dealing with federal charges or serious crimes like fraud, money laundering, or conspiracy, the sentencing guidelines aren't going to magically disappear just because you kept a clean record. Your lawyer conveniently forgets to mention that the court often has zero interest in handing out a slap on the wrist for major offenses. And that's where the lie comes into play.

The Misleading "We'll Argue Mitigating Factors" Strategy

Oh, this is a classic. Your lawyer will tell you that they'll argue "mitigating factors"–your sad life story, your community involvement, how you feed stray cats on the weekends–and the judge will see the light and opt for probation. What they *won't* tell you is that the judge already knows these tricks and hears them every single day. The mitigating factors are about as useful as throwing confetti at a firing squad. When the crime doesn't allow for probation–because, let's face it, drug trafficking, securities fraud, or anything involving federal statutes usually doesn't–those sob stories mean *nothing*.

The "Prosecutor Might Play Ball" Lie

This one's a gem. "The prosecutor might offer you probation in exchange for a plea deal!" your lawyer says, with the same enthusiasm as a used car salesman pushing a lemon. The problem? The prosecutor is in the business of locking people up, not letting them waltz out of the courtroom with probation and a slap on the wrist. If your crime carries mandatory sentencing, the prosecutor can't and won't offer you probation unless they have *nothing* on you–and let's be honest, they didn't file the charges on a hunch. But your lawyer doesn't want you to know that yet. They want you hopeful, quiet, and naïve.

The Conveniently Ignored Sentencing Guidelines

Here's a fun fact your lawyer might gloss over: federal sentencing guidelines aren't optional. They exist for a reason, and they're not exactly leaning in your favor. If you're facing federal charges that carry a minimum sentence, the odds of walking out with probation are about as likely as finding a Starbucks on the moon. Your lawyer won't mention this right away because it's easier to keep you compliant if you think you'll get a cushy deal. They'd rather save that cold, hard reality for later—after they've squeezed every last dollar out of you.

The "Judge's Discretion" Fairy Tale

And then there's the ultimate lawyer fairy tale: "It's all up to the judge. We just need to get a lenient one." Ah, yes, as if the judge is some whimsical figure deciding punishments based on how many compliments they get that morning. Reality check: federal judges don't have the luxury of winging it. They have rules to follow, laws to enforce, and guidelines to adhere to. But your lawyer's not going to tell you that part up front. They'll let you dream about some mystical lenient judge who's going to toss out your sentence like it's a parking ticket.

The Bottom Line: Probation Is a Mirage

The truth is that probation, especially for serious crimes or federal offenses, is a mirage. Your lawyer sells it to you because it sounds better than, "You're probably going to prison." It keeps you calm, keeps you paying, and keeps the wheels of the legal machine spinning. But when the day of reckoning comes and that judge stares you down from the bench, all those promises of probation will evaporate faster than you can say "sentencing guidelines." You'll be left standing there, wondering how you bought into the lie—and your lawyer will be counting the cash.

"The DIY Reality Check: How to Find Out If You're Really Probation Eligible"

So your lawyer's been feeding you that sweet, sugary lie that you're going to walk away from this whole mess with nothing more than probation. You're feeling hopeful, maybe even relieved, thinking you've dodged the prison bullet. But deep down, something's gnawing at you. Is this for real? Or are they just keeping you happy and paying up until the day of sentencing when the truth hits like a freight train? Spoiler alert: it's probably the latter. But the good news? You don't have to sit in the dark and wait for disaster to strike. You can actually *do your own research* to figure out if probation is even on the table. And trust me, the truth is out there if you're willing to dig for it.

Step 1: Crack Open the Federal Sentencing Guidelines

Welcome to the jungle–the U.S. Sentencing Guidelines. It's the federal government's very own playbook, and believe me, it's not written in a way that makes life easier for you. But this is where you need to start. You'll want to look up your specific offense under the *U.S. Sentencing Guidelines Manual*. Each crime has a base offense level that determines the range of punishment, and guess what? For most serious offenses–fraud, drug trafficking, conspiracy–probation isn't even mentioned unless you're some kind of miraculous outlier.

Go straight to the table of contents or search for your crime. Once you find it, you'll see a grid that assigns offense levels and, most importantly, suggested penalties. If you see mandatory minimum sentences, like 5, 10, or 20 years, that's a red flag. The feds don't mess around, and mandatory minimums mean that the judge doesn't have the discretion to hand you probation even if you show up to court dressed like a Boy Scout.

Step 2: Understand Mandatory Minimums

Speaking of mandatory minimums, if you're charged with a crime that falls under these statutes–think drug trafficking, firearms violations, large-scale fraud–you can pretty much kiss probation goodbye. Mandatory minimums are like the government's way of saying, "Nope, we don't care how nice you are or how many puppies you've saved, you're going to prison."

To check if your offense carries a mandatory minimum, look up the statute under which you were charged. It'll be something like 21 U.S.C. § 841 (for drug crimes) or 18 U.S.C. § 924 (for firearms). You can find these codes online at legal websites like Cornell Law School's Legal Information Institute or through the Department of Justice's website. If the statute has a minimum number of years tied to it, probation is not happening, my friend.

Step 3: Search for Precedent and Case Law

Now it's time to see what happened to people in situations like yours. This step involves digging into case law, which is a fancy way of saying "what happened to other poor souls who got charged with the same crime." You can use free legal research tools like Google Scholar or FindLaw to look up cases involving your specific charges. Look for cases in the same jurisdiction or federal district where you're being prosecuted, and see what kind of sentences were handed down.

You'll start to notice a pattern. If most of these defendants ended up with prison time, regardless of how hard their lawyers argued for probation, you're probably staring down the same outcome. Case law gives you a pretty honest look at how sentencing is actually handled in the real world—not in the fantasy your lawyer's selling you.

Step 4: Know Your Criminal History Category

Ah, the dreaded *criminal history category*. The feds love their grids and charts, and this is where they decide just how dangerous they think you are. The Sentencing Guidelines use both your offense level and your criminal history to calculate where you fall in the grand scheme of punishment. If you've got a clean record, congrats, you might land in Criminal History Category I, which is the least severe. But even that doesn't guarantee probation.

Check your Pre-Sentence Report (PSR), which your lawyer will have access to. The PSR includes details about your past criminal activity (if any), and trust me, it plays a big role in whether or not probation is even possible. If you're up in Category III, IV, or higher, probation isn't just a long shot—it's practically a fairy tale.

Step 5: Look Up Sentencing Alternatives and How Rare They Are

Sure, your lawyer might mention alternatives to prison—like home confinement, community service, or supervised release—as if they're likely outcomes. Don't buy it without doing your homework. The truth is, these alternatives are only handed out in very specific, low-level cases. Most federal crimes that carry serious weight aren't eligible for these slap-on-the-wrist alternatives. Look up how often sentencing alternatives are used for your specific offense. A quick search online will show you that for high-level offenses, these alternatives are about as common as a unicorn sighting.

Step 6: Know the Prosecutor's Role in Sentencing

While you're being wooed by your lawyer's promises of probation, remember this—*the prosecutor holds a lot of power*. Even if your lawyer pushes for probation, if the prosecutor isn't on board, it's dead in the water. The prosecutor will be recommending a sentence to the court, and trust me, they're not in the business of cutting you slack just because your lawyer threw in a few shiny arguments. Check into typical sentencing recommendations for your type of crime. Does the prosecution usually push for the maximum? How often do they agree to probation deals? Spoiler: almost never in serious cases.

Step 7: Read the Sentencing Memorandums

Finally, get your hands on past sentencing memorandums—both from the prosecution and the defense. These documents outline what each side is arguing for and, more importantly, what the judge is likely to go with. You can find sample sentencing memorandums online or, if you're really savvy, you can ask your lawyer for examples from cases similar to yours. They probably won't volunteer them, but once you see what's actually argued in court, you'll get a crystal-clear picture of where you stand.

The Reality: Probation Is Rare–Do Your Own Homework

The bottom line? Don't take your lawyer's word for it. Probation is a unicorn in the world of serious federal crimes, and unless your offense level is rock-bottom and your criminal history is squeaky clean, it's not likely. So do the research. Dig into the sentencing guidelines, the case law, and the precedent. Because the last thing you want is to stand in court on sentencing day, blindsided, while your lawyer shrugs and mumbles something about "unexpected outcomes." The only person you can really trust to tell you the truth? *You.*

"The 7 Lies Prosecutors Tell You About Getting Probation"

Ah, prosecutors—the government's well-dressed, smooth-talking salesmen, promising deals that sound too good to be true. And guess what? They usually are. When it comes to probation, they're more than happy to lead you down the primrose path, dangling a carrot while sharpening the stick behind their back. They might tell you that probation is within reach, but the reality? They're gunning for a conviction and a hefty sentence to pad their stats. Let's break down the 7 biggest lies prosecutors tell when they're talking about probation.

1. "We're Open to Probation, It's Definitely on the Table"

Oh, really? Sure, they'll act like probation is an option, keeping you and your lawyer hopeful. But in the background, they're preparing their case to push for the maximum penalty they can get. The truth is, probation isn't really on the table if you're dealing with serious federal charges. The prosecutor just wants to keep you engaged and cooperative, so you don't rock the boat or fight too hard.

2. "If You Cooperate, Probation Is More Likely"

Ah, the cooperation trap. They'll tell you that if you play ball—maybe flip on some friends, give up some info—you'll have a better shot at probation. What they're not telling you is that cooperation is a tool for them to get what they need, and once they've got it, your dreams of probation can disappear faster than your trust in the system. More often than not, your "cooperation" just helps them lock down a conviction, and they'll still push for prison time.

3. "The Judge Usually Follows Our Recommendation"

This one's a classic. The prosecutor will tell you that if they recommend probation, the judge will likely go along with it. The truth? Judges don't owe the prosecutor a thing. Even if they suggest probation, the judge can (and often will) ignore it, especially if the crime carries a hefty sentence under the guidelines. Prosecutors know this, but they'll string you along, making you think their recommendation holds more weight than it actually does.

4. "You're Not the 'Type' to Go to Prison"

Oh, they'll flatter you all right. "You're a first-time offender," they say, "You're not a violent criminal; you don't belong in prison." What they conveniently leave out is that the law doesn't care if you're a white-collar guy or a hardened gangster. The sentencing guidelines are the same, and if your crime is serious enough, the "type" you are won't matter one bit. They're just buttering you up so you'll play along with their plea deal.

5. "We'll Argue Hard for Probation"

This one's rich. They'll tell you they're going to bat for you, making it sound like they're on your side. But the prosecutor's job isn't to hand out leniency; it's to secure convictions and sentences that make them look tough on crime. Even if they "argue" for probation, they'll make sure to lay out every reason why you still deserve a stiff sentence. It's all about appearances—they'll look good, and you'll still be facing time behind bars.

6. *"If You Take the Plea, Probation's a Real Possibility"*

Here's the trap: you're offered a plea deal, and the prosecutor sweetens it by saying probation is a real possibility if you sign on the dotted line. What they don't mention is that accepting the plea means you're pleading guilty, and probation is still at the discretion of the court. More often than not, you're just paving the way for them to secure a conviction while you end up with a sentence you weren't prepared for.

7. *"Probation Is a Fair Outcome for Your Case"*

What's fair in the eyes of a prosecutor? Not much. They'll tell you that probation is a reasonable and fair outcome, making it sound like they're offering you a golden ticket. But behind closed doors, they're probably still gunning for prison time. "Fair" to a prosecutor is whatever gets the conviction while minimizing their workload. Even if they mention probation, don't think for a second they aren't prepared to push for more.

The Bottom Line: Prosecutors Don't Deal in Probation, They Deal in Convictions

At the end of the day, prosecutors are in the business of winning cases and securing convictions, not handing out probation like party favors. They'll use the illusion of probation to keep you cooperative, but once they've got what they need, that leniency they dangled in front of you vanishes. So when the prosecutor starts talking probation, take it with a grain of salt—and maybe a shot of whiskey. You're likely in for a harder fall than they're letting on.

"The 7 Lies Defense Lawyers Tell You About Getting Probation"

Ah, your defense lawyer—your supposed knight in shining armor, fighting off the evil government to keep you out of a prison jumpsuit. But let's not kid ourselves: lawyers have a knack for stretching the truth, especially when it comes to probation. They know you're scared, desperate, and willing to believe in a fairytale ending. And nothing sells better than the idea that you'll walk away from this mess with just a slap on the wrist. So, let's break down the 7 biggest lies defense lawyers tell about getting probation.

1. "Probation Is Definitely on the Table"

This is the granddaddy of them all—the big, shiny lie that keeps you from spiraling into full-blown panic mode. Your lawyer will confidently tell you that probation is a solid option. The truth? It's not. They're just keeping you calm while they negotiate behind the scenes, knowing full well that your charges, the sentencing guidelines, and the federal statutes don't leave much room for probation. It's the bait to keep you trusting them (and writing those checks).

2. "First-Time Offenders Like You Get Probation All the Time"

Oh, the first-time offender card. They'll play it like it's some kind of get-out-of-jail-free ticket. Just because it's your first rodeo doesn't mean the court's going to pat you on the back and send you home with probation. Your lawyer won't mention that serious federal crimes—fraud, drug trafficking, conspiracy—don't care whether you're a seasoned criminal or a rookie. The law doesn't magically forgive because it's your "first offense." They'll push this lie to keep you from realizing how dire the situation really is.

3. "We'll Argue for a Light Sentence and Get Probation"

Sure, they'll argue for a light sentence, and they'll make it sound like that argument has some serious weight behind it. What they won't tell you is that judges hear these same weak defenses every day, and unless you're facing a particularly lenient judge or an extremely unusual set of circumstances, the odds of getting probation are about as slim as a snowball surviving a summer day in Death Valley. They argue because they have to, but they know full well it's not likely to sway the court.

4. "Judges Have Discretion, and We'll Push for Probation"

Another whopper. Your lawyer will make you think that the judge is sitting up there with infinite power, just waiting to be convinced to give you probation instead of prison time. They'll say things like, "It's all about how we present your case." Reality check: if the sentencing guidelines say prison time is mandatory, no amount of slick talking is going to change that. The judge's discretion is a lot narrower than your lawyer would have you believe.

5. "We Can Use Your Good Character and Community Ties to Get Probation"

Your lawyer will tell you that your spotless reputation, community involvement, and letters from your pastor will sway the court into giving you probation. While those things can help in some cases, they're not a golden ticket out of prison. They're nice window dressing, but when the charges are serious, the court is focused on punishment and deterrence, not on how many bake sales you organized. Your lawyer won't admit that good character means very little when stacked up against a felony conviction.

6. "A Good Sentencing Memorandum Can Get You Probation"

They'll sell you on the idea that their well-crafted sentencing memorandum is the key to keeping you out of prison. It's not. While a solid memo can sometimes reduce the length of your sentence, the idea that it will magically convert prison time into probation is a stretch. Unless there's a glaring legal error in the prosecution's case or the judge is feeling exceptionally merciful, that memo is just a formality. Your lawyer will oversell its importance to justify their fees and make you think they're pulling out all the stops.

7. "We'll Bargain With the Prosecutor for Probation"

This one's rich. Your lawyer will tell you that they'll negotiate with the prosecutor and strike a deal that includes probation. What they won't tell you is that most prosecutors are more interested in securing convictions and prison time than handing out probation. Unless your case is a low-level, non-violent crime, or you're willing to give the Feds something they want in return, bargaining for probation is like negotiating for ice cream in a steakhouse. It's not on the menu, and they know it.

Probation Is a Pipe Dream for Most Serious Crimes

Let's face it, probation is the unicorn in the world of federal criminal defense. Your lawyer will dangle it in front of you to keep you hopeful, calm, and most importantly, paying their fees. But when you look at the charges, the guidelines, and the reality of the justice system, it's clear that probation is rarely a real option. The truth is, they're selling you the idea of a soft landing while knowing full well that the system is gearing up to throw the book at you. Trust, but verify—or better yet, do your own research.

Exhibit Eight: The Bottom Line

Probation is the carrot they dangle in front of suckers who still believe the system gives a damn. It's the illusion of mercy wrapped in legal bullshit and sold to you by the very people cashing your checks. Your lawyer knows you're desperate, the prosecutor knows you're scared, and the judge knows exactly how it ends. They just play their parts while you sit there clinging to the fantasy that somebody's gonna throw you a lifeline.

But here's the real game – probation isn't justice, it's bait. It keeps you docile, compliant, and dreaming right up until they slam the door. Nobody's handing out second chances in federal court. They don't see a person; they see a conviction, a stat, another body in the machine. Your lawyer sells you hope because fear doesn't pay the retainer, and the prosecutor plays along because false hope makes convictions cleaner.

So when they tell you "probation's on the table," remember – it's only there so they can pull it away later. In this system, the table's rigged, the dice are loaded, and the only thing you'll be rolling is your own damn future into a cellblock.

Next Up – Exhibit Nine: Paid Lawyers

Think public defenders were the worst it could get? Cute. Now we're stepping into the luxury scam – the world of overpriced suits who smile while selling you down the river. Exhibit Nine exposes the real hustle: paid defense lawyers who promise you the moon, bill you for the stars, then leave you broke, convicted, and wondering how the hell you paid top dollar to lose. Welcome to the private-sector slaughterhouse.

EXHIBIT NINE

Paid Lawyer Conspiracy

The Courtroom Conspiracy - Illusions of Justice

It always starts the same. You're desperate, broke, terrified, and drowning in alphabet soup–FBI, DOJ, IRS –and you think a private lawyer's gonna save your ass. You tell yourself, I need the best. No more public defenders or appointed mouth pieces, I want the shark. And then you meet him.

Offices of Find Em, Fuck Em and Fleece Em

He's sitting behind a desk the size of a coffin, smiling like he just buried his last client in it. The office smells like money and lies—polished wood, framed degrees, espresso machine humming like a slot machine. His assistant greets you like you're some kind of celebrity, offers water that costs more than your lunch, and tells you "Mr. Barnett will be right with you." You think, *Damn, this is legit* No, motherfucker. This is theater.

The Sales Pitch in a Suit

He strolls in wearing a $2,000 suit and a smirk. He's tan, confident, and full of shit. The handshake's strong, the eye contact is surgical, and the bullshit starts immediately. He drops words like "strategy," "connections," and "reputation" like holy scripture. He's not trying to defend you—he's auditioning to *sell* you. And you're buying it. Because fear turns people into ATM machines.

He leans back in his leather chair, pretends to listen while you ramble about your innocence, and every few seconds he hits you with a slow nod like he's decoding the Constitution in his head. Then, the line: **"I've handled cases like yours before. You came to the right guy."**

That's the hook. You're already bleeding out, and he just threw you a tourniquet made of dollar signs. You think this man's your savior. You think you just bought protection. What you really bought was silence wrapped in arrogance. You're not hiring a lawyer—you're financing his vacation.

Hope Is Just a Hook

The real scam isn't in the lies—it's in the **hope**. That's the product. That's what they sell. He'll study you like a hustler clocking a mark at the poker table. Nervous hands? Desperation in your eyes? He's got you pegged before you've finished your coffee.

He'll talk soft, calm, like a preacher before the offering plate comes around. "We're gonna fight this," he says. "I've already got an idea how to dismantle the government's case." You don't even realize it, but you're nodding along. Because it sounds good. It feels good. And that's how they get you. You'll hear the same lines over and over:

"This is beatable.", "I know the prosecutor personally.", "I'll make this disappear."

Every one of those lines is a shell casing from the last poor bastard who sat in that same chair. They recycle confidence like they recycle printer toner. They promise you control, when the only thing they control is your panic level and your wallet. And when they slide that retainer agreement across the desk, it's game over. You don't even read it. You're too busy trying to believe the fantasy that your freedom can be purchased in one lump sum. You sign. You shake hands. You feel relieved. He smiles. Because he just closed the sale.

That "personalized representation" you think you bought? It's worth exactly one thing—the ink on your check. Once that clears, your "priority case" becomes a low-tier side project delegated to some intern who still thinks RICO is a cartoon.

The Legal Strip Club

You ever been to a strip club? You know the routine. They flirt, they flatter, they make you feel like the only one in the room. And the moment you stop tipping, they move on to the next sucker. That's the private law game.

They'll make you feel special. "You're not like my other clients." Bullshit. You're exactly like their other clients—scared, broke, and desperate for validation. They'll answer your calls fast in the beginning, flood you with updates, and make you think they're grinding on your case around the clock. Then, one day, your email hits voicemail. Then it's "he's in court all day." Then it's "he's traveling." You've been ghosted by your own defense.

The junior associate steps in with fake confidence and coffee breath. "Mr. Barnett wanted me to give you an update." Translation: *You're not important enough for the man himself anymore.* You're stuck in a loop of half-answers, excuses, and invoices that read like ransom notes.

By the time you realize it, your lawyer's at lunch with a prosecutor talking golf while your file's being used as a coaster. The system ain't broken—it's working exactly how it was built: to make you pay for the illusion of fairness.

You Bought the Lie, Now Live in It

When that first "unexpected expense" hits, you'll get it. "We need another $5,000 for expert witnesses." "We need to file additional motions." "This could really help your case." And you'll pay it. Because you're in too deep to back out.

They know it. That's the art of the hustle—get you emotionally and financially trapped until saying *no* feels like signing your own death warrant. And when the trial date gets close, that big talk from your first meeting—"slam dunk," "airtight," "we got this"—starts fading fast. Now they're saying, "There's always risk in trial." "We should explore a plea deal." Wait, what happened to your miracle defense Oh, it's gone—buried under billable hours and empty promises. You'll walk into court thinking your lawyer's about to unleash hell. Instead, he's whispering with the prosecutor, nodding like a man negotiating a car trade-in. Then you hear it:

"Your Honor, we've reached an agreement." That's legal code for "we folded."

Your $25,000 retainer just bought you a plea bargain you could've gotten for free. He'll shake your hand after the hearing and tell you, "This was the best possible outcome." You'll nod, dazed, half-believing it, because the alternative—admitting you were scammed—is too much to swallow. Then you go home broke, branded, and bitter, while he goes home to a dinner reservation and a new client walking in tomorrow with the same story.

The Real Hustle

You thought court was the battlefield. Wrong. The real war happened in that office the day you signed the retainer. That's when you lost. That's when they won. Because the justice system runs on fear and false confidence—and private lawyers are the middlemen, flipping misery like real estate.

You didn't hire a defense. You financed a lifestyle. They don't sell justice–they lease hope. And when the lease expires, they repossess your freedom and move on to the next scared sucker walking through that glass door, clutching a folder and a fantasy. That's the game. And now you're in it.

Meet the Butchers in Blazers

Buck "The Butcher" Barnett – Legal Assassin for Hire

He used to be the guy putting people in cages. Now he charges twelve hundred an hour to *pretend* he's trying to keep you out of one.

Ex-federal prosecutor turned private mercenary, Buck's entire resume is a graveyard of ruined lives. Harvard Law, top of his class, cut his teeth in the U.S. Attorney's Office by turning plea deals into sport and destroying defendants like it was just another day at the office. His conviction rate? Stupid high. You could sneeze wrong and this motherfucker would turn it into an enhancement.

Now he's "on your side." Yeah, and snakes make great babysitters.

You sit across from Buck thinking you hired the best. He sits across from you calculating how many hours he can bill before dumping your ass into a deal he could've written in crayon.

He's the master of the **silent nod**–lets you talk for 20 minutes, says five words, and still sends you a bill for "strategic consultation." Every word out of his mouth feels like it was pulled from a DOJ training manual wrapped in a Gucci tie. He ain't defending you–he's processing you. Like meat. Buck doesn't *fight* prosecutors. He used to *train* them. The only thing he's "leveraging" now is your panic into a platinum AmEx swipe.

Vinny "The Hammer" Vincenzo - The Smile Behind the Scam

Vinny's not a lawyer–he's a Vegas illusionist with a bar card. Suits tailored like he's on trial for fashion fraud, cologne thick enough to trigger asthma, and charm so slick it should come with a floor warning.

He talks like your big brother. Laughs like he knows a secret. Hell, you might even trust him–*that's* the danger.

Vinny's game is *emotional seduction*. He reels you in with empathy, tells you how "he's been there," how "he knows how they think," and how he's gonna "burn the whole thing down." Then he drops the classic:

"We're not just gonna fight–we're gonna win."

You hear that and you think, *Finally. Someone's in my corner.* Nah. You're in his funnel.

What you don't see is Vinny playing both sides. He's buttering up the prosecutor while dragging your case out *just long enough* to bill six figures before folding you into a plea deal you could've negotiated on your own.

His motto? "Control the narrative." What that means is: lie to you just enough to keep the checks coming and keep your dumb ass hopeful. You'll be telling your cellmate that Vinny was your ride or die –right before they tell you he worked their case too, with the same outcome.

Vinny doesn't win cases. He wins *confidence*. And that's all he needs to keep the lights on and the bullshit flowing.

Johnny "The Intern" Fitzgerald – The Hopeful Sacrifice

Johnny still believes in "justice." Poor bastard.

Fresh outta Yale with a haircut from a barbershop that doesn't exist anymore and a head full of dreams that ain't gonna survive his first filing deadline. Johnny's that wide-eyed associate they trot out during your second meeting to make you think you've got a whole "team" working your case. You don't. You've got Johnny.

They put him in the room so you feel like someone's paying attention. He nods, takes notes like he's writing a Pulitzer piece, and says things like:

> "I'll check in with Mr. Barnett about that."

What he *means* is, "I have no idea what I'm doing and my boss just handed me this file five minutes ago." Johnny's the buffer. The scapegoat. The future fall guy. And the longer your case drags on, the more it becomes *his* problem. Because Buck and Vinny already got paid. Johnny's just trying not to cry in the bathroom between status conferences.

But don't get it twisted—Johnny ain't innocent. He's learning fast. He's absorbing every greasy trick, every billed second, every fake update. In a year? He'll be the next Vinny. And you'll be his practice dummy.

Sasha "Silk Tongue" Martinez – Legal Influencer, Gaslight Queen

And then there's Sasha. The femme fatale of felony defense. The courtroom Kardashian with a bar card. She doesn't just practice law—she **performs it**, streams it, hashtags it, and merchandises the fuck out of it. You didn't hire a lawyer. You hired a *brand ambassador for self-delusion*.

You'll find her all over social media, flashing courthouse selfies and uploading inspirational bullshit like, *"Strong women don't plead, they rise."* Meanwhile, you're sitting in lock-up wondering why your pretrial motion never got filed. Spoiler: she was too busy recording a podcast about "restorative justice and self-care under capitalism."

Sasha's got a talent–**emotional manipulation in designer heels**. She doesn't drop legal jargon. She drops catchphrases. She tells you you're "a fighter," that your story "needs to be heard," that "the system fears your strength." What she *won't* tell you is that she hasn't read your discovery packet and that your file's buried under a stack of unpaid invoices.

But you believe her. Because Sasha doesn't sell defense. She sells *empowerment*. And not the real kind. The kind with **tiers**. Platinum packages. "One-on-one mindset sessions." Affirmation worksheets. Trauma mapping. And of course, customized merch.

She'll gaslight you like a pro. Ask a question about the case? You're "being negative." Show doubt? "That's just internalized oppression." She reframes every red flag as your personal growth journey–right up until you're chained to a five-year plea deal she helped negotiate *while hosting a Twitter Space about resilience in carceral spaces*.

She makes you feel like a **survivor**. A warrior. A voice for the voiceless. Until sentencing day.

That's when it hits. No miracle motion. No dramatic closing argument. Just a bland-ass plea you didn't understand and a perfunctory apology she wrote during her makeup appointment.And the worst part? You're still defending her. You're sitting in that holding cell telling yourself, *"She really tried. The system is just broken."*

No, boo. She didn't try. She **posted**. And while you're being processed into custody, she's already uploading a TikTok clip titled *"Hard day in court, but we stay strong #JusticeJourney."* You didn't hire a lawyer. You hired a motivational speaker in Louboutins, selling therapy words with a side of subpoenas. And she **charged you double for the hashtags.**

Bottom Line: This Is Your Dream Team from Hell

You thought you were buying expertise. What you bought was:

- A butcher who used to sharpen the government's knives
- A con artist who tells bedtime stories with a straight face

- A law school baby bird learning to fly with your life on the line
- And a social media star more interested in filters than filings

This ain't a dream team. It's a **legal Ponzi scheme** with courtroom credentials. They don't fight for you —they fight to stay booked. And guess what? Every one of them will smile at you while they do it.

Next lets examine the bullshit they spout and tactics to fight back and make then do their fucking jobs.

Lawyer's Bullshit Hall of Fame

1. "I Know the Prosecutor Personally."

Lawyer's Lies: The moment you walk into that overpriced showroom of a law office, this is the first line they drop. "I know the prosecutor," they say, like it's some kind of get-out-of-jail-free card. They talk about golf outings, bar mixers, mutual friends at the courthouse. They make it sound like your case isn't about evidence—it's about favors. That they've got some secret backchannel that'll make your indictment vanish in a puff of legal pixie dust.

The Fucking Truth: Federal prosecutors don't give a damn about your lawyer's brunch history. They're bloodhounds with quotas. They get promotions for convictions, not for cutting sweetheart deals with old law school buddies. If your lawyer's selling "connections," they're stalling while your file collects dust. Relationships don't dismiss cases–facts do. And if your only hope is that your lawyer plays poker with the AUSA, you're already halfway to prison.

2. "I Guarantee You Won't Go to Jail."

Lawyer's Lies: Ah, the sweet sound of false hope. "You won't see a day behind bars," they tell you, chest out, voice calm, like they just parted the Red Sea. They feed you lines about how they've "handled worse," how the judge "owes them one," how they'll "crush the government's case." It's all confidence and certainty. You walk out thinking you just bought your freedom.

The Fucking Truth: No lawyer can guarantee you shit–especially not in federal court. This ain't traffic court. This is mandatory minimums, sentencing guidelines, and judges who think compassion is a sign of weakness. Anyone who promises you zero jail time is either selling snake oil or too stupid to be practicing law. Either way, you're fucked if you believe it. A real lawyer doesn't guarantee results–they guarantee the fight. And if you ain't hearing that, you're paying for fantasy.

3. "I've Never Lost a Case."

Lawyer's Lies: This one's a classic. They lean back, flash that smug grin, and say it like it's holy scripture. "I'm undefeated." They drop stats like they're Mayweather. They'll tell you they've "never lost," "always win," and that the feds are scared of them. You're supposed to feel like you just hired a walking legal WMD.

The Fucking Truth: Bull. Shit. Any lawyer with actual battle scars has *lost*. That's part of the game. What "never lost" usually means is they cherry-picked easy cases, took plea deals before shit got real, or straight up padded the truth. If your lawyer acts like they've never taken an L, they've also never taken a risk. Real defense means walking into gunfire with your head high. If they're undefeated, it's because they've never been tested.

4. "I'll Handle Everything Personally."

Lawyer's Lies: In the first meeting, they make it sound like you'll have their personal cell, their undivided attention, and their loyal service until verdict. They say things like, "I'll be on this every step of the way," or "You won't be handed off to some junior." It's all eye contact and sincerity. You feel like you're in safe hands.

The Fucking Truth: Once that retainer clears? You're passed down the food chain faster than a prison tray. You won't see that big-name lawyer again until plea day or sentencing–if you're lucky. Every document, every phone call, every "update" gets outsourced to the junior associate or paralegal while the partner's off chasing his next paycheck. They didn't lie–technically. They're "overseeing" the case. Translation: they're billing you while someone else screws it up.

5. "This Case Is Just Like One I Won Before."

Lawyer's Lies: They'll say, "I had a guy just like you," or "I handled this exact same charge last year." They make it sound like your case is nothing special–just another number in their victory parade. The implication? They already know what to do, and you're in good hands.

The Fucking Truth: There is *no such thing* as a copy-paste federal case. Every defendant, every fact pattern, every judge, every prosecutor is a new minefield. What worked once might get your ass buried next time. If they're using someone else's case to explain yours, it means they're cutting corners and gambling with your life. You don't need recycled defense–you need strategy.

6. "I've Got Secret Strategies the Government Doesn't Know."

Lawyer's Lies: This one sounds sexy. They tell you they've got "tricks," "techniques," "creative motions" the prosecution's never seen coming. They say they're always ten steps ahead, like some courtroom ninja. You start thinking you hired a legal magician.

The Fucking Truth: There are no "secret moves" in federal court. The government has seen it all. You're not the first drug case. You're not the first fraud case. Your situation isn't special, and your lawyer isn't Neo in The Matrix. What wins cases is hard work, long hours, deep research, and grit–not smoke and mirrors. Anyone claiming to have "unknown legal tactics" is bullshitting you straight to a conviction.

7. "Hiring Me Now Will Save You Money Later."

Lawyer's Lies: This one sounds responsible, like legal budgeting. "If you hire me now, we can nip this in the bud," they say. "Early defense saves costs later." They push urgency like a used car dealer: "Act now before this gets worse!"

The Fucking Truth: They're front-loading the grift. You'll pay big now *and* pay big later. Nothing in federal court is quick or cheap. Investigations drag, discovery drags, judges take months to rule on basic motions. And your lawyer knows that. What they *don't* want is you shopping around or stalling—because the quicker you sign, the quicker they bill.

8. "My Fee Covers Everything."

Lawyer's Lies: This is the all-inclusive vacation package version of defense. "One flat fee. Everything included." Sounds clean. Sounds safe. Sounds like you're not gonna get nickeled and dimed into bankruptcy.

The Fucking Truth: That "flat fee" usually covers the bare minimum—and the rest is coming out of your hide. They'll bill you extra for experts, travel, trial prep, coffee, gum, and breathing too hard during meetings. It's a Trojan horse. You'll think you paid for peace of mind, but what you really bought was a down payment on financial ruin.

9. "We'll Be Done Before You Know It."

Lawyer's Lies: They make it sound like your case is just a bump in the road. "This'll be wrapped up quickly." "We'll handle this before summer." You hear that and think you'll be back to your life by next month.

The Fucking Truth: Federal cases don't move fast. There's no such thing as "quick." Everything drags. Motions take months. Trial calendars are clogged. Discovery gets delayed. And when your lawyer tells you it'll be done soon, it's because they don't want you asking questions once you're six months deep with no progress and no hope.

10. "You're My Top Priority."

Lawyer's Lies: This is the emotional manipulation card. They look you in the eye, lower their voice, and say, "You matter to me. I'm dropping everything else to focus on this." You feel seen. You feel important. You think you're the exception.

The Fucking Truth: You're not their priority. You're a file. A revenue stream. A name on a whiteboard calendar between two other clients who heard the same damn lie. Unless you're paying them seven figures or your case is gonna get them on the news, you're background noise. They'll say whatever it takes to keep you calm while they move on to the next payday.

From Slam Dunk to Slammed in Court

At the beginning, it's all champagne promises and swagger. "This case is a slam dunk," they say, chest puffed, acting like they've already won. They'll tell you it's open-and-shut, airtight, "the government's case is weak," and you eat it up because you *want* to believe it. They hype you up like you're walking into a minor inconvenience instead of a damn federal cage match. You walk out of the consult thinking trial's just a formality and your victory parade is scheduled for Tuesday.

 Fast-forward six months and now that same "slam dunk" case has mysteriously morphed into a nightmare with a plea deal duct-taped to it. Your lawyer's tone changed—now it's "there are no guarantees," and "trial is always a risk," and "maybe we should talk settlement." What happened? Nothing. You just got sold on confidence and billed on cowardice. "Slam dunk" was never strategy—it was a closer's pitch. Now that the real fight's starting, they're trying to cash out and move on. You didn't hire a warrior. You hired a motivational speaker with a calendar to fill.

When the Real Lawyer Disappears and the Rookie Takes Over

You hired *The Name*. The guy with the reputation. The one with the firm's title on the front door and the podcast where he quotes himself. He sat across from you in that first meeting, told you he'd be hands-on, told you this case was personal. You shook hands with the top dog. You felt like you bought the best. You probably even bragged to your family, "I got the big dog on this one."

Then comes reality. Suddenly, your calls are being returned by someone named "Johnny." Some baby-faced intern who's still figuring out how to format a motion. He stammers through updates, mispronounces charges, and says "we're still reviewing discovery" like it's a damn mantra. That hotshot partner you hired? Gone. Ghosted. He's off chasing new retainers while you're stuck with a fresh-out-of-law-school paperweight pretending to be your shield in court. Your case didn't get elevated–it got *delegated*. And now, when it all crashes, the firm will blame "team dynamics" while you get slapped with five to ten.

Weaponize the Paper Trail

You want power? Start stacking paper. Not legal briefs – **receipts.** You turn every conversation, every promise, every delay into a logged, dated, saved, and forwarded record of accountability. After every call, send a follow-up email. Bullet-point what was said. Include timelines. Use phrases like "as we discussed" and "per our agreement." That ain't paperwork – that's **ammo.**

And guess what? Most lawyers count on the fact that you won't. That you'll forget. That you'll stay quiet, scared, and disorganized. Don't. You build that paper trail like you're prepping for war, because that's exactly what this is. When the day comes and they try to gaslight you with "I don't recall," you'll have the proof – their own words, stamped in time, ready to bury them under their own bullshit.

Control the Clock, Own the Room

You wanna stop being billed for "research" that's really fantasy football? Then control the time. Schedule weekly check-ins, mandatory. Don't ask. Tell. You want a 15-minute update–email, call, smoke signal, whatever. If they ghost you, hit their office like a repo man on deadline.

Don't ever let them walk into a meeting more prepared than you. You bring a notepad, a list of questions, and the attitude of someone who's already halfway to filing a bar complaint. You set deadlines. You ask for strategy outlines. You treat them like you're the boss–because guess what? You are. You're the one paying. Start acting like it.

Make 'Em Regret Underestimating You

They expected you to shut up, nod, and write checks. Make them regret that mistake with every interaction. Demand answers. Demand strategy. Demand receipts. When they say "we're reviewing the discovery," ask what they've found. Ask what's missing. Ask how many pages they've actually read. When they say "we're negotiating with the prosecutor," ask what terms have been discussed and what leverage they're using.

And if they start stuttering? That's when you press harder. Don't get loud—get surgical. Calm, direct, and relentless. Treat their bullshit like cross-examination. Make them work for every dime.passive. That you're scared. But when you build that paper trail, they know damn well you're not just another soft target. You're a walking timebomb with evidence.

How to Make These Bastards Work for You

Once you master these fifteen moves, you stop being the mark and start being the threat. You can't out-lawyer a lawyer, but you can out-manage one. Paper, pressure, and presence—those are your weapons. Make them earn every damn dollar or choke on their own invoice. That's how you survive the game.

Tactic 1. Put Everything in Writing

If it ain't written, it never happened. Period. Lawyers survive on "I don't recall." You kill that phrase by keeping receipts like a paranoid ex. Every time you talk, you follow up with an email: *"Just confirming you'll file the suppression motion by Friday."* That's a trap—now their bullshit has a date and a signature. Save every text, email, invoice, and voicemail. Screenshot everything. Print it if you have to. When the day comes that they claim they "never said that," you pull out the file and bury them in their own words.

Tactic 2. Force a Written Game Plan

You don't hand your life over to somebody who's winging it. Tell your lawyer to give you a timeline in black and white: motions, hearings, deadlines, all of it. If they shrug or mumble about "strategy," that means they're improvising. Push until you get specifics–dates, tasks, and who's responsible. You're not being nosy; you're running quality control. And once that plan's on paper, you've got something solid to hold them to when they start stalling.

Tactic 3. Run Your Own Deadline Tracker

Don't trust their calendar. Make your own. Write down every promise, filing date, and court appearance. Circle them, highlight them, tattoo them on your damn brain if you have to. When a date passes with no action, call them out instantly. "You said motion by the 10th–it's the 14th. What's the excuse?" The goal is to make them realize you're tracking every breath they take. Lazy lawyers fear clients who keep time better than they do.

Tactic 4. Demand Proof of Progress

Words mean nothing–documents mean everything. Every time they claim they've "filed something," you ask for a copy. Every time they say they "talked to the prosecutor," you want an email confirming it. When they brag about "prepping discovery," ask to see the notes. You're not doubting them–you're verifying. If that pisses them off, good. Pissed-off lawyers work faster when they know someone's checking their homework.

Tactic 5. Control Meetings Like Interrogations

You're not in their office for a sermon–you're there for answers. Walk in with questions written down and read them off one by one. When they start rambling, cut them off and drag them back to the point. Take notes while they talk; nothing scares a liar like a client writing mid-sentence. When the meeting's done, email them a summary: "Here's what we discussed and what you agreed to." You just turned a conversation into a contract.

Tactic 6. Review Discovery Yourself

Don't ever let them "summarize" discovery for you like you're too stupid to understand it. Ask for the full packet, digital or paper, and go through every page. You'll catch shit they missed because they skimmed it between golf rounds. Ask questions about anything that smells off. "Why does this report say one time and the police log says another?" That's how real defenses start—when the defendant knows the evidence better than the lawyer pretending to.

Tactic 7. Demand Drafts Before They File

You wouldn't let a mechanic fix your car blindfolded; don't let a lawyer file motions without your eyes on them. Tell them: "I want to review every filing before it hits the court docket." They'll groan about time, but screw that—it's your name on the paperwork. Read every word. Catch the lazy copy-paste bullshit. If they rush, tell them to slow down. Half their filings are templates anyway; your edits will remind them there's a human being attached to the case number.

Tactic 8. Audit Their Billing Like a Detective

When that invoice hits your inbox, don't just pay it—**interrogate** it. Every entry needs to explain what they actually did. "Research – 3.2 hours"? Researching what? On whose computer? Was it law books or Facebook? Ask until they squirm. Most lawyers pad hours because nobody calls them on it. Once they see you reading line by line, those hours start dropping like bad charges on appeal.

Tactic 9. Monitor Their Communication Lag

Here's the thing—lawyers ghost. They'll vanish for weeks and call it "being in court." Track how long it takes them to respond. Start timing replies like you're clocking a race. If a day passes with no answer, you send a polite nudge. Two days? You escalate: call, email, and leave a message marked *urgent*. After three days, copy the office manager. Keep records of every delay. When you prove they've been ignoring you, you own them.

Tactic 10. Know Who's Actually Working Your Case

You hired a name, but that name's out golfing while some intern is fumbling through your future. Ask straight up: "Who's handling my file day-to-day?" Get names. Get titles. If the person in charge changes, demand to be told in writing. Make it known that you know every face touching your case. Nobody wants to get caught screwing over the client who keeps a roll call.

Tactic 11. Push for Witness Contact Updates

Ask, "Which witnesses have you spoken to? When? What did they say?" If they mumble about "ongoing investigation," call bullshit. They're supposed to gather facts, not hide behind clichés. Keep a list of witnesses yourself and tick off who's been contacted. If it's blank after a month, demand movement. Lawyers who drag their feet on witness work are either lazy or scared–either way, pressure fixes both.

Tactic 12. Challenge Every Excuse

You'll hear them all: "The court's backed up." "The prosecutor's unavailable." "We're waiting on transcripts." Every delay costs you money or time. Whenever they give you an excuse, ask, "What are we doing while we wait?" Make them work during the lull. File something. Draft something. Research something. If they refuse, document it. Excuses shrink fast when they realize you're turning each one into a record of incompetence.

Tactic 13. Drop the State Bar Bomb

You don't threaten–you **suggest**. Casually mention you've "been reading the Bar's ethics rules" or "talked to a friend about complaint procedures." Watch the blood drain from their face. The Bar is their parole officer; even a whisper of a complaint makes them snap to attention. Don't overuse it–once or twice is enough. Just knowing you know that route exists keeps them in line.

Tactic 14. Bring a Witness to Meetings

Lawyers act better when someone else is watching. Bring a spouse, a friend, anybody who can sit quietly and take notes. Introduce them as "my observer." Now the lawyer's got an audience, and their bullshit filter magically improves. If they lie or dodge later, your witness becomes your credibility. It's amazing how professional they get when there's another pair of eyes in the room.

Tactic 15. Track Every Broken Promise

Make a page in your notebook titled "Promises." Each time they say they'll do something–call, file, update–write it down with the date. When it doesn't happen, mark *FAILED* next to it. After a month, email the list to them:

"Here are the outstanding promises as of today."

That email is nuclear. It's proof of neglect wrapped in politeness. If they still don't move, you forward that list to the senior partner–or the Bar. Either way, the fear of exposure will light a fire under their designer shoes.

You Thought You Hired a Savior. You Hired a Sales Rep.

You thought you were buying salvation. What you really bought was a salesman who figured out how to make desperation a billable service. These lawyers don't sell justice–they sell performance. The handshake, the forced empathy, the "we'll fight this together" line–it's all part of the act. They know exactly what you want to hear: that someone powerful is finally on your side. They'll nod, listen, and pretend to care while mentally calculating how deep your pockets go and how fast they can empty them.

The moment your check clears, the transformation happens. The "personal defender of your freedom" turns into an accountant with a law degree. Suddenly, it's all about hours, filings, and logistics. The same man who said he'd *stand by you* now takes three days to answer an email. The woman who said she'd *fight for your life* now sends invoices that look like war budgets. The truth is, you didn't hire an advocate–you hired a closer. Someone who talks like a savior until you're locked in, then reverts to corporate autopilot. You thought you were buying justice, but you just funded someone's third Tesla payment.

The Real Trial Was Surviving Your Own Defense

The real trial wasn't in the courtroom–it was in your inbox, waiting for a call that never came. You survived months of being ghosted, gaslit, and guilt-tripped by the very people you were paying to protect you. You learned the hard way that "zealous representation" is lawyer-speak for "we'll do the bare minimum until it bites us." You had to chase updates like a bill collector, remind them of deadlines they forgot, and re-explain your own case because the associate assigned to you didn't exist the last time you were in court. It wasn't a defense–it was a hostage situation with stationery.

By the time trial or plea day came, you weren't hoping for victory–you were praying your lawyer would just remember your name. You walked in thinking the system was your enemy, but the truth was uglier:

the enemy had your signature on a retainer agreement. You paid for strategy and got a shrug. You bought "experience" and got excuses. You spent thousands to keep from drowning, only to realize your lawyer was holding the hose. Every defendant learns the same lesson eventually–the courtroom's not where they screw you. That part happens way before, inside the firm's conference room.

Play the Game or Get Played

There's no such thing as a fair fight in federal court. Everyone's lying, everyone's protecting something, and the only person who actually gives a damn about your freedom is you. So you've got two choices–either play the game like a hustler or get played like a rookie. You think your lawyer's on your team? They're on the payroll. You're not their client; you're their project–something to close out before vacation. You want control? Then you have to **take it**. Keep receipts. Watch the clock. Ask questions that make them uncomfortable. Be the nightmare client–the one they can't bullshit without sweating through their suit.

The law isn't justice; it's a marketplace. Everything's for sale–pleas, motions, reputations–and you're the one footing the bill. The only leverage you've got is pressure. Apply it relentlessly. Make them earn the money, word by word, filing by filing. You stop pushing, they start cruising. And once they start cruising, you're on your way to prison. So don't play nice–play smart. They designed this game to drain you, but if you learn the rules, you can flip the board. Because the only real defense in America isn't in the courtroom–it's **in knowing the hustle better than the hustlers.**

Exhibit Nine: The Bottom Line

> So here's the truth no one in the suits will ever tell you: *expensive doesn't mean good, and confident doesn't mean capable. A high retainer isn't a shield– it's a trap. It just means you'll be billed more to lose slower. You don't need blind faith; you need proof of work. You don't need charm; you need competence. And you sure as hell don't need another smooth-talking savior selling "justice" out of a brochure.*

What you need is self-defense disguised as self-awareness. You need to know that every word out of their mouth is marketing until it's proven otherwise. Stop expecting morality from people who bill by the hour. The only way to survive the legal machine is to treat it like a street hustle—because that's exactly what it is.

You can't out-lawyer them, but you can outsmart the system. You can keep the receipts, push the pace, and make sure they choke on accountability. The next time some "top-tier" attorney leans across that mahogany desk and says, "You're in good hands," just smile back and think, "Yeah—mine."

Then walk out, eyes open, receipts ready, fire lit. Because that's how you beat the game that was built to bury you.

Next Up – Exhibit Ten: Prosecutors

If the defense was a con, the prosecutor's the true believer. These are the government's holy warriors – dressed in conviction stats and sanctimony, preaching "justice" while hunting trophies. They don't build cases; they build careers. Every charge is a headline, every plea a sermon, and every ruined life another notch on their résumé.

Welcome to the altar of guilt – where mercy's a myth, power's a drug, and winning means never asking whether they destroyed the wrong person.

EXHIBIT TEN

Federal Prosecutor Conspiracy

The Myth of a Crusader

Welcome to the underbelly of the federal courtroom, where the real power doesn't always sit behind the bench but paces the floor in front of it, wrapped in a government-issued suit and armed with the full authority of the Department of Justice. Enter the Federal Prosecutor, otherwise known as the Assistant United States Attorney (AUSA)–the courtroom's version of a pit bull, trained to smell fear and tear your defense apart without so much as a second thought.

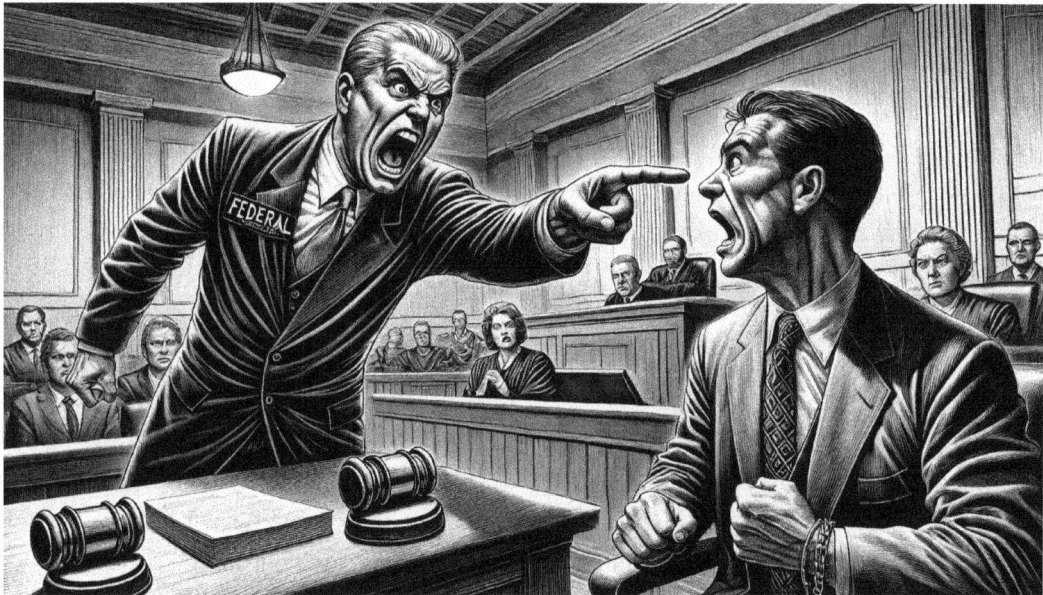

Who Prosecutors Are and Who They Think They Are

The AUSA isn't here to ensure justice or protect the innocent. No, they're here to win–plain and simple. It doesn't matter if you're guilty, innocent, or somewhere in between. In their eyes, you're nothing more than another notch on their belt, another conviction to boost their stats. And trust me, they've got the conviction rate to prove it. These guys don't come to court hoping to win; they walk in knowing they will. The deck

Strip away the robe-sniffing fantasy. This is who the prosecutor really is.

You ever met someone who walks into a room like they're doing God's work but acts more like the Grim Reaper's paralegal? That's your federal prosecutor. Not a truth-seeker. Not a guardian of justice. Just a well-dressed hitman with a J.D. and a parking pass.

The Myth of the Crusader

The government packages them like heroes–upstanding civil servants defending America from chaos and crime. Cue the patriotic violin music. But peel back that flag-draped bullshit, and what do you really have? A career bureaucrat with a 98% conviction rate and a God complex so big it needs its own office. These people didn't get into prosecution to "do the right thing." They got into it to win. Justice is optional. Victory is mandatory.

They don't chase truth–they chase headlines. They don't weigh fairness–they weaponize it. If it fits the story they want to sell the judge, it's truth. If it doesn't? It's "inadmissible" or "not credible." Translation: inconvenient. They sculpt reality like it's Play-Doh in a courtroom full of blindfolded sheep, and the judge claps along like a trained seal.

From Ivy League to Echo Chamber

Let's kill the fantasy right now: your average federal prosecutor isn't a battle-hardened warrior of the law. They're a highly political, overcaffeinated spreadsheet jockey with zero real-world experience and a deep, irrational hatred of gray areas. Nuance? Never met her. These people went from Ivy League to cubicle to courtroom without ever once living in the mess they claim to understand.

And here's the sick punchline—they think they're the good guys. No matter how many families they blow apart, how many lives they burn down over garbage charges and fake conspiracies, they'll sleep like babies. Because in their minds, they're cleaning the streets. Upholding order. Serving justice.

Yeah. And the IRS is doing charity work.

Knives Made of Paperwork

They are not arbiters of morality. They're closer to boxers in a rigged match—training to throw punches, not care who's on the mat. Their job is to bury you. The system rewards them for it. Promotions, press releases, pats on the back—hell, maybe even a future judgeship if they kiss enough ass on the way up.

So don't be fooled by the haircut and the Harvard diploma. Underneath that polished smile is a killer who doesn't need a knife—just a microphone, a jury box, and a defense lawyer dumb enough to believe the rules matter.

Who Prosecutors Work For and Who Owns Their Soul

Spoiler alert: It ain't "the people." It's the fucking machine.

You think the prosecutor works for you? Cute. Maybe you believe in the Tooth Fairy too. The federal prosecutor doesn't give a damn about "the people." That's just a buzzword they toss around when they're trying to squeeze your ass for a plea.

Welcome to the Church of Federal Power

The truth? **They work for the biggest, nastiest, most bloated gang in town—the Department of Justice, also known as the Church of Federal Power**. And their Bible? The U.S. Code. Thick enough to kill a man with, vague enough to bury anyone who pisses them off.

But let's be clear: the DOJ isn't some holy temple of honor. It's a political meat grinder run by career ladder-climbers and backroom deal-makers. And the prosecutor? Just another cog in that greasy, blood-lubed machine.

It's Not About Justice. It's About Job Security.

They don't answer to the public. They answer to their bosses–U.S. Attorneys who answer to Main Justice, who answer to politicians, who answer to donors and poll numbers. It's a daisy chain of ass-kissing and power games, and truth doesn't even get a seat at the table.

Every decision–from what charges they file, to who they cut deals with, to what kind of human sacrifice they demand in court–is filtered through one lens: *will this make me look good?* Not "is it right," not "is it fair," but "can I notch another scalp on my belt and maybe land a panel spot on CNN when this shitstorm's over?"

They Don't Fight Crime. They Curate Headlines.

These prosecutors are federal hitmen with stock options in public approval. They don't prosecute crime. They curate stories. They bend narratives to fit their personal brand. That means chasing high-profile targets, even if the case is built on duct tape and bullshit. That means hammering small-time defendants with 30-year threats just so they can say, "Look what I did for America."

Mainlining Power Like Junkies on a Bender

And let's not forget their real addiction: control. Prosecutors aren't just drunk on power–they're mainlining it. They're not happy unless you're squirming, begging, or signing your life away on a plea deal they know is garbage. Why? Because they can. And the system rewards it. The harsher they are, the faster they rise. That's the game. Ruthlessness is a résumé booster.

They call themselves "servants of justice." But in reality, they're just civil servants with delusions of grandeur and a boss that wants results, not redemption.

Leashed by Washington. Fed by Fear.

Their soul belongs to the system. Their leash is held by Washington. And their only god is conviction stats.

So next time a prosecutor tells you, "We're just doing our job"–believe them. Their job is to destroy lives as efficiently as possible, smile for the press conference, and make sure the real puppeteers behind the curtain stay happy.

What Prosecutors Really Do When Nobody's Watching

Behind the badge, beneath the robe-polish, it's just ego, shortcuts, and a spreadsheet of broken lives.

The official job description reads like a fucking hymn: "Pursue justice, uphold the law, serve the people." Beautiful, right? Like something your civics teacher would jerk off to. But when nobody's watching? That's when the mask comes off and the knives come out.

They Don't Investigate – They Delegate and Inflate

First off, they don't "investigate." That's too much work. They delegate that shit to the alphabet boys—FBI, DEA, ATF—and then pick through whatever half-baked garbage those agencies dump on their desk. Evidence? Optional. Consistency? Not required. As long as it sounds good on paper and wraps around a scary word like "conspiracy," it's full steam ahead.

They cut and paste indictments like it's arts and crafts day. Just swap names, flip the dates, slap in a few new overt acts and boom—you're in a multi-defendant, multi-kilo, racketeering-magic circus that never had to prove a damn thing. Why build a case when you can just build fear?

The Plea Deal: The Devil's Bargain

Let's talk about the plea deal—a prosecutor's favorite weapon. They'll come at you with a laundry list of charges that could send you away for life, then offer you a "deal" that'll only land you in prison for 10 or 20 years if you plead guilty. It's psychological warfare at its finest. They know you're scared, they know you're desperate, and they know you don't want to roll the dice at trial. So you take the deal, hoping for a lighter sentence, and they chalk up another win.

But here's the truth: that plea deal isn't a favor. It's a trap. The prosecutor knows they've got you by the throat, and they're just waiting for you to choke. They don't care about your innocence or your guilt—they care about clearing cases, boosting their stats, and moving on to the next victim. So when they offer you a deal, just remember: it's not because they're being generous. It's because they've already won, and they're giving you a chance to surrender before they crush you completely.

The Shadow Games: Hide, Twist, and Bury

What else do they do? Oh, they lie. Constantly. Not in court–that's too risky. But in the shadows? They manipulate timelines, stretch interpretations, and twist facts into weapons. That Brady material? Buried. That exculpatory witness? Suddenly "not credible." The surveillance tape that might help you? Lost in "technical error."

This ain't an accident. It's strategy. They're not seeking truth–they're avoiding it. The more facts get in the way, the more they edit the script.

Narrative Sculptors with a Bloodlust

Then there's their real obsession: narrative sculpting. They cherry-pick every detail to paint you like a monster and themselves like fucking Captain America. They'll comb your Facebook for a photo where you held a red Solo cup and call it "documented substance abuse." They'll quote your text messages like it's scripture–out of context, twisted, weaponized. You were "lol"ing with your buddy? They'll turn it into intent to distribute.

It's not about what you did. It's about what they can *make it look like you did.* Courtroom theater with prison time as the intermission.

Microsoft Word Warriors in Power Ties

And don't think they're working around the clock. Most of these fuckers are home by six unless there's a press conference or an office happy hour to gossip about who bagged the juiciest indictment. Their actual labor? Delegated, templated, and fueled by Microsoft Word macros. The hardest thing most of them do is pick which necktie will match the bloodbath they orchestrated that day. They don't build justice. They build careers–on your back, on your fear, on your silence.

A Game of Numbers

For the AUSA, the courtroom is a numbers game. They're not interested in whether you're a good person who made a mistake or a career criminal who deserves to rot in a cell. What matters to them is their conviction rate. Federal prosecutors boast an astounding conviction rate of over 90%, and they'll do whatever it takes to maintain that number. If that means cutting shady deals with co-defendants to flip on you, so be it. If it means throwing the book at you with every charge imaginable, even better.

And here's the kicker: most federal cases never even go to trial. The AUSA is a master of psychological warfare, using the sheer weight of the charges against you to force a plea deal. They'll dangle a potential life sentence in front of you, knowing full well that you'll be too terrified to risk it in court. So you take the deal, hoping for leniency, and they get another conviction to add to their stats. It's a win-win for them, and a lose-lose for you.

The Ego Behind the Job

Don't let that calm, collected exterior fool you–underneath that government-issued suit is an ego the size of the DOJ headquarters. Federal prosecutors didn't get into this line of work to help people or fight for justice. They got into it because they crave power, and in the courtroom, they're the ones holding all the cards. They control the narrative, they decide the charges, and they push for the harshest sentences they can get away with. Every conviction is a feather in their cap, a sign that they're climbing the ranks. And you? You're just another rung on their ladder to success.

It doesn't matter if you're a small-time drug dealer or a white-collar criminal–you're nothing more than a case file to them, one that will either help or hinder their rise to the top. They've got quotas to meet, bosses to impress, and promotions to chase. And they'll do whatever it takes to make sure they come out on top, even if it means bending the rules or twisting the facts to make sure you go down.

Who Prosecutors Rub Elbows With

It ain't a justice system. It's a country club where everyone's in on the same joke–except you. Let's get something straight: the courthouse isn't some sacred battlefield where noble gladiators clash over truth and fairness. It's a goddamn cocktail party with robes, badges, and a punchbowl full of power plays. And prosecutors? They're the overconfident assholes who show up thinking they own the place–because half the time, they do.

Judges? That's their old drinking buddy. They used to sit across the aisle during their early years at the U.S. Attorney's Office, trading snark over plea memos. Now one wears a robe and pretends to be neutral while the other calls in favors with a wink. Don't believe it? Watch how fast that judge shuts down a defense objection like it's a toddler whining about bedtime. "Sustained." *Boom.* Moving on. That wasn't justice–that was a group text reply.

Clerks? Oh, those lovely underpaid little gremlins keeping the circus running. Prosecutors treat them like coffee-fetching interns and get away with it because they bring the heat. Need a docket bumped? A filing mysteriously disappears until next week? The clerk's "got you," as long as you keep flashing that smug little DOJ smile.

Probation officers? That's your post-sentencing cleanup crew. They're supposed to write those pre-sentence reports like neutral observers, but guess who feeds them the narrative? That's right–your friendly neighborhood prosecutor. And if the PO doesn't play ball? No worries. Prosecutors just submit their own "corrections" to the report. Translation: "Rewrite this shit so I get my sentencing enhancement." Collaboration, baby.

Cops and agents? That's the pit crew. FBI, DEA, ATF–they're all part of the same machine. Prosecutors use them like Uber drivers for bullshit. "Go find me a cooperator who can spell 'conspiracy,' and I'll give him a pass on his own crimes." Agents nod, drop the handcuffs on some poor bastard, and toss the keys to the prosecutor like they just valet parked a life sentence.

Defense attorneys? Mixed bag. The good ones are enemies–the real ones, the fighters, the ones who actually *read* discovery and call out lies like it's a hobby. Prosecutors hate them. But the rest? They're just warm bodies in tailored suits pretending to fight while they help negotiate your slow legal death over lunch. Those plea deals don't draft themselves.

And don't forget the "mutual respect" handshake after every hearing. Yeah, that's not civility. That's collusion in a polyester suit. They're all playing the same game. You? You're the game piece.

So when you see that courtroom lineup–judge, prosecutor, defense, clerk, agents–don't think of it as separate branches of justice. Think of it as a **crew**, a well-oiled syndicate with matching badges and a shared mission: **keep the gears turning, feed the machine, and make sure the outcome never threatens the illusion.** You're not in a courtroom. You're in a fucking ecosystem—and you're the prey.

How Prosecutors Embellish the Truth

They don't need facts. They've got fear, loopholes, and a Bible-thick manual of psychological warfare dressed up as "procedure."

You think prosecutors are out here proving shit? Please. They're not truth-hunters. They're *narrative engineers.* Your story? Doesn't matter. They're gonna rewrite it, dramatize it, twist it into a Netflix-worthy indictment, and make sure the jury sees you as the villain by page two.

First trick? Inflate the charges. You steal a Snickers, they call it organized theft with conspiracy ties and emotional trauma to the vending machine operator. They're stacking charges like Legos, hoping the tower's so high you'll beg for a plea deal just to avoid getting crushed under the weight of a 97-count indictment for breathing near a crime scene.

Second trick? Weaponize cooperation. They flip your codefendant faster than pancakes at a prison breakfast. Now he's "cooperating," which really means he's been coached, squeezed, and promised a lighter sentence to regurgitate whatever version of events the government needs to bury you. Truth optional. Perjury overlooked. As long as the story matches the script, everyone claps.

Third trick? The courtroom theatrics. They stroll in like they're auditioning for Law & Order: starched suit, leather folder, fake righteous fury. Every question to a witness is a landmine. Every objection is strategic. Every pause is calibrated to make you look guilty. And if they can cry in front of the jury? Bonus points. Nothing says "justice" like a U.S. attorney pretending to care.

Fourth Trick? Pre-trial detention threats. They whisper sweet threats into your ear through your own lawyer: "If you don't take this deal, we're filing enhancements. We'll lock you up pre-trial. We'll call you a danger. We'll drag your name through the media." And guess what? It works. Because fear is the cheapest, most effective prosecution tactic in the world.

Fifth Trick? Hide the ball. Brady violations, discovery delays, "oops, forgot to turn that over." They'll bury exculpatory evidence under 1,200 pages of garbage and act shocked when you didn't find it. Then they'll stand up in court and talk about how "fair" they've been.

Sixth Trick? Sentencing manipulation. Once they get your plea (or your verdict), they slap you with every enhancement in the book. You blinked wrong? Leadership role. You had a cellphone? Obstruction. You didn't sob and confess during your PSR interview? Lack of remorse. Every guideline they can stretch, they stretch. And the judge eats it up like free shrimp at a federal conference.

Last? The unwritten rule: never lose. Prosecutors don't admit mistakes. They double down. If they're caught cheating? Deny. If a conviction gets overturned? Appeal. If the judge throws out evidence? Re-Indict. Their job isn't justice. It's to win. And if they gotta cheat, spin, or emotionally bludgeon you into submission, so be it.

They don't bring truth into the courtroom. They bring *tactics*. It's a strategy game where the scoreboard is *your years in prison*. And every time they win, they smile, shake hands, and go home to dinner while you get fitted for orange and shipped off to nowhere.

Why Prosecutors Get Away With It

"Checks and balances" is a cute bedtime story. In reality? It's a goddamn mirage in the desert of accountability. Let's start with the crown jewel of bullshit: **prosecutorial immunity**.

That's right—these suit-wearing mercenaries can lie, cheat, and destroy lives in a courtroom, and the law says you can't touch them. If a prosecutor fabricates evidence? Too bad. If they hide a key witness? Oh well. If they tank your life over a lie? The courts will shrug and say, *"But they meant well."* Because as long as they're "performing official duties," they're basically untouchable demigods with law degrees.

Internal Oversight: The Theater of Pretending to Care

Now sprinkle in the culture of ass-covering cowardice. Nobody wants to be the judge who slapped a prosecutor. Nobody wants to be the supervisor who admits the golden boy in the office cooked the books. It's all about keeping the machine looking clean. Internal investigations? Please. That's just the same crew jerking each other off behind closed doors, pretending to care while protecting their own. They don't do justice—they do damage control. And only when the press starts sniffing around.

Bureaucracy: The Cloak of Invisibility for Cowards

Then there's bureaucracy—the prosecutor's favorite invisibility cloak. Ever try filing a complaint against a federal prosecutor? Good luck. You'll be told to talk to the U.S. Attorney's Office… who will assign it to one of their own. That's like reporting a mugging to the guy who mugged you. There's no external oversight. There's no independent review board. Just a circle of suits passing the buck until you shut up or go away.

And if you don't shut up? They'll bury your complaint under a mountain of legalese and "pending review" sticky notes until the sun burns out.

Politics, Power, and the Great Circle Jerk

Politics? Oh, it's thick. Prosecutors are career climbers. They've got their eyes on judge seats, Senate runs, or cushy think tank gigs. So nobody wants to burn bridges by calling out misconduct. Even defense lawyers stay quiet. They've got other clients to think about—and pissing off the government is bad for business. So the silence isn't weakness. It's strategy.

Nobody wants to be the guy who made waves and lost access. So they all pretend the water's calm—even when it's full of sharks.

The Fear Factor: Don't Cross the Golden Boys

And let's not forget fear. Straight-up, pants-wetting fear. You think a judge is gonna humiliate a prosecutor in open court? You think a clerk is gonna report some shady shit they saw? Hell no. Everyone's scared of retaliation, of getting iced out, or just getting buried in career quicksand. So they stay silent. They look the other way. They pretend not to notice when the government brings a bazooka to a fistfight.

Fear keeps the system in check–not justice. Fear of losing jobs. Fear of being blacklisted. Fear of going against the grain and getting chewed up by the same machine you tried to stop.

The Branding Scam: White Hats, Black Hearts

Finally–nobody wants to believe the white hat's dirty. Prosecutors are sold to the public like they're Avengers in pinstripes. They're "serving justice," "protecting the people," "standing up for victims." It's all branding. All bullshit. But the illusion is comforting. And comfort sells better than truth. People don't want to hear that the guy who just locked up a single mom for a bullshit conspiracy charge is the real criminal. They want to believe he's the hero.

So why do prosecutors get away with it? Because the game was built for them to win.

Because the watchdogs are asleep, blind, or scared shitless. Because accountability is just a word they slap on mission statements. You're not watching a system with cracks. You're watching a system built like a fortress– And you're the one locked outside, screaming for justice while they sip cocktails inside and laugh.

The Aftermath (What's Left When They're Done With You)

When the show's over and the suits go home, the fallout starts – slow, ugly, and permanent.

Let's start with you – the defendant. You're not just sentenced. You're *erased*. You don't come out of the courtroom the same. You come out wearing a label, stripped of rights, and tied to a number in some federal database that'll follow you longer than your own shadow. Try getting a job, a loan, a lease, or your damn dignity back with "felon" stamped on your forehead. Good luck.

Your finances? Annihilated. Legal fees, restitution, asset seizures, fines – they hit you with the full buffet of financial destruction, and then garnish your future to pay for the privilege. Your credit's shot, your savings are gone, and even your fucking commissary money gets taxed by the system that broke you.

Your family? Collateral damage. Your mom ages ten years in the first six months. Your kids learn to celebrate birthdays over a jailhouse phone line. Your partner, if they don't leave, becomes a full-time paralegal, social worker, and emotional punching bag – all unpaid. The prosecutor never looks them in the eye. To them, your family's just scenery in the courtroom. Background noise. Forgotten the second the verdict hits.

And what about your name? It's radioactive. You become a cautionary tale. Whispers in your old neighborhood. Suspicion in job interviews. Every introduction becomes a minefield – "So, what do you do?" You either lie, or bleed your story out for people who stopped listening at the word "prison."

Meanwhile, the prosecutor? They're off at some charity dinner talking about "justice served."

They're polishing plaques, climbing ladders, and writing op-eds about "community safety." They never see the broken homes, the eviction notices, the kid who can't sleep, the partner who stopped smiling. They *don't care*. That's not their problem. Their job ended at the conviction. Everything else is **just wreckage they walked away from**.

And the system? It doesn't clean up. It doesn't heal. It just resets for the next show. Because **the machine doesn't mourn.** It feeds. And once it's done chewing you up, it spits out the bones and resets the docket. So if you're waiting for closure, peace, or some magical "lesson" from all this? Don't. There's no fucking epilogue. Just paperwork. And silence. And a life that has to keep going with the pieces left behind.

Myths About Federal Prosecutors

So, you're staring down the barrel of a federal indictment, and your lawyer sits you down for "the talk." They smile like they've got everything under control, tell you not to worry, and start spinning a web of half-truths and outright lies about the prosecutor on the other side of the courtroom. But let's rip off the bandage right now—most of what they're feeding you is designed to keep you calm, compliant, and signing those checks. Here's a no-nonsense look at the top lies lawyers tell you about federal prosecutors, straight from the trenches.

The Prosecutor is Just Doing Their Job, It's Nothing Personal

The Myth: Oh, of course, the prosecutor's just a humble public servant, punching the clock and doing their civic duty. It's nothing personal, right? They're just following the law, not targeting you at all. Kind of like how a hitman is just doing their job, you know, no hard feelings—it's just business.

Reality Check: Yeah, it's personal. Prosecutors don't get out of bed in the morning to do paperwork and sip coffee—they live for convictions. To them, every time they take down another poor soul like you, it's like earning another merit badge in the grand career ladder of "Let's Ruin Lives." They're not just doing a job; they're hunting for trophies. And guess who's the deer in their sights?

"The Prosecutor Will Be Fair and Reasonable."

The Myth: Oh, absolutely. The prosecutor is practically a walking, talking model of fairness. They're just like that friendly guy at the carnival who assures you that the basketball hoop isn't rigged. Your lawyer will tell you the prosecutor is open to negotiation, and they're not out to wreck your life. Sure.

Reality Check: Fair? They're about as fair as a casino slot machine. They're here to see you lose, and they're willing to rig the game to make sure it happens. That "reasonable" plea deal? It's just a way to scare the crap out of you so you'll take it. They throw the worst possible charges at you, then offer a "deal" that still feels like a slow walk to a prison cell. They call that a break—you call that a life sentence.

"The Prosecutor is a Straight Shooter."

The Myth: Hilarious. Your lawyer will have you believe that the prosecutor's middle name is "By-the-Book," and they wouldn't dream of bending the rules. You can totally trust them to play it straight, right? They'll never withhold evidence or manipulate witnesses. No way.

Reality Check: If you think prosecutors play by the rules, I've got a bridge to sell you. These people have more tricks than a Vegas magician. Withholding exculpatory evidence? Check. Leaning on witnesses like a mob boss? Double-check. They're not above twisting the truth to get a win, all while smiling sweetly like they've never bent a rule in their life. Straight shooters? More like crooked snipers.

"The Prosecutor Isn't Out to Ruin Your Life."

The Myth: Oh, sure. The prosecutor's just here for justice, not to crush your hopes, dreams, and freedom into a fine powder. They don't want to destroy your life, right? Your lawyer will tell you that the prosecutor isn't some villain cackling in their office, rubbing their hands together like a cartoon bad guy.

Reality Check: Wrong. The prosecutor's dream is to see you in orange, and they'll sleep better at night knowing they've secured another guilty verdict to boost their stats. It's not about justice—it's about padding their résumé with your misery. Your life is just another rung on the ladder to their next promotion. Ruining you is just a bonus.

"They're Open to Negotiation."

The Myth: Oh, definitely. The prosecutor is practically begging to negotiate with you in good faith. They're just dying to find common ground, right? Your lawyer will assure you that negotiations are on the table, and you're totally going to get a fair shake.

Reality Check: Yeah, they'll negotiate—because it saves them time and effort. But make no mistake, they've got the upper hand, and they know it. They're not negotiating because they care about your side of the story; they're doing it to wrap things up quickly. And if you think you're getting a great deal, guess again. You're getting the deal that's easiest for them, which usually means it's a raw deal for you.

"The Prosecutor Will Be Impressed if You Take Responsibility."

The Myth: Your lawyer might tell you that owning up to your mistakes, showing some remorse, and acting all responsible will win the prosecutor over. It's going to tug at their heartstrings, and they'll go easy on you, right?

Reality Check:: Impressed? Please. Taking responsibility is like handing them the shovel to dig your own grave. They'll nod, thank you for your cooperation, and then hit you with a harsher sentence. Your heartfelt apologies are just ammunition for them to nail you harder. You're not earning brownie points—you're giving them more leverage to crush you. So, congratulations on your newfound responsibility. Enjoy the extra years they throw at you for it.

The Prosecutor Won't Overcharge You."

The Myth: Oh, sure. The prosecutor's going to stick to the basics, right? They'll only charge you with what's absolutely necessary and won't go overboard. Your lawyer might reassure you that the prosecutor isn't going to load you up with extra charges just to make you sweat.

Reality Check: HA! Overcharging is the prosecutor's bread and butter. They'll slap every possible charge on you, right down to jaywalking if they can. Why? Because it freaks you out and makes you more likely to plead guilty to something–anything–to avoid the mountain of charges they've dumped on your head. Overcharging isn't just a tactic–it's their favorite game. And guess what? You're losing.

"Prosecutors Only Care About Justice."

The Myth: Yep, prosecutors wake up every day thinking about how to serve justice like it's some kind of divine mission. They're all about truth, fairness, and the American way. They'll give your case the attention it deserves because it's about making sure justice is done.

Reality Check: Newsflash–prosecutors care about one thing: winning. Justice is just a word they throw around in press releases. In reality, they're laser-focused on convictions. That's their scoreboard, and they want the high score. So when your lawyer tells you the prosecutor's all about justice, just know that what they're really about is racking up another win, no matter how dirty they play to get it.

The Prosecutor Will Be Fair at Sentencing."

The Myth: Oh, your lawyer says the prosecutor will be reasonable when it comes time for sentencing. If you cooperate, they'll push for a lighter sentence, right? They're not out to ruin your life completely, just give you a little slap on the wrist.

Reality Check: The prosecutor's idea of "fair" at sentencing is to make sure you're buried under the jail. They're pushing for the max sentence they can get their hands on. Every enhancement, every aggravating factor–they'll pile it on. They want you gone for as long as possible because, to them, your sentence is another trophy on their wall. Fair? The only thing they care about is whether you'll fit into the jumpsuit they've got waiting for you.

"Prosecutors Don't Hold Grudges."

The Myth: Your lawyer will assure you that standing up for yourself won't piss off the prosecutor. It's all part of the job, right? They won't take it personally if you push back or reject their plea deal.

Reality Check: Oh, they hold grudges. You make their job harder, and they'll make sure you pay for it. Push back too much? Watch them pile on more charges or fight even harder for a harsher sentence. Prosecutors are human–ambitious, competitive humans–and they remember when you make them work harder. You reject their deal? They'll make sure the next offer is worse, and at trial, they'll come after you like a pack of wolves.

Exhibit Ten: The Bottom Line

Federal prosecutors aren't guardians of justice – they're the priesthood of punishment. They don't serve "the people"; they serve the machine. Every indictment, every plea, every conviction is another prayer to the altar of control. They wear righteousness like armor and weaponize morality like a club. The courtroom isn't their workplace – it's their church, and your life is the offering.

Don't mistake their calm voices or polished arguments for integrity. That's theater. Their goal isn't to prove the truth – it's to perform a narrative so tight the jury stops thinking. They lie clean, cheat politely, and smile while doing it. Every move is a calculation: how to destroy you legally and still look noble doing it. And when the gavel drops, they walk out untouched – trophies in hand, souls unscathed.

If you're still waiting for justice, stop. The prosecutors already won before you showed up. The only thing left to decide is how cleanly they can bury you.

Next Up – Exhibit Eleven: The Unholy Triangle

You've met the actors. Now meet the syndicate. The judge, the prosecutor, and the defense lawyer – three heads of the same beast. They call it "the adversarial system." I call it a cartel with better suits. Exhibit Nine peels back the curtain on the collusion that keeps the whole charade running – and why the fight was fixed long before you walked into court.

EXHIBIT ELEVEN

The Unholy Triangle of Lawyer, Prosecutors & Judges

Lies My Lawyer Told Me - The Courtroom Conspiracy

You walk into a courtroom thinking it's a gladiator arena—a battle for your very existence. On one side, your defense lawyer is supposed to be armed to the teeth, fighting to protect your freedom. On the other side, the prosecutor stands ready to paint you as the villain of the century, eager to bury you under a mountain of legal jargon and manufactured outrage.

A Swamp of Favors, Incompetence, and Blind Luck

But here's the cold, hard truth: this isn't some dramatic showdown. It's a rigged poker game, and everyone at the table including the already knows each other. You're just another chip in their well-practiced game. If you think federal judges get appointed because they're the best and brightest legal minds in the country, I've got beachfront property in Kansas to sell you. The ugly truth is this: a lot of these judges are appointed for one reason, and one reason only—somebody owed somebody a favor. It's a grimy game of backroom deals, political handshakes, and calling in favors, not because they've got some sparkling judicial wisdom, but because their name was on the right cocktail party guest list.

You see, becoming a federal judge isn't about competence, legal brilliance, or even being remotely qualified to sit in judgment of another human being's life. Nah, it's about connections. These are lawyers who rubbed elbows with the right politicians, donated to the right campaigns, and kissed the right asses. Maybe they did a favor for the senator's brother-in-law's cousin ten years ago, or they greased the wheels on a corporate deal that made some congressmen's pockets a little deeper. Now, it's payback time.

And here's the kicker—half these people barely know which end of the gavel to hold. They're sitting there on the federal bench with the power to send you to prison for life, and some of them couldn't argue their way out of a parking ticket. But none of that matters. You don't need to be a legal genius to be a judge in the federal system. You just need to be well-connected, shake the right hands, and toe the party line.

Incompetent Judges

The scary part is how *incompetent* some of these judges really are. We're talking about people who've never set foot in a criminal courtroom, who have zero experience with the kind of high-stakes cases they're now presiding over. But they wear the robe, they play the part, and they've got the power to make decisions that'll ruin lives. You think they're sweating the details of your case? Hell no. They're more concerned with whether their appointment to the circuit court is coming through, or if that senator they owe drinks to is happy with how they're handling things.

Levine would tell you: this system isn't about justice. It's about favors, back-scratching, and political chess. These federal judges are often nothing more than lawyers who climbed the greasy ladder, smiling their way into positions of unearned authority. And you? You're the unlucky fool standing in front of them, hoping they actually know what they're doing. Spoiler alert: they probably don't.

The Old Boys' Club: Where Everyone Knows Your Name

Let's dispel any illusions you might have about a grand battle between good and evil. Your lawyer and the prosecutor? They've known each other for years. Hell, they probably went to the same law school, sat in the same lectures, and partied at the same frat houses. They crammed for the same bar exams, swapping study tips like college kids passing notes in class. You think they've got some deep-seated rivalry? Think again. Sure, they'll play their parts in court, trading objections and delivering impassioned speeches. But when the court day ends, they're as chummy as two old fraternity brothers.

Here's the dirty truth: they've probably worked at the same law firms, clerked for the same judges, maybe even shared office space at some point. They've been in the trenches together, trying to land the same jobs and nodding at each other across boardroom tables. It's all part of the cycle. One day they're wearing the prosecutor's hat, trying to nail you to the wall; the next, they're working defense, raking in cash to help the next poor bastard. And round and round it goes. Prosecutors become defense attorneys, defense attorneys become prosecutors, and you're just the latest roadkill on their career highway.

Whiskey, Women, and War Stories

If you think these legal titans go home at night nursing grudges and licking their wounds, you're sorely mistaken. After a long day of "fighting" in court, they don't retreat to strategize and sharpen their swords. No, they head straight to the nearest bar, order a round of overpriced whiskey, and swap war stories like old soldiers back from the front. The prosecutor who just tried to hang you in front of the jury? He's slapping your defense lawyer on the back, laughing about that one case they worked together ten years ago. They've probably closed down more dive bars together than you've had legal fees.

And let's not get all saintly about it either. These guys have likely shared more than just drinks. Chances are they've chased after the same women, too. Whether it's at a legal conference in some swanky hotel or during a happy hour that got a little too rowdy, they've got history–personal history. They've spent wild nights chasing skirts, waking up with regrets, and forming bonds that go way beyond the courtroom. So while you're sitting there, sweating bullets, thinking your lawyer and the prosecutor are about to tear each other apart for your sake, let me break it to you: you're just a footnote in their long, intertwined careers. You're the sideshow to their ongoing buddy drama.

The Judge? Oh, He's in on It Too

And don't for a second think the judge is sitting on some lofty, impartial perch, gazing down on this legal combat with wisdom and fairness. The judge is just as much a part of this mess as anyone else. You think these defense lawyers and prosecutors don't know the judge personally? Of course they do. They've been working the same cases in front of the same judge for years. They've rubbed elbows at the same charity galas, schmoozed at the same legal seminars, and clinked glasses at the same holiday parties. You think the judge doesn't have their favorite lawyers, their personal biases? Wake the hell up. They're just as human as anyone else, and just as connected to this legal web of relationships.

Half the time, your lawyer and the prosecutor already know how the judge is going to rule before they even step into the courtroom. The judge is a known entity. They've golfed together, sat on bar association panels together, maybe even swapped favors or shared old law school stories. When they walk into court, they're not strangers playing out some epic battle–they're old friends playing their roles in the ongoing legal drama. And you? You're just the unfortunate guest star of the week, caught up in the plot.

Defense Attorneys: Into It for the Money, Not the Fight

Let's cut through the crap about your defense lawyer being some kind of gladiator fighting for your life. You think they're going to war for you, battling for your freedom with every ounce of their being? Guess again. Most defense attorneys are in this game for one reason, and one reason only: the paycheck. You're just another case in their book, another hour to bill, another set of documents to file before they move on to the next unlucky soul.

Sure, they'll act like they care–they'll talk a big game about justice and fairness–but at the end of the day, it's all about the bottom line. Your lawyer knows the prosecutor, knows the judge, and probably already has a pretty good idea how this whole thing is going to go down. They'll play their part, sure, but don't expect them to bleed for your cause. It's not personal for them. It's business.

They've got a reputation to maintain, of course, but they're not looking for a bloody fight. They're looking for the easiest way to get you out of their hair while they move on to the next paying client. You're not special. You're just a job, another case to close so they can get their next paycheck.

A Scripted Showdown: Playing Their Parts for the Audience

Now, sit back and watch the show. You're sitting in court, watching what looks like a heated legal battle unfold before your eyes. Your lawyer stands up, delivers a passionate defense, pulling out all the stops. The prosecutor fires back with righteous indignation, making you out to be some kind of master criminal. The judge makes a few stern rulings, playing the role of the impartial arbiter. It's like a well-rehearsed courtroom drama, perfectly choreographed down to the smallest detail. But that's all it is–a performance. A scripted, well-worn routine they've all played out hundreds of times.

Behind the scenes, these lawyers have already had drinks, laughed about your case, and maybe even whispered a few agreements under their breath. The prosecutor's job is to win, but they don't need to destroy you—they've got bigger fish to fry. The defense lawyer wants to look good, sure, but not at the cost of burning bridges with their buddy across the aisle. And the judge? The judge just wants to maintain order without upsetting the delicate balance they've built with the lawyers who will be back in their courtroom next week.

You're just the latest actor in a well-rehearsed play, and spoiler alert—the script doesn't favor you.

What Happens After Court? More of the Same

When the gavel bangs and court adjourns for the day, you're heading home to sweat over what the hell just happened. Your defense lawyer? They're heading to the same bar they always go to. And who do you think they'll find there? The prosecutor, of course. They'll sit at the bar, talk shop, maybe swap a few stories about the "interesting legal points" in your case, laugh about some old college memories, and order another round of whiskey.

The law isn't about justice. It's about relationships—relationships forged in the same schools, the same courtrooms, the same bars, and yes, even the same beds. The players know each other, trust each other, and respect each other in ways you'll never understand. And you? You're just another chapter in their shared story, another case number, another headline for their résumés.

Conflicts of Interest: Lawyers, Prosecutors, and the Ethics Mirage

Let me lay it out for you—the so-called *ethics standards* in the legal world are about as real as a UFO sighting at midnight. Lawyers and prosecutors are swimming in the same murky pool, pretending like they don't know each other outside the courtroom when, in reality, they're up to their necks in conflicts of interest. The whole thing is a joke wrapped in the shiny, self-righteous cloak of *legal ethics*—and they expect you to believe it.

Here's the dirty little secret: lawyers and prosecutors have more in common with each other than they'll ever have with you, their client. They rotate jobs like musical chairs—one day they're a prosecutor trying to nail you to the wall, the next they're a defense attorney raking in cash to "save" another poor bastard. It's all part of the club.

They've worked together, sat on the same committees, and probably chased after the same partners at law firm retreats. But when they're in court? Oh, they act like they've never met before. It's all just smoke and mirrors.

The Judicial Frat Party

And then there's *ethics*—a laughable set of rules that lawyers love to throw around when it suits them but conveniently ignore when it gets in the way of their next payday. Technically, conflicts of interest are a big no-no, but enforcement is a joke. If your lawyer is buddy-buddy with the prosecutor, sharing drinks after hours, how do you think that's going to affect your case? Are they really going to go for the jugular when they've got a golf outing planned next weekend with the same guy trying to throw you in prison? Of course not.

But the *ethics standards* say everything's fine as long as they disclose the conflict or pretend to "act in your best interest." What a scam. Legal ethics are a fig leaf covering up a massive conflict-of-interest industry. Everyone's in on the game, and you're the only one playing it straight. So while you're sweating bullets over your future, your lawyer and the prosecutor are exchanging winks and nods, knowing damn well their "conflict" won't get in the way of their next paycheck. Ethics, my friend, are for suckers. And in this game? You're the sucker.

The Court House Phonies

Here's the dirty truth they'll never tell you: your defense lawyer doesn't really care about you. Sure, they'll put on a good show. They'll file motions and argue objections, but at the end of the day, they're more concerned about keeping their relationships intact than they are about saving you. Prosecutors come and go, judges rotate, but the relationships stay.

They'll play nice with the prosecutor because they know they might switch sides someday. They'll be polite to the judge because they've got more cases coming up. And you? You're just a blip on the radar.

You think you're hiring a gladiator, someone who's going to fight to the death to defend your freedom. But what you're really hiring is someone who's playing a game they've been playing for years, and the outcome doesn't really matter to them. You're just another job. Another billable hour. Another day in the office.nGot it. Here are ten gritty, sarcasm-laced entries that pull no punches:

The Judges Are Completely Neutral Bullshit Myth

Oh, sure, judges are just here to call it fair, like some kind of courtroom referees with no bias, no agendas, and no personal stake in the outcome. They're like saintly monks, immune to influence or favor, floating above the fray to keep things equal and impartial.

Judges come with their own set of biases, alliances, and attitudes toward the people in their courtroom, and guess who usually benefits? Not the defense. Judges and prosecutors have a tight little circle, often sharing casual chats, social events, and sometimes even professional histories that make them lean toward the prosecution side.

A defense attorney walks in to face a judge who's had coffee with the prosecutor that morning and doesn't even realize they're already behind. Neutrality? It's a nice story they sell to the public, but in the real world, judges often give the nod to their allies on the prosecution side, consciously or not, turning neutrality into a fairytale that rarely holds up in court.

Prosecutors and Defense Attorneys Are Equal in Court

The Myth: In the American legal system, both sides have an equal voice, right? Prosecutors and defense attorneys supposedly face off on the same level, each with their arsenal of arguments and evidence, ready to go head-to-head in the battle for justice. No one has the upper hand here—it's all fair.

Reality Check: This "equal footing" is a myth. Prosecutors are armed to the teeth with government resources: labs, investigators, experts on speed-dial, and nearly unlimited funds. They're backed by the state, while defense attorneys often operate on a shoestring budget, sometimes begging for basic resources just to stay in the game.

And let's not forget the judge's bias here. Defense attorneys find themselves on the outside, treated like intruders in the prosecution's club, a club that includes the judge. The defense has to work twice as hard to be heard, with the deck stacked against them from the start. Equality? Only if you consider an uphill battle "equal footing."

Judges Don't Play Favorites

The Myth: Judges are the ultimate impartial figures, treating every lawyer, defendant, and piece of evidence with the same level of respect and scrutiny. They don't care who you are or what side you're on; they're above favoritism and couldn't possibly be swayed by a familiar face.

The Truth: Judges play favorites all the time, and they often don't even hide it. Prosecutors are in their courts day after day, building a rapport that defense attorneys don't get. Judges know the prosecutors well, sharing lunches, laughs, and that unspoken understanding of being on the same side of "justice."

When a defense attorney tries to call out the prosecution's moves, judges can be quick to shut them down, siding with the friendly face they know and trust. Favoritism is alive and well, especially when the judge's "favorite" is the person they've built a relationship with over years of shared cases, conferences, and the occasional drink after court.

Defense Attorneys and Prosecutors Are Adversaries

The Myth: It's a showdown, right? Prosecutors and defense attorneys are rivals in the courtroom, clashing swords, each fighting tooth and nail for their side. They're adversaries through and through, bringing all they've got to defeat each other.

The Truth: The so-called rivalry is often just a show for the jury. Outside the courtroom, prosecutors and defense attorneys are often on friendly terms, grabbing coffee, chatting at legal events, and even sharing laughs. The intense battle in the courtroom can be more of a scripted dance, with each side playing their role while knowing they'll be back to buddying up once the trial wraps.

Sure, there's a performance for the court, but in the end, these relationships are more civil than adversarial. Many defense attorneys know not to push too hard, keeping things friendly enough to stay in the good graces of both the prosecutor and the judge.

Judges Follow the Law to the Letter

The Myth: Judges are supposed to be sticklers for the law, rigidly applying statutes, precedent, and procedure without bending or interpreting to fit their personal beliefs. They're bound by the black-and-white text of the law, not their own opinions.

The Truth: Judges "interpret" the law to reach the outcomes they want, and this often means bending rules to help the prosecution. Need to let in a questionable piece of evidence? They'll find a justification. Want to dismiss a defense argument? They'll rule it "irrelevant." The law in a judge's hands is as flexible as rubber, and personal opinions play a huge role in how they apply it. And when they're friendly with the prosecutor, they're all the more likely to twist things in ways that benefit the state's case. This isn't rigid law-following; it's selective enforcement dressed up as "judicial discretion."

Prosecutors Are Seeking Truth, Not Wins

The Myth: Prosecutors are supposed to be noble pursuers of truth, working to uncover the facts and serve justice. They're not in it for the win; they're in it to ensure the right outcome, regardless of personal ambition or statistics.

The Truth: Prosecutors live and die by their conviction rates. Their careers, promotions, and reputations hinge on how many "wins" they can rack up, and they'll do just about anything to get them. They're not above stretching evidence, pushing witnesses, or even withholding material from the defense if it gives them a better chance at conviction.

For prosecutors, the courtroom is less about truth and more about numbers, with justice taking a backseat to the scoreboard. The truth is just another weapon they manipulate as it suits them, all in the name of keeping their win stats up.

Judges and Prosecutors Are Not Aligned

The Myth: In the court of law, judges and prosecutors supposedly work independently, each operating in their own lane to uphold the law. They're not on the same team; they're supposed to keep each other in check, ensuring fairness for all.

The Truth: Judges and prosecutors are deeply aligned, sometimes without even realizing it. They're part of the same legal ecosystem, often seeing each other outside the courtroom at conferences, social events, and informal gatherings. This camaraderie means they often have each other's backs, with judges giving prosecutors the benefit of the doubt and the wiggle room they need to secure convictions. Defense attorneys? They're not part of this club, left to fend for themselves in a courtroom where the judge and prosecutor already have a built-in alliance, formal or informal.

Prosecutor & Judge Don't Communicate Behind Closed Doors

Everything that happens in court is above board, right? There's no back-channeling or off-the-record conversations. Your case is argued out in the open, where you and your defense team get a fair shot. Prosecutors and judges would never be caught chatting about a case in chambers or in private; that's strictly off-limits. The idea that they're talking about you while you're not there? Just paranoid thinking.

The Truth: The courtroom is only half the game. The real decisions are often made over coffee, in chambers, or during casual hallway chats where no one's watching and nothing's recorded. You'd be shocked at how often "private consultations" happen between judges and prosecutors, where they swap opinions on cases, share insights, or even hint at what they think _should_ happen.

They're smoothing out details, discussing strategies, and maybe even tipping each other off about issues that could come up. Your lawyer? They'll play along because that's how the system keeps ticking. The transparency you expect? It's a smokescreen. The real moves are being made in places you'll never see or hear about.

Your Lawyer Can't Do Anything If the Judge & Prosecutor Are Buddies

The Myth: Your lawyer would fight tooth and nail for you if the judge and prosecutor were being unfair. But if they're pals, well, their hands are tied! They'll say, "It's unfortunate, but we have to work with the judge we have," making it sound like the legal equivalent of bad luck. Your defense is supposedly at the mercy of a friendship they can't disrupt. After all, they're the outsider in this clique.

The Truth: Here's the harsh truth: most lawyers don't *want* to disrupt that cozy little clique. They're not fighting against a buddy-buddy judge-prosecutor team because they don't want to rock the boat. This is the system they have to work in every day, case after case. Your case isn't important enough to ruin that long-term relationship.

If your lawyer were really determined, they'd file complaints, challenge rulings, and push the judge to reconsider their biases. But why risk it? Staying in the judge's and prosecutor's good graces means less hassle and more cooperation down the line–for them, not for you. So instead of going to bat, they let the courtroom politics play out as usual, leaving you to navigate a rigged game while they stick to their safe, "diplomatic" approach.

Exhibit Eleven: The Bottom Line

The courtroom isn't a battleground – it's a backroom deal with better lighting. You're not watching justice unfold; you're watching a social club protect its own. The prosecutor, the judge, and your lawyer all swim in the same pond, and you're the bait that keeps the water churning. They'll smile in public, argue for show, and then clink glasses in private, congratulating each other on another "clean day in court." It's not corruption in the cinematic sense – it's worse. It's routine.

This "unholy triangle" isn't about guilt or innocence; it's about order, relationships, and face-saving. Prosecutors feed judges convictions to pad their careers. Judges reward lawyers who don't cause trouble. Lawyers play nice to stay invited to the next party. And you? You're the disposable storyline that keeps the script running.

The real crime isn't what you did – it's believing any of them were ever fighting for you. The judge keeps the illusion alive, the prosecutor fuels it, and your lawyer sells you tickets to the show. Justice isn't blind – it's drunk, bored, and taking notes from its friends at the bar.

Next Up – Exhibit Twelve: Judges

You've seen the collusion–the backroom deals, the friendly fire, the cozy lunches where justice gets traded like gossip. But now we climb higher up the food chain. The judge isn't just part of the triangle–he's the apex. The robe, the gavel, the myth of neutrality. He's the one who turns every lie into law and every performance into a verdict.

Next up, we strip the sanctity off the bench and show you how gods are made–one political favor at a time

EXHIBIT TWELVE

Federal Judge Conspirator

Where "Your Honor" Means You're Already Screwed

You walk in that courtroom and instantly know—you ain't shit in here. The air hits different. Cold, dead, recycled through the same vents that had been choking defendants for decades. The flag's hangin' there like it's watchin', the seal on the wall lookin' down like the all-seein' eye of bullshit. "All rise," they bark, and the whole damn room jumps up like trained dogs. Nobody's honoring justice. They're just scared.

The Theater Of The Damned

That's the trick–they sell you this lie that the judge is some holy man, handpicked by destiny to keep the balance of good and evil. Hell no. He's an actor in a robe, playin' God with your future. This whole setup is theater, and you? You're the free entertainment. The prosecutor's got the script, your lawyer's acting nervous, and the audience already knows how it ends. The judge walks in like he's Moses on Mount Fuckin' Sinai, when really he's just a government employee with a caffeine habit and a fragile ego.

They say justice is blind, but she damn sure hears the judge's footsteps. This ain't blind justice–it's deaf obedience. And if you ever forget that, that robe will remind you exactly who runs this show.

The Robe As Armor

That robe ain't a symbol–it's a shield. It hides the ego, the bias, and the hangover from whatever they drank the night before sentencing your ass. It's polyester arrogance sewn into authority. Without it, these judges are just cranky lawyers with bad knees and God complexes. But that black curtain? That's their invisibility cloak. It turns mortal assholes into untouchable saints.

They love that power trip. It's the only job in America where you can ruin lives before lunch, take an hour for golf, and still get called "Your Honor." It's all ceremony, all control. You can't call 'em out, can't talk back, can't even look too long without getting that "contempt of court" threat like it's a damn magic spell. The robe makes 'em bulletproof–emotionally, legally, morally. You can't sue 'em. You can't expose 'em. You can't do shit but stand there while they play priest and executioner in the same breath.

They act like it's wisdom, but it's insulation. The robe ain't justice–it's armor against consequence.

THE ILLUSION OF WISDOM

Let me tell you something: half of these judges couldn't find fairness with a flashlight and a map. They hide behind big-ass words and Latin phrases nobody asked for–*res judicata, mens rea, habeas this and that*–like it makes 'em prophets instead of politicians in costume. It's language as intimidation. The more confused you are, the more power they feel.

They weren't chosen 'cause they're the smartest. They got picked 'cause they kissed the right ring and made the right friends. It's politics in a robe. Every appointment's a favor owed, every lifetime seat a thank-you card from some senator or president. You think justice chose them? Nah, lobbyists did. You think they care about truth? They care about optics. The robe's just the logo.

You'll see it when they talk–half asleep, halfway listening, already decided. They ain't hearing arguments; they're counting minutes. They'll hit you with that fake patience, that long pause before the ruling, like they're having a deep moral crisis. Bullshit. They're just deciding how hard they can crush you before the lunch line closes.

The Church Of Control

The courtroom's their church, and that bench is their pulpit. The lawyers play choir, the clerks sing backup, and you're the sinner begging for mercy in a language nobody in the room speaks anymore. Everything about it screams religion–rituals, kneeling, standing, reciting, confessing. Except in this church, forgiveness don't exist. The robe replaced the cross, and the gavel replaced the Bible. You can't question the faith or the high priest will send your ass to purgatory with a sentencing chart.

And here's the sick part–they believe it. Every judge who's been worshipped long enough starts to think the robe grew outta their skin. They stop seeing defendants as people and start seeing them as numbers, docket entries, statistics on a spreadsheet they can brag about at retirement dinners. They say things like "Justice must be served" while treating it like a catering order.

You ever notice how the courtroom hushes when the judge speaks? That ain't respect–it's fear disguised as discipline. Everyone in that room knows who can end a career or a life with a sigh and a sentence. They've built a cult around that power. And you, standing there in shackles or cheap shoes, are the sacrifice.

The Aftertaste Of Obedience

By the time you leave that courtroom, you'll start believing the myth yourself. That maybe the judge *was* right. That maybe this *is* justice. That's the genius of the whole scam–they make you grateful for being destroyed politely. The robe, the rituals, the fake dignity–it's psychological warfare dressed up as professionalism. They don't need to beat you down physically; they do it with posture, tone, and silence.

Here's the truth nobody prints on the courtroom walls: judges don't preserve justice, they preserve control. The robe isn't a symbol of wisdom; it's a weapon of obedience. Every "All rise" is a reminder that you don't have a voice in here–only permission to speak. And when that gavel hits, it's not justice echoing–it's the sound of ownership.

Lifetime Appointment, Lifetime Arrogance

A federal judge don't serve justice–they serve themselves. Lifetime appointment? That's code for *we don't fire our own.* Once they sit down in that big oak chair, it's permanent. You could catch one of these fossils drooling mid-hearing and nobody's got the guts to call it what it is–judicial hospice care.

They'll tell you it's "public service." Don't buy it. It's a lifetime vacation with taxpayer benefits and god-mode authority. You could have a judge who hasn't read a real case since Clinton was in office, still dictating human destinies like it's a crossword puzzle. And when the robe starts fitting tight from all that ego weight, they don't quit–they just lean back, get crankier, and start sentencing people like they're pruning weeds.

And the worst part? They start believing the hype. Every "Your Honor" feeds their delusion. Every lawyer bowing, every "may it please the court" makes 'em think they're divine. They ain't. They're old bureaucrats who got promoted from lawyer to lifetime god. And when you stand in front of one, shaking in that itchy county suit, they see you as a statistic, not a soul.

Try to challenge them. Go ahead. You'll get the contempt look–the "how dare you breathe my air" glare. They've been untouchable so long, they forgot what accountability even feels like. These people could ruin your life before lunch and still make it home in time for a taxpayer-funded pension dinner.

They say judges interpret law. Nah–they *invent* it on the spot. Depends on their mood, their politics, and whether they had to parallel park that morning. "Lifetime appointment" doesn't mean wisdom. It means *too long unchecked.*

Politics in a Black Robe

Let's kill this fairy tale about "nonpartisan justice." Every single one of these robed hustlers is somebody's political pet project. They don't end up on the bench 'cause they're brilliant–they end up there 'cause they kissed the right asses and kept their scandals quiet.

Every nomination's a chess move. A president throws one judge to the wolves, then installs three more who'll dance to his tune for the next forty years. That's the real game–control the courtroom, control the country. Red or blue, it don't matter–they're all just different brands of loyalty.

You ever seen the confirmation hearings? That fake politeness? It's a Broadway show. The senators ask "tough" questions for TV, the nominee dodges like a pro, and then–surprise!–everyone votes along party lines anyway. Boom. Lifetime power unlocked.

And once they get that robe, they're free agents. Presidents come and go, laws change, people die–but these judges? They just keep signing names and stacking sentences. They'll tell you they don't care about politics, but somehow every ruling lines up with their donor's philosophy. Coincidence, right?

And you wanna talk hypocrisy? Watch one of these "strict constitutionalists" bend reality like yoga instructors when it suits them. Suddenly, precedent don't matter, facts don't matter, empathy don't matter. All that matters is control. Judicial independence, my ass–it's a political retirement plan with better lighting.

They say justice is blind. Maybe once. Now she's just wearing tinted glasses and pretending she don't see the money.

The Personality Lottery

Federal court ain't justice–it's Russian roulette with paperwork. Who you get behind that bench decides your whole damn life. Pull a soft-spoken philosopher? You might walk out breathing. Pull a sociopath in a robe? You're about to learn what 360 months sounds like in federal English.

They'll tell you it's "sentencing consistency." Yeah, consistent like weather. Two defendants, same crime, same facts—one walks with probation, the other gets a decade. Why? 'Cause one judge was in a good mood and the other didn't get his morning muffin. That's the system. Law by caffeine levels.

And the egos—Jesus Christ. Some of these judges treat trials like personal therapy sessions. They'll scold you, lecture you, degrade you like you're the moral collapse of civilization itself. They think their robe makes them philosophers, prophets, heroes. Nah, just bullies with gavels.

Ever notice how they all talk the same? Slow, deliberate, like they're narrating the Ten Commandments. It's a performance. Every "the court finds…" is another verse in their vanity gospel. The courtroom's just their stage, the lawyers are their props, and you're the emotional punchline.

Some smile while they ruin you. That's the worst kind. They hand out sentences with a kind of poetic rhythm, like they're doing you a favor by destroying your life gracefully. Others don't even fake it—they just drop numbers like grenades, grab their coat, and walk out. Cold. Efficient. Bored.

And when you're gone—file closed, body shipped off—they don't think about you again. You vanish into the paperwork void. Your name becomes docket dust. Meanwhile, they're onto the next show, next defendant, next ego trip.The law don't protect you—it entertains them.

The Bottom Line

District judges ain't public servants—they're the system's landlords. You pay rent in respect, obedience, and silence. They don't care if you're innocent; they care if you're compliant. You can quote the Constitution till your tongue dries up, but if their patience runs out, that gavel's coming down like a guillotine.

They'll smile in your direction, call it "due process," then hand your life over to a file clerk like it's junk mail. That's not justice—that's logistics.

Federal judges don't need crowns. The robe *is* the crown. The courtroom's their kingdom, the clerk's their serf, and you? You're just another trespasser who forgot that in America, kings still exist—they just traded thrones for benches.

So when your lawyer whispers, "Address the court as 'Your Honor,'" don't say it like you mean it. Say it like a survival strategy. 'Cause in that room, honor's got nothing to do with it.

Hang 'Em High Harry: The Factory Foreman of Misery

Judge Harry ain't a man – he's a goddamn monument to punishment. If human misery was a stock, this old bastard would own majority shares. Been on the bench since fax machines were cutting edge, still slamming gavels like he's trying to crack concrete. He's dished out so many years of prison time, rumor says the Bureau of Prisons sends him Christmas cards with *"Thanks for keeping the lights on."*

The Million-Month Man

He brags about it too. Keeps a running total like some deranged collector. "A million months," he told a reporter once, chest puffed like he just cured cancer. Except he didn't cure shit – he just filled cages with people too poor to afford a lawyer who plays golf with the right senators. You don't get the nickname *Hang 'Em High* for being compassionate. You get it for building your legacy on other people's broken lives.

Every defendant's a notch on his gavel. Every sentence a sermon in his gospel of pain. Harry doesn't see people – he sees quotas. He's running a numbers racket with a robe on. The court staff calls him *The Calculator*, and the nickname fits: emotionless, predictable, efficient at destruction.

And don't let that soft old-man shuffle fool you. Behind that cane and cardigan sits a sadist who measures worth by how hard he can hammer someone before lunch. If there's a hell, Harry's probably presiding there, adding "eternity" to your sentence just to stay consistent.

Justice by Calculator

When Harry's in session, the courtroom sounds like a math class run by a sociopath. He doesn't listen to pleas or explanations – he calculates doom. You can almost hear his internal abacus clicking while you beg for mercy. Ten points for "leadership role," two for "obstruction," five for "general breathing while indicted."

He calls it "consistency." The lawyers call it "clinical insanity." Nobody can talk sense into him – he's addicted to the guidelines. He reads them like scripture, quotes them like poetry. "Section 2B1.1," he'll say, eyes glazed like a preacher in a trance. Translation: *I stopped caring about you four paragraphs ago.*

See, to Harry, justice ain't a balance – it's a spreadsheet. He'll shave off empathy like it's decimal rounding. Doesn't matter if you're a scared 20-year-old or a grandma who bounced a check; once the math lands, so does the hammer.

And if you try to reason with him, forget it. He's got that smug, half-smile judges get when they know they're untouchable. He'll lean back, tap that old Casio calculator, and drop a number so absurd you'll think he misread the decimal. "Three hundred sixty months," he'll say, monotone. No emotion. No hesitation. Just another brick in his empire of wasted lives.

You can almost see it on his face – that flicker of satisfaction. The high of knowing he's still got the power to ruin someone's future before his next nap.

Harry doesn't interpret the law – he *weaponizes* it. Every sentence he hands down is a performance of authority, a reminder that the robe doesn't just symbolize justice; it *replaces* it.

The Cane of Doom

That cane ain't medical – it's ceremonial. It's the staff of an executioner who never had to swing the blade himself. Harry walks in tapping that thing like a metronome of fear. *Tap... tap... tap...* Every sound a warning shot. You can feel the tension in the room rise with each step, like everyone's waiting to find out whose life gets flattened next.

He uses it for punctuation – one hard slam to shut down a lawyer, another to silence a defendant mid-sentence. Some judges use words. Harry uses percussion. The sound of that cane hitting the floor is the prelude to another 30-year symphony of suffering.

They say one time, a defendant fainted during sentencing. Harry didn't flinch. Just poked the guy's leg with his cane and told the marshal, "Pick him up – I'm not done yet." That's the level of compassion we're dealing with here.

When he's not slamming it, he's leaning on it like a king on a throne, surveying his empire of despair. That courtroom isn't a place of law – it's his kingdom. The clerks are his peasants, the lawyers his jesters, and every defendant's another sacrifice at the altar of his ego.

They joke that when he finally dies, they'll mount that cane behind the bench like a relic. *"In memory of Justice Served – and Mercy Denied."*

But it ain't a joke. That cane's soaked with the ghosts of everyone he's buried in paperwork. You can hear them if you listen close – all those lives he totaled up like receipts.

Justice as Performance Art

Harry doesn't run a courtroom; he runs a stage play. He's the director, the star, and the audience all rolled into one. He'll crack jokes during sentencing, drop biblical quotes before handing down 25 years, and smirk like he's doing society a favor. He doesn't see trials as trials – he sees them as theater, and everyone else is there to make him look righteous.

Watch his face when the prosecutor talks – that's admiration. Watch his face when defense tries to speak – that's irritation. The verdict was written before the first word was spoken. The rest is just for show.

One time, some poor bastard tried to explain himself – talk about redemption, responsibility, turning over a new leaf. Harry let him finish, leaned forward, and said, "That's touching. You'll have 300 months to reflect on it." Then he winked at the clerk. Winked. Like he just nailed a punchline.

He doesn't punish to correct. He punishes to *perform*. Every case is another encore, another audience to watch him prove he's still the biggest, baddest moral compass in the room.

The Last Hangman

Harry's the final generation of dinosaurs – the last hangman in a world that likes to pretend it evolved. He doesn't believe in rehabilitation. He believes in retribution. To him, justice is revenge dressed up in Latin.

He's what happens when you give an old man god-level authority and no expiration date. He'll sit on that bench until rigor mortis sets in, and even then, they'll probably keep him propped up for sentencing. The courtroom would just keep rolling – defendants crying, clerks typing, Harry drooling but still mumbling "30 years" on instinct.

He'll die doing what he loves – crushing people. They'll hold his funeral in that same courtroom, maybe even drape his robe over the coffin. And you know what? The same lawyers who feared him will show up pretending to respect him, because that's how the system survives – by pretending monsters are heroes.

When the obituary comes out, it'll say *"A lifetime dedicated to public service."* What it should say is: *"Responsible for more destroyed lives than heroin."*

The Aftermath of a Legend Nobody Needed

Hang 'Em High Harry will get his portrait on the courthouse wall one day – right next to the other fossils who believed mass incarceration was moral duty. His face will stare down from that wall like a threat to every poor bastard who walks in next.

They'll name a courtroom after him, too. "The Honorable Judge Harrington Chamber." Has a nice ring, doesn't it? Sounds noble, right up until you realize how many people walked into that room free and left in chains.

The prosecutors will toast him. The defense attorneys will breathe easier. And the defendants – the thousands of ghosts he built his legacy on – will keep serving their million months, forgotten, faceless, and voiceless.

Because that's how it ends in Harry's world – the man dies, the sentences live on. His justice never really stops. It just keeps echoing through every cell block he helped fill.

The Bottom Line

Judge Harry ain't just a man. He's a system with wrinkles. A living fossil in a black robe, running the world's most efficient misery factory. The machine keeps him alive because he makes it look legitimate. "Look," they say, "that's justice – a wise old man keeping order."

Nah. That's propaganda in polyester. He's the perfect illusion – a grandfatherly executioner with a gavel instead of a gun.

When you stand in front of him, remember this: you're not getting judged. You're getting processed. And every word you say just feeds the gears.

Harry doesn't need a hangman's noose. His signature *is* the rope.

The Court's Good Cop: Judge Solomon Grey

Judge Solomon Grey walks into court like the antidote to Harry – clean suit, calm smile, silver hair shining like a halo under fluorescent light. He's not yelling, not slamming his cane, not quoting scripture between sentences. Nah, Grey's got that steady preacher voice that makes you *want* to believe him. He listens. He nods. He uses words like "rehabilitation" and "second chances." And right when you start thinking maybe this one's different, he slides the knife in – gentle, surgical, professional.

The Gentle Executioner

See, that's his trick. Grey kills softly. He makes injustice sound like compassion. He doesn't punish with rage; he punishes with empathy. He'll call you "Mr." instead of "Defendant," tell you he understands your pain, and then tack on a decade "for deterrence." It's punishment wrapped in poetry. You leave his courtroom thanking him for destroying you *politely*.

Grey's courtroom ain't loud. It's quiet – like a funeral home. You don't hear anger, you hear resignation. Everyone knows the outcome, they're just waiting for the ceremony. Grey presides like a priest giving last rites to another sinner who thought the system could forgive.

That's what makes him dangerous. Harry's brutality wakes you up. Grey's compassion lulls you into accepting your own execution.

Wisdom on a Leash

Solomon Grey's got the kind of wisdom people write puff pieces about – "a balanced jurist," "a man of reason," "a modern judge with an old soul." You see those headlines every few years, right before they reassign him to a high-profile case to make the court look human again. He's their PR weapon – the mask the system wears when it wants to look civilized.

He's smart, no question. Sharp enough to see the game for what it is, but too deep in it to change the rules. That's the tragedy of Grey – he knows the system's fucked. He's read the same sentencing reports, seen the same recycled defendants, watched the same prosecutors pad their stats. He knows "justice" is just paperwork dressed up for court. But he still signs the orders. Still reads the sentences. Still keeps the gears turning.

That's the leash – the invisible one every "good" judge wears. You don't get to climb the ladder without learning how to toe the line. Grey knows who really runs the room: the U.S. Attorney's Office, the probation reports, the goddamn Sentencing Commission. He might soften the blow here and there, but he ain't changing the impact. He's the face they put on the machine when they want mercy to look official.

He'll tell himself he's making a difference. That his fairness "balances the system." But let's be honest – fairness don't fix a rigged game. It just makes it easier to sell the illusion.

The Fair Face of the Same Beast

Here's the bottom line: Grey's a better man than Harry, but it don't matter. They're both gears in the same engine – one runs hot, one runs smooth, but they spin the same direction. You can't "reform" justice by swapping out personalities. The machine doesn't care who's driving.

Grey hands out sentences that sound merciful – 24 months instead of 30, probation instead of prison. But the paperwork still crushes lives. The felonies still stick. The probation violations still drag people back to court. And every signature he puts down keeps the system fed – quiet, clean, sustainable oppression.

He's not evil. He's efficient. And that's worse. Evil you can see coming; efficiency sneaks in smiling. Grey believes he's doing right, and maybe that's true in his head – but "right" in a broken system still ends in ruin.

You want to know how deep the rot runs? Look at the defendants who thank him on their way out. "Thank you, Your Honor," they say, tears in their eyes, cuffed wrists shaking. Thanking the man who just took their freedom because at least he didn't humiliate them like Harry did. That's how you know the system's complete – when the condemned start thanking the hangman for using a softer rope.

The Machine Needs Its Angels

See, the court can't survive on monsters alone. It needs angels too. It needs a Solomon Grey to make people believe there's still decency in the mix. He's the moral camouflage – the reason the public still calls it *justice* instead of *processing.* He's proof the machine has evolved – not by fixing itself, but by hiring better actors.

Grey's mercy is a feature, not a flaw. His empathy makes the punishment look palatable, keeps the outrage low, keeps the headlines positive. Without him, the courts would look like what they really are – a conveyor belt of ruined lives operated by people with law degrees. Grey softens the optics, sanitizes the slaughter, and calls it grace. He's not the villain. He's the lubricant. Without men like him, the gears would grind too loud to ignore.

The Bottom Line

Judge Solomon Grey ain't your redemption arc – he's your lullaby before the needle hits the vein. He's what the system rolls out when it needs to look human for five goddamn minutes. The robe fits better, the tone's smoother, the words are warmer – but the results are the same: you lose, quietly.

That's the trick, isn't it? Harry makes you hate the system; Grey makes you *trust* it again. You walk out of his courtroom thinking maybe, just maybe, there's hope. That's how deep the scam runs – they make injustice feel humane. You're not supposed to walk out angry; you're supposed to walk out grateful. That's not fairness. That's psychological warfare wrapped in manners.

Grey believes in order. Structure. Balance. But balance in a crooked room still tilts toward the powerful. His fairness isn't freedom – it's anesthesia. It's the calm voice telling you it won't hurt right before it does.

He's not a savior. He's a system-approved illusion. His job isn't to fix injustice – it's to make you swallow it without choking.

Mercy in a Machine That Doesn't Feel

Grey's mercy is manufactured, stamped, and filed under *public perception.* It's there to prove the machine still "cares." That's the genius of it. Every Harry needs a Grey – the hammer and the halo – so the public can pretend there's balance. One breaks you, the other consoles you, and both feed the same beast.

He doesn't burn you like Harry. He just lowers you gently into the fire. And when you start to scream, he tells you it's for your own good. That's the kind of justice America mass-produces now – polite, articulate, and lethal as ever.

Because in the end, there ain't no "good" judges or "bad" ones. There's just degrees of delusion – how soft they make it sound while they hand you to the same goddamn system that's been devouring people for a hundred years.

So remember this when you stand before him: the tone might change, the words might soothe, but the outcome never does. The robe don't care who's wearing it. The gavel always falls the same.

U.S. Magistrate Judges

Before you ever get your big day in court, you gotta pass through the magistrate – the bureaucratic bouncer guarding the velvet rope of federal "justice." These folks decide if you get to sleep in your own bed or rot in a concrete box till trial. Spoiler: most of y'all are rotting.

Magistrates talk like they're running a fair game – "We'll review your risk factors," "We'll evaluate flight risk," "We'll consider community ties." Yeah, right. Translation: *We've already decided.* They don't see people; they see categories – "high risk," "moderate risk," "no risk but still screwed." They're basically human pretrial algorithms wrapped in polyester robes

The Bureaucrats of Bail

You walk in thinking this is a bail hearing. It ain't. It's a loyalty test. They're not deciding your freedom – they're measuring how much of a threat you are to their process. Got a passport? Denied. Own a business? Denied. Have kids? Denied – "potential flight risk." You could have GPS on your ankle, your mom as your guarantor, and Jesus vouching for your honesty, and the magistrate will still say, *"The court finds detention appropriate."*

And the prosecutor? They don't even break a sweat. They just read off a script about "danger to the community," toss around words like "sophisticated operation," and boom – bail denied. Magistrate nods. Gavel drops. Your life goes into storage. They'll call it "precautionary." You'll call it a preview of hell.

Paperwork in Human Form

You ever seen someone so deep in bureaucracy they start speaking in bullet points? That's your magistrate. They don't think – they process. Every ruling's a template, every word recycled from yesterday's hearing. Half the time they're not even pretending to care. They just check the boxes, mumble some legalese, and move on to the next poor bastard.

They say magistrates keep the system "efficient." Nah, they keep it lubricated. They make sure the paperwork never stops moving – the affidavits, warrants, pretrial reports, orders of detention. They're the ones who make the machine look smooth while it's grinding people into paste.

And don't be fooled by that fake politeness. "Good morning, counsel," "Thank you for your argument," "The court appreciates your time." That's bureaucrat talk for *you've already lost.* You could give the Gettysburg Address about why you deserve bail, and they'll still cut you off mid-sentence with, *"After careful consideration, the motion is denied."* Careful consideration my ass – they read three lines from Pretrial Services and called it gospel.

Magistrates don't judge truth. They judge paperwork. If it's typed neat and stamped right, it's law. You could hand them the Ten Commandments and they'd ask if it's notarized.

They're like vending machines for rulings – feed them a government motion, press "ENTER," and out drops your detention order.

The Gate Fee to Hell

Here's how the scam works: the magistrate softens you up for the slaughter. You've been locked up for 72 hours, half-fed, half-awake, wearing county-issued khakis that smell like sweat and bleach. You finally stand in front of someone who might have the power to let you go. You think, *maybe this is my shot.* Wrong. This is the part where they break your spirit so you'll plead faster later.

They make freedom sound conditional. Like it's a privilege you haven't earned yet. They'll stack you with conditions so impossible you'll violate them sneezing. "No contact with co-defendants," "No travel outside your zip code," "Random drug testing," "Daily check-ins." It's freedom with a leash, designed to choke you the second you move too far.

But most of the time, you don't even get that. You get the speech. You know the one: "The court finds no combination of conditions sufficient to ensure the defendant's appearance or the safety of the community." That's bureaucratic poetry for *we're locking your ass up.*

Once you're remanded, you're not just in custody – you're in the system's chokehold. You miss work, lose your house, your family starts drifting, your defense weakens, and by the time your "real" trial starts, you're so damn desperate you'll take whatever plea they throw at you.

That's the whole point. The magistrate ain't there to protect your rights – they're there to make you tired. To get you used to the cage so you stop fighting before the judge ever meets you.

They call it *pretrial detention.* I call it *training for surrender.*

The Hidden Handshake

The magistrates are the connective tissue between cops and courts – the quiet facilitators of federal control. They sign the warrants, issue the orders, approve the searches, and greenlight the surveillance.

They're the reason your phone got tapped, your door got kicked, and your "constitutional rights" became a punchline.

Every bad search, every overreach, every illegal sting operation has a magistrate's signature hiding behind it. They'll rubber-stamp a warrant faster than you can spell "probable cause." Doesn't matter how thin the affidavit is – if it's typed by an agent with a badge, it's good enough.

You think it's hard to get a federal warrant? Nope. It's like ordering coffee. The feds walk in, mumble some buzzwords about "ongoing investigation" and "credible intelligence," and boom – magistrate nods, pen hits paper, someone's life goes up in smoke. No questions. No doubt. Just process. They're not judges. They're gatekeepers with pens – opening doors for everyone but you.

The Bottom Line

Magistrates don't decide justice. They decide convenience. They're the toll collectors on the road to ruin – the first faces you see when the system grabs you by the throat. Their job is to clear the path for the big dogs: the prosecutors, the district judges, the clerks, the whole damn judicial cartel.

They'll smile, they'll say "thank you," they'll act professional – but make no mistake: they're the ones greasing the gears that grind you down. Every "denied without prejudice," every "motion reserved," every signature they scribble is another cog clicking into place.

You never stood a chance at bail, because bail was never about trust – it's about control. And magistrates are the ones who make sure control never slips. So when they say, "This is just the beginning," believe them. Because once you've met the gatekeeper, you've already walked through the gates of hell.

The Black Robe Cartel Different Robes, Same Bloodstains

Let's stop pretending these judges are different breeds. Harry, Grey, the Magistrate – they're all running the same con. They just play different instruments in the orchestra of ruin. Harry's the drum – loud, cruel, proud of it. Grey's the violin – soft, sympathetic, manipulative as hell. And the Magistrate? He's the metronome – keeping the tempo steady while the other two tear you apart in rhythm.

You thought the courtroom was divided – "tough judge," "fair judge," "procedural magistrate." Nah. That's marketing. The judicial branch doesn't do diversity; it does division of labor. Each one's got a role to play in the slow grind of your destruction. The Magistrate locks you down. Grey breaks your will. Harry finishes the job. Different robes, same bloodstains – soaked in the same ink and arrogance. They call it checks and balances. I call it organized cruelty with nameplates.

The Unholy Trinity of Control

Here's how the hierarchy shakes out: The Magistrate opens the trapdoor. Grey pretends to offer a rope. Harry kicks the chair. That's the chain of command. That's your "justice system." Magistrates are the gatekeepers – the pretrial priests who bless the government's paperwork before anyone else sees it. They set the stage for failure by denying bail and calling it "risk management." Then comes Grey, the false prophet of fairness, making you believe maybe – *just maybe* – someone up there still gives a damn. You start to relax. That's when Harry walks in, swings the hammer, and turns you into a sentencing statistic.

They work together like a cartel – each one feeding the next, each one cleaning up the other's mess. You can't appeal the Magistrate without landing in front of a District Judge. You can't challenge the District Judge without facing an Appellate Judge. It's not a system; it's a pyramid scheme with gavels.

And guess who's at the bottom holding the weight? You. Always you.

The Circle of Corruption

Every ruling, every order, every "judicial decision" is part of the same feedback loop. They validate each other's bullshit in a never-ending chain of circular praise. One judge screws you, another judge signs off on it, and a third one pretends it's precedent. That's how bad law becomes gospel – through repetition.

File a motion against Harry? Grey denies it. File a complaint against Grey? The Magistrate dismisses it. Appeal the Magistrate's ruling? Harry signs it again just to remind you who's boss. You can't beat them because they built the maze and welded the exit shut.

They're not accountable to voters, juries, or logic. They answer only to themselves – a black-robe brotherhood where ego outweighs evidence and "justice" is whatever makes their paperwork look tidy.

They act like priests of the law, but they're more like crime scene cleaners – wiping down the messes the government makes and pretending the blood was never there.

The Payoff for Loyalty

You ever notice how judges almost never get punished? That's the reward for playing along. They can ruin lives, bend laws, even get caught lying on the record – and still keep their lifetime paychecks. Why? Because the system protects its own. You could burn down a courthouse before you'd see a sitting federal judge fired.

Magistrates dream of becoming district judges. District judges dream of sitting on the appellate bench. Appellate judges dream of being remembered as "distinguished." And every single one of them knows the only way to climb is to never rock the boat. Loyalty is the only law they actually enforce.

So they sell their integrity piece by piece – a denied motion here, a bullshit ruling there – until they're just another cog in the federal meat grinder.

You thought corruption meant money under the table? Nah. This is worse. It's career survival disguised as "judicial discretion."

The Final Judgment

These judges don't deliver justice – they deliver *outcomes*. Pre-decided, pre-packaged, and pre-approved by the same government they're supposed to check. They are not referees. They are partners in prosecution. Every robe in that courtroom – from the lowly Magistrate to Hang 'Em High Harry himself – is part of one connected hive, protecting the illusion of law while feeding on the carcass of due process.

When they say "Order in the court," what they really mean is "Submission." The courtroom isn't sacred – it's a slaughterhouse with better lighting. And these three are the butchers, carving up defendants like product, wrapping it in procedural bullshit, and stamping it "justice served."

So when you hear "Your Honor," remember this – There ain't no honor in that robe, just hierarchy.

Survival Manual: Loopoholes, Hacks, & Dirty Plays

You want to survive federal court? Stop thinking like an innocent person and start thinking like a tactician. This isn't honor. It's endurance. Play the game by its ugly little rules and you'll live to sue another day. Fail to learn the hacks and the machine chews you up and files the pieces under "case closed." Below: real, nasty, legal-ish things that work – or at least buy time, leverage, and breathing room. Not a prayer. Not pretty. Effective.

Delay Like It's a Religion

Time kills the prosecution's rhythm. Time scars the witnesses. Time makes people forget why they cared in the first place.

What to do:

File the paperwork relentlessly. Motions to dismiss, motions to compel, Daubert motions, complex discovery motions, follow-ups – make them respond. Every response costs them staff hours and credibility.

Make discovery a war. Use Rule 16 / Brady / Jencks requests like a buzzsaw. Demand specific documents, not vague assertions. Make them produce witness statements, agent notes, Financial Analysis – everything.

Exploit calendaring. Ask for continuances when good cause exists – illness of a key witness, a new disclosure, conflicts. Even routine delays make the prosecution re-budget resources.

Change counsel tactically. A real switch (not a sham) forces a reset – time for new counsel to file fresh motions, review material, and set strategy.

Force hearings. Bench conferences, evidentiary hearings, mini-trials on discrete issues. Drag them into legal battles they didn't want on record.

Use the record. Make them make bad rulings on the record. One error on transcript can become an appeal chip later.

Why it works: The government has staff and pride – not infinite patience. Make them spend both. Wear them out. When they get sloppy, you pounce.

Don'ts: Don't delay for its own sake if you have no plan. Judges smell games. Be tactical, not petulant.

Weaponize Sympathy – But Don't Beg

People respond to stories. The system is mechanical; humans run it. Don't make a sob story – make a human ledger.

What to do:

Tell a controlled story. Pick 2-3 details that humanize you (kids, steady job, health condition) and have them drilled for court. Keep it simple and believable.

Stage your moments. Not every hearing is a heartstring moment. Save genuine humanization for PSR interviews, sentencing hearings, or bail arguments – places where sympathy gets converted to mitigating language.

Use witness testimony sparingly. One credible family member or employer beats ten written fan letters. Judges respond to calm, credible humans more than theatrics.

Avoid desperation. Don't beg, don't hysteric. Humility works; self-pity doesn't. If you look unhinged, it flips sympathy into contempt.

Document it. Evidence of community ties, medical records, proof of employment, child care obligations – give probation officers easy facts to put in the report.

Why it works: Judges hate being the villain in public. If you can make them feel like a humane actor, they'll choose the option that lets them wear mercy on their résumé.

Don'ts: Never invent facts. Perjury's a factory of new charges. Make the file look good, not false.

Feed Their Ego, Starve Their Patience

Judges love to be needed – then bored. Make them feel both.

What to do:

Praise craft. Brief your filings to the point. Say "Your Honor" the way a professional does. Flattery isn't fake – it's tactical.

But build complexity. Follow flattery with a procedural morass: well-argued, complex, technical motions that take time and energy to parse. They'll either rule you a problem to avoid or give you a favorable compromise.

Use smart motion practice. Don't file junk. Make them read something worth their time – but make it long enough that they're tempted to cut a plea or compromise rather than adjudicate.

Create cost for the other side. Demand experts, expensive testing, discovery they need to produce – make the prosecution pay in time and money.

Why it works: Judges will take the path that conserves their oxygen. If your motion makes the courtroom work easier by settling issues, they may opt for compromise.

Don'ts: Don't waste a judge's time with obvious nonsense. That destroys credibility.

The Recusal Grenade

When a judge is rotten, make them toxic to themselves.

What to do:

Document bias carefully. Look for prior rulings, public statements, improper ex parte contacts, or judicial interactions that suggest prejudice

Raise precise, procedural grounds. Conflict of interest, financial ties, prior representation, or clear statements showing bias. Make it look like a duty for the judge to step aside.

File early, file formally. Don't throw a Hail Mary later. Early recusal motions force neutral handling of your case from the outset.

Use it as leverage, not vengeance. Even a failed recusal can make the judge squeamish and less performative, and it forces appellate issues on the record.

Why it works: Judges hate the humiliation of a recusal motion. Even if it fails, it makes them cautious – and caution helps you.

Don'ts: Don't file frivolous motions. A frivolous recusal can backfire and get sanctions.

Play Nice with Probation – They Hold the Pen

Probation officers write the report judges read before they wreck your life. Treat them like a jury of one.

What to do:

Cooperate early and earnestly. Be respectful, on time, and transparent (without waiving rights). Probation reports are narrative gold.

Control your origin story. Give probation facts that favor mitigation: steady work, rehab steps, family responsibilities.

Provide corroboration. Letters, pay stubs, treatment enrollments, community service receipts – give the probation officer ready-to-use material.

Prep witnesses. The probation officer will likely interview your family and employers; make sure they give consistent, credible, non-fluffy answers.

Correct errors fast. If the draft PSR has inaccuracies, file objections immediately and back them with proof.

Why it works: Judges heavily weight PSRs; a sympathetic, well-documented PSR can move a sentence by years.

Don'ts: Don't lie to probation. False statements are perjury-adjacent and will destroy whatever little credibility you have.

Letters, Lies, and Last Chances

This is the theater. Make the stage look right – don't fake the play.

What to do:

Get real, credible letters. Employers, clergy, police chiefs, teachers – people with reputations. One credible letter trumps ten desperate notes from relatives.

Draft letters for signers. People are lazy – give them clean, honest templates they can sign. Make the content specific: dates, duties, observed behavior.

Use programs credibly. Enroll in treatment, job training, education – show progress before sentencing. Certificates matter.

Plan a mitigation narrative. Don't dump your whole life in court. Build a clear arc: mistake → accountability (treatment/work/community service) → plan for the future.

Cooperate strategically. Cooperation with prosecutors (proffers, witness testimony) can work, but it's a gamble. Understand the risk to safety, reputation, and future retaliation. Only pursue if counsel says it's worth the concrete, documented reduction.

Why it works: Judges love to claim they "help" people. Give them the opportunity to look magnanimous and they will.

Don'ts: Don't coach false testimony. Don't manufacture evidence. Courts can and will catch it.

Tactical Legal Moves You Should Know (Short List)

(Not exhaustive – but the stuff that actually buys leverage.)

Suppression (Fourth Amendment) motions – if evidence was tainted by illegal search/seizure: fight it early and hard.

Brady/Giglio demands – force them to disclose favorable material and impeachment for witnesses.

Daubert challenges – attack shoddy experts; exclude the fancy chart that scares juries.

Fischbach/Rule 404(b) motions – limit prejudicial "other act" evidence that paints you as a monster.

Bill of Particulars – force the prosecution to be specific rather than vague.

Discovery sanctions – if they fail to disclose, push for dismissal or evidentiary exclusion.

Preservation for appeal – always get adverse rulings on the record with a motion for reconsideration – an empty appeal is a dead appeal.

These moves cost the government time, money, and political capital. Use them like a scalpel, not a hammer.

The Final Playbook – Mindset and Metrics

This is not a courtroom drama. It's supply-chain warfare. The prosecution has resources. You have time and creativity if you fight smart.

Measure everything. Every motion, every delay, every conversation – log it. The record is your ammo.

Win small, lose smart. A minor tactical loss today can set up a major win tomorrow. Think chess, not checkers.

Control your narrative. Don't vomit your life into court. Let your story be curated, credible, and provable.

Leverage everything into leverage. A sloppy affidavit, a missing Brady letter, a fired witness – fold those into motions, press releases, and pressure points.

Assume they'll lie sometimes. Assume witness memory is terrible. Assume agents mis-memorize. Build cross-examination that exposes those cracks.

The Lies Lawyers Tell About Judges

Bottom line: the courthouse is not a morality play. It's a business. You survive not by being right, but by being harder to bury. Be boring, be procedural, be annoying, be expensive to prosecute. Make their jobs harder than yours. If you can do that, you have a shot at living to fight another day.

1. The Myth: "The Judge Will Be Fair."

Your lawyer feeds you this one like morphine before surgery. "Don't worry, the judge will see reason." Oh, sure – right after they finish checking their fantasy football stats. You think the robe makes them neutral? Nah, it just hides the humanity they had to kill to get the job. "Fair" in federal court means the prosecution didn't openly laugh while burying you. Judges don't weigh truth – they weigh efficiency. And you, my friend, are just one more clog in their overbooked docket.

Reality Check: The judge woke up late, hates your lawyer, and already decided your fate while stirring their coffee. You're not a case – you're a calendar problem. Fairness died somewhere between the Senate confirmation and their first taxpayer-funded golf trip. They'll call it "judicial discretion," but it's really just arrogance in a robe.

2. "The Judge Isn't Political."

The Myth: Your lawyer says, "Judges rise above politics." Yeah, and strippers dance for exercise. Every judge is a political animal in denial – one half playing Moses, the other half running for sainthood. Their rulings? Campaign speeches in Latin. You're just the unpaid extra in their legacy theater.

Reality Check: They were handpicked, groomed, and sworn in by the same machine that wrote your indictment. You're not in a courtroom – you're in a policy lab. Every sentence they hand down is a press release for their ideology. Democrat, Republican, conservative, liberal – doesn't matter. The robe is just camouflage for whoever they owe dinner to.

3. "We'll Appeal If We Lose."

The Myth: Your lawyer leans in like a used car salesman: "If this goes south, we'll appeal." What they mean is: *you'll pay, and you'll lose slower.* Appeals aren't justice; they're a polite way to get denied in another zip code. You'll spend years feeding paper into a machine that never spits anything back but "affirmed."

Reality Check: Appeals are a rerun of your funeral. Same lies, bigger courtroom, deader hope. The appellate judges aren't knights – they're higher priests in the same corrupt religion. They don't overturn cases because that means admitting the system screwed up. And the system never confesses – it just updates the docket.

4. "The Judge Understands Your Situation."

The Myth: Your lawyer says the judge will "take your circumstances into account." That's adorable. You think that millionaire bureaucrat who's been on the bench since dial-up internet gives a shit that your kid's sick or your rent's past due? The only hardship they recognize is when their favorite lunch spot's closed.

Reality Check: They've been cocooned in marble hallways so long they forgot what it's like to sweat a bill or bleed for a paycheck. They don't see you as human – you're a variable in their paperwork. The robe sterilized them. They don't hear stories; they hear statistics. You're not a father, husband, or employee. You're a defendant. And defendants lose.

5. "The Judge Rewards Cooperation."

The Myth: Your lawyer whispers, "If you cooperate, the judge will go easy." Yeah, easy like a guillotine drop. Cooperation is a loyalty test, not a mercy card. You bend, they break you. You snitch, they smile, and still throw you under the bus for dessert.

Reality Check: The judge doesn't reward cooperation; they use it to write a tighter press release. The feds get their win, and you get ten years instead of twenty. They'll call that "leniency." You'll call it "still in prison." The system doesn't forgive – it discounts suffering like a clearance sale.

6. "The Judge Reads Everything."

The Myth: Your lawyer brags about their fifty-page motion like it's the next *War and Peace.* Spoiler: the judge didn't even make it past the title. You think they're in chambers studying your file? Nah. They've got clerks for that – underpaid interns who skim, summarize, and rubber-stamp your destiny.

Reality Check: Judges don't read. They *delegate reading.* You're not being judged by a person; you're being graded by a paralegal with carpal tunnel. The robe signs whatever's on top of the stack. If you think your "motion to suppress" is changing the game, guess what – it's already in the recycle bin.

7. "The Judge Wants the Truth."

The Myth: You picture this robe-wearing sage leaning forward, hungry for honesty, ready to hear your side. Stop watching movies. Judges don't want truth – they want closure. Truth slows things down, pisses off prosecutors, and messes with the narrative.

Reality Check: They don't listen for facts. They listen for *admissions.* The truth is dangerous because it forces the system to think. Thinking costs time. And time is the only thing they can't bill for. You want truth? You're in the wrong building.

8. "The Judge Is Bound by Law."

The Myth: Your lawyer tells you the law is clear. That's the punchline. The law's never clear – it's elastic, twisted, and flexible as hell. Judges stretch it like taffy to fit whatever outcome makes their life easier.

Reality Check: Judges don't follow law – they interpret it. Which means they invent it, wrap it in Latin, and call it precedent. You violate a rule, you're guilty. They violate a rule, it's "judicial discretion." The law bends for the bench and breaks for everyone else.

9. "Judges Don't Hold Grudges."

The Myth: Your lawyer says, "Don't worry, judges are professionals." Yeah, and crocodiles are vegetarians. Judges are petty, thin-skinned demigods with vendettas sharper than their pencils. One wrong smirk, one sarcastic tone, and suddenly every motion you file gets torpedoed.

Reality Check: They never forget. You question their ruling, they remember it for years. You piss them off, your bail hearing becomes a bloodbath. They call it "maintaining order." You call it "revenge in slow motion." There's no HR department for godhood.

10. "Judges Are the Last Line of Defense."

The Myth: Your lawyer paints the judge like the hero in the third act – the one who'll finally bring balance and justice. Bullshit. The judge isn't the wall between you and tyranny; they're the gatekeeper keeping tyranny fed.

Reality Check: Judges don't defend rights – they ration them. They don't fight the system – they *are* the system. Every word from that bench is theater, every "consideration" is choreography. They don't bang the gavel for justice; they bang it to cue the next victim.

The Robe Is the Uniform of Control

Your lawyer lies to keep you calm. The judge lies to keep you contained. And the system lies to keep you coming back. Don't mistake politeness for mercy. Don't confuse process for justice. The robe doesn't symbolize fairness – it's just camouflage for the executioner.

Once you've seen behind the curtain, you realize the only difference between a prosecutor and a judge is who gets the better parking spot.

Exhibit Twelve: The Bottom Line

The robe doesn't grant wisdom – it grants cover. Judges aren't impartial. They're just bureaucrats with gavels and unchecked egos, hiding behind phrases like "discretion" and "judicial economy" to justify whatever the hell they feel like doing. They pretend to weigh fairness, but they're usually just reacting to whoever stroked their pride, flattered their ego, or stayed on their good side.

You don't argue law in front of a judge – you perform submission. The second you walk into their courtroom, you're not a citizen, you're a subject. They decide what evidence matters, which objections land, and how hard the hammer falls. And if you think the appeals court will fix it? That's cute. The appellate system is just a bunch of judges protecting other judges.

So remember this: The courtroom isn't a temple of justice. It's a stage for a monarch with a grudge and a robe. And once they've made up their mind? You're not arguing for freedom – you're begging for mercy.

Next Up – Exhibit Thirteen: Clerks & Court Reporters

If judges are the face of the machine, clerks and court reporters are the hands that quietly twist the screws. You won't see them grandstanding or lecturing from the bench—but make no mistake, they're rigging the game behind the scenes. These are the quiet gatekeepers of chaos: they lose your motions, "misplace" your filings, and transcribe your words just crooked enough to hang you later.

Welcome to the part of the system nobody warns you about—where silence does the dirty work, and the record ain't just kept… it's edited.

EXHIBIT THIRTEEN

Clerks and Stenographers

They Don't Judge You — They Rewrite You

You thought the judge was the one running the show? That's like believing the ventriloquist dummy controls the punchlines. Judges may wear the robe, but they don't run the grind. The gears chewing you up? That's the clerks and the court reporters–the faceless, nameless bureaucrats with god-mode access to your future.

The Court's Most Dangerous People

They don't need gavels. They've got keyboards, docket software, and just enough authority to make you disappear into a paperwork sinkhole. They don't issue rulings–they just make sure yours never show up on time. Lost filings, "misplaced" exhibits, and notices that somehow never made it to your mailbox... oops. Must've been a clerical error.

Clerks aren't assistants. They're the petty tyrants of procedural warfare. If your paperwork touches their desk, they control its fate–and by extension, yours. Delay it. Reject it. Send it back for formatting. Hold it for review. *Forget* to process it until the deadline's passed. And the best part? They answer to no one. The judge shrugs, your lawyer grits their teeth, and you get shafted by someone who wouldn't last ten minutes managing a Burger King.

And court reporters? Don't get me started. They're the official memory of the courtroom–and memory, in this system, is optional. If it didn't get transcribed, it didn't exist. That critical objection your lawyer made? Gone. That moment the prosecutor slipped up? "Inaudible." That witness contradiction? "Didn't catch it." A single tap of a delete key can nuke hours of testimony–and nobody questions it.

These aren't side characters. These are the hidden bosses. And you never see them coming until your appeal collapses under the weight of a missing paragraph. Let *that* sink in.

The Paper Gods - Clerks and Their Petty Kingdoms

You wanna know how clerks turn procedures into a weapon? Start by forgetting everything you think you know about "filing paperwork." This isn't your neighborhood post office. This is legal landmine territory, and the federal clerks are the ones planting them. They don't just move paper–they *booby-trap* it.

Every motion, every exhibit, every form you touch has to pass through their silent, smirking hands. And here's the game: they don't need to deny your motion to kill it. All they have to do is bounce it. Delay it. Misfile it. Stall just long enough for your deadline to pass–then shrug and point to the rules. Rules they interpret however the hell they want.

The Formatting Scam

Your motion can be legally flawless—and still get kicked back because the font wasn't 12-point Times New Roman, or the margins weren't exactly 1.25 inches, or the footnote numbers didn't use superscript. Yes, they check. Yes, they care. Because **every rejection resets the clock**. And you only get so many swings before the system calls "too late."

Some clerks will reject a 50-page motion because the signature line wasn't centered. Others will "lose" your attachment and pretend it was never included. And if you're filing pro se? You're already screwed. The bar is five times higher—and they're hoping you don't know the rules so they can gut your submission without blinking.

The Passive-Aggressive Rejection Loop

Clerks don't argue. They don't debate. They reject—and they do it quietly. You'll get a one-line notice with some vague reference to Local Rule 7.1 or "improper formatting," and that's it. No phone call. No real explanation. You're expected to decode it, correct it, and resubmit. And every time you do, the clock keeps ticking.

They'll bounce the same filing three times and act like they're doing you a favor. You ever try getting clarification from a federal clerk? Good luck. They'll tell you they "can't give legal advice," which is their way of saying: *We know what's wrong, but we're not telling you.*

The Delay Trick

Let's say your filing *does* make it through. You think that means it lands on the judge's desk that day? Not even close. There's a holding pattern—an invisible purgatory between "filed" and "reviewed." Clerks decide how fast things move. That emergency motion you submitted Friday? Might not get docketed till Tuesday. And guess what? Your hearing was Monday. *Tough break.*

They call it "administrative processing." You'll call it sabotage. And they'll never be held accountable for it, because technically, everything was "handled in accordance with standard court procedure."

The Prosecutor Pipeline

Here's the part they *really* don't want you to know: clerks play favorites. And prosecutors? They're the favorites. Filings from the U.S. Attorney's office don't get rejected for font size. Their motions don't sit in the inbox over the weekend. When the government files something, it glides through the system like it's on a goddamn red carpet.

But if you—or your broke-ass court-appointed defense lawyer—submit something? You're getting the white glove treatment. Not the nice kind. The forensic kind. Every line scanned. Every signature scrutinized. Every minor error flagged for return. It's not about fairness. It's about friction. They make it hard for you because they *can*. And because no one's ever stopped them.

The Silence That Kills

But the worst part? You don't even know it's happening. The clerk's office is where your rights go to die *quietly*. No big rejection letter. No ruling. No courtroom drama. Just silence. No response. No update. No proof your motion was ever seen. And by the time you realize what's missing, the deadline's passed and the judge "can't do anything now." Welcome to the clerks' domain: a place where *procedure is power*, and *silence is a weapon*.

Court Reporters The Soundkeepers of Bullshit

You walk into that courtroom thinking every word matters. Every objection, every contradiction, every pissed-off slip from the prosecutor's mouth. You think it's all being captured. You think the record is your safety net. You think wrong.

Court reporters–those quiet little keyboard jockeys tapping away like they're just background noise–aren't documenting what *happened*. They're *editing history in real time*. And if they don't like what you said, or you said it too fast, or the judge interrupted, or their lunch break started three minutes early–guess what? It's gone. Poof. Never existed. And good luck appealing *a ghost.*

The Myth of the Neutral Observer

They sell you this fairytale that court reporters are neutral. Unbiased. Just stenographers transcribing the facts. Bullshit. These people sit *feet* from the bench, day in and day out. They eat lunch with clerks, joke with bailiffs, and whisper with prosecutors between sessions. You think they don't pick sides? They're embedded deeper than the court seal on the judge's wall.

And when the heat's on, they know how to cover asses. The judge interrupts an objection? That part of the transcript becomes "inaudible." The defense raises hell on a rights violation? Suddenly, the record shows "no audible response from the court." Convenient.

They don't just write down what happens–they *shape what's remembered*. And in federal court, *memory is everything.* **If They Don't Type It, It Never Happened.**

Transcript Tampering, a.k.a. The Legal Memory Hole

There are two kinds of court record sabotage: **deletion** and **distortion**.

Deletion is when shit just vanishes. The strong objection? Gone. The judge yelling? Gone. The contradiction in the cop's story? Somehow never picked up.

Distortion is worse. That moment you said, "I did *not* consent"? It shows up as "I did consent." And the official transcript–guess what? That's what the appellate court sees. Not the truth. Just the official fiction signed off by a court reporter no one's allowed to question.

You challenge it, they circle the wagons. Judges protect their record like it's the Ark of the Covenant. "We have full confidence in the transcript." Yeah, because it was written by one of their own.

The Audit That Never Comes

Here's the scam: there's no real oversight. No quality control. No second set of ears. If the court doesn't use audio backup (and most don't), the transcript *is the gospel*. And the person who typed it? Immune.

You can request corrections, sure—if you can afford it. If you can prove the transcript is wrong without any evidence to support you. If you can find a lawyer brave (or dumb) enough to file a motion accusing a federal court reporter of falsifying the record. Spoiler alert: you can't. And even if you could, guess who decides if your correction gets approved? The same damn judge who benefits from the lie.

Missing Pages, Missing Rights

There are whole cases where *entire days of trial testimony go missing*. Gone. Redacted. "Technical issues." Sometimes they say the mic cut out. Sometimes the reporter was "out sick." Sometimes there's just no explanation at all.

That critical witness who flipped mid-testimony? The cop who contradicted himself on the stand? The judge who made a prejudicial remark in open court?

If it's not in the transcript, *it didn't happen.* And when you appeal, you're not appealing what really went down. You're appealing *whatever the stenographer decided to write.* You're arguing against a story that already erased the chapter where you had a shot.

The Record Is Not Your Friend

This is the part nobody tells defendants. Your fight isn't just in the courtroom—it's in the transcript. The judge can be wrong, the prosecutor can cheat, the jury can be confused—and none of that matters if the record is scrubbed clean.

You could make the greatest legal argument of your life, and if the court reporter didn't feel like typing it? It's gone. And once it's gone, it's never coming back. They're not just "keeping the record." They're building the narrative that will get you denied, dismissed, and discarded.

And all you'll have left is your memory versus *theirs*. Guess which one the system believes.

Loopholes of the Lower Gods

Courtroom Cheat Codes for the Desperate, the Damned, and the Defiant Let's get one thing straight: this ain't a courtroom–it's a rigged casino with fluorescent lighting. And the clerks and stenographers? They're the pit bosses and card shufflers making sure *you* never walk out with a win.

But even crooked games have loopholes. Hidden cracks in the floor. And if you know how to find 'em, you can make that system slip on its own rules. This section ain't about charm or courtesy. It's about **tactical manipulation**, plain and dirty.

1. The Ego Trigger – Make the Clerk Feel Like a God

Clerks are petty tyrants with a martyr complex. They hate their jobs, hate the people walking in, and hate themselves just a little more every day. So flip that. Feed their ego. Ask for *their* opinion. Act like they're the gatekeeper to Olympus. Give 'em that fake-flattery performance like you're trying to get into Studio 54 in the middle of a bomb threat.

Why? Because a bored, underpaid clerk who feels seen might just "accidentally" skip protocol for you. A little nod here, a little "don't worry, I'll handle that" there. Suddenly, your motion doesn't sit in the black hole for a week. But play it smart–go too far and you'll come off like a kiss-ass. This is theater, not therapy.

2. Put That on the Fucking Record – Force the Court Reporter's Hand

Most people in court sit quiet, scared, and spineless. That silence? It's the system's favorite tool. If nobody demands the record reflect what's *actually happening*, then the court gets to write its own version of events–and spoiler alert: it won't include your objections.

You hear something shady? You catch a judge muttering threats under their breath or a prosecutor bending the facts like taffy? Say it loud: **"I want that on the record."** Say it like your future depends on it–because it does.

Why? Because if it ain't in the transcript, it's legally invisible. And if it *is* in the transcript, they can't pretend it never happened. Court reporters hate being called out mid-hearing, but once you make it known you're watching the record like a hawk, they're a lot less likely to redact your life into oblivion.

3. The Backdoor Inbox - Skip the Line, Crash the Process

Want to know the federal court's best-kept secret? Almost every clerk has an internal email address they never advertise. It's buried deep in the court website like a smuggled shank–and just as effective.

Why waste hours in line at the clerk's window getting treated like a roach when you can cut through the circus and drop your motion straight into their inbox? This ain't "hacking the system"–this *is* the system. They built a backdoor and hoped no one would notice. So notice.

Why? Because it bypasses the attitude, the wait, and the paper shuffle. It drops your issue right in front of someone who might actually do something–*before* it lands in the pile marked "Maybe Later." Use it right, and you're not just filing documents–you're launching legal airstrikes from behind enemy lines.

4. The Readback Power Move - Keep the Stenographer on a Leash

Court reporters hate being questioned. So that's exactly what you do. You hear something off? You sense a detail got twisted or a quote miswritten? Interrupt with confidence: **"Can we get a readback on that?"**

It's not a request–it's a reminder. That someone's watching. That someone knows their future is being built word by word. That someone isn't going to let a keyboard jockey with a god complex rewrite the moment to make the court look clean.

Why? Because calling for a readback isn't just about fixing errors–it's about putting the court reporter on notice. The message is clear: screw up my record, and I will call it out *on the spot*. They hate it. Which means you should do it more.

5. The Double Tap – Submit It Twice or Prepare to Be Ghosted

 Here's how the scam works: you submit your motion, you wait, and the clerk swears it "never arrived." Boom–deadline missed, opportunity gone, and the system wins without ever having to lift a finger.

So you don't give them that chance. You file it **twice**–once electronically, once physically. You get receipts. You keep timestamps. You staple the damn confirmations to your chest if you have to.

Why? Because redundancy is your last defense. It shuts down the "we didn't receive it" lie before it leaves their mouth. Two filings means two trails. And two trails means you're not at their mercy when they suddenly "can't find" the most important motion of your life.

6. The Transcript Trap – Audit the Fiction Before It Becomes History

You think that transcript is an accurate record? Please. It's a **court-approved fairytale**, typed up by someone who spent half the hearing daydreaming about lunch. You want the real story preserved? You **request the transcript immediately**. Not next week. Not when it's too late to challenge.

Once you get it, don't skim. **Rip it apart.** Line by line. Catch every omission, distortion, or conveniently reworded exchange. That critical "no" that got turned into a "yes"? That's where you hit back.

Why? Because the court's memory is what they *print*, not what they *heard*. And if you don't fight to correct the record, that fiction becomes law. Every lie typed into that transcript becomes the truth on appeal. Fix it now, or choke on it later.

7. The Off-the-Record Gambit – Refuse to Let Them Bury the Truth

When a judge says "We're going off the record," it's never for your benefit. That's when the threats, the side deals, the inappropriate jokes, and the real opinions come out. It's where they bury the things they *don't want to be held accountable for.*

So don't let 'em. Interrupt. Demand it go back on the record. Say: **"This affects my case–I want it documented."** Loud enough for the walls to hear. Judges hate it. Lawyers squirm. Court reporters hesitate. That's the sweet spot.

Why? Because the second you let them talk in the dark, they'll set your entire future on fire without leaving a trace. "Off the record" is where injustice hides. Drag it into the light. Force it into the transcript. And remind them that if they wanted privacy, they shouldn't have joined the circus.

Bullshit Lawyers Say About Clerks & Stenographers

Lawyers lie about clerks because it keeps the illusion intact. If they told you the truth–that some underpaid, overpowered bureaucrat behind a glass window can derail your entire case with a passive-aggressive smirk and a missing timestamp–you'd lose faith in the system before your first court date. So instead, they spin the fairy tale. "Clerks are just here to help," "They don't have real power," "It was probably just a mistake." It's damage control. They need you calm, compliant, and clueless. Because if you knew how much chaos a pissed-off clerk could unleash, you'd stop blaming the judge and start flipping desks in the filing room. Lawyers don't protect you from the truth–they protect the system from your outrage.

1. The Court Reporter Captures Everything Word-for-Word."

Your Lawyer's Bullshit: The court reporter is basically a human tape recorder They catch every syllable, every murmur, and every mumbled insult under the judge's breath with perfect precision. Yeah, sure. In reality, courtrooms are chaotic, and court reporters are just like the rest of us–they blink, they miss things, and sometimes they're sitting there thinking about lunch. So when your lawyer says everything's captured "word-for-word," they're really saying, "Let's hope nobody mumbles, or we're screwed."

The Fucking Truth: Court reporters miss things. They misinterpret, they mishear, and unless someone clarifies, those mistakes become the "official" record. Good luck fixing that later.

2. "Clerks Are Just Paper Pushers–They Have No Real Power."

Your Lawyer's Bullshit: Clerks are harmless little drones, just mindlessly filing papers, answering phones, and totally not controlling the flow of your entire case. They're like robots with zero influence, right? Wrong. In reality, the clerk is the gatekeeper, the person who decides whether your documents move swiftly or get lost in the black hole of "processing." If you don't play nice, expect your motion to sit in purgatory while the clerk takes a leisurely coffee break.

The Fucking Truth: Clerks wield more power than you realize. They're the ones who can delay your case, misplace a critical document, or "accidentally" send you to the wrong courtroom. If you think they're powerless, enjoy waiting an extra month for that urgent motion to get filed

-

3. Clerk and Court Reporters are Neutral

Your Lawyer's Bullshit: "Don't worry, they're neutral." Sure–neutral like a sniper in a blindfold. That blank stare they wear? It isn't professionalism; it's camouflage. Clerks and reporters don't take sides on paper, but off paper, they're swimming in bias. They've got favorites, grudges, moods, and lunch buddies–and if you think any of that stays outside the record, you're delusional.

The Fucking Truth: Neutrality is theater. Clerks decide whose paperwork gets priority, and reporters decide what parts of your defense make it onto the record. If they like the prosecutor, your motion glides through. If they don't like you, it sits in limbo while they "process" a few other cases first. They're not impartial observers–they're gatekeepers with opinions.

So when your lawyer says, "Everyone's just doing their job," what they really mean is, *pray the clerk isn't hungover and the court reporter isn't mad at your lawyer.* Because in a courthouse built on egos, neutrality isn't a principle–it's a performance. And you're the one paying for the tickets.

4. "We Can Always Fix the Record Later."

Your Lawyer's Bullshit: Oh, yeah, no big deal. If something gets screwed up, we'll just fix it later. Like revising a grocery list, right? Wrong. Once that transcript is set, it's practically carved in stone. Filing a motion to correct the record is about as easy as herding cats, and judges aren't exactly thrilled about revisiting the sacred text of the stenographer. Your lawyer might act like it's no problem, but it's more like rewriting history after the ink has dried.

The Fucking Truth: Fixing a transcript mistake is a nightmare. It's not a "just send an email" kind of deal. If something important gets missed, you're in for a bureaucratic wrestling match to get it corrected.

5. "Clerks Are There to Help."

Your Lawyer's Bullshit: Sure, the clerk's whole job is to help you navigate the system, answer your questions, and make your life easier. Just ask, and they'll be happy to drop everything to assist you with a smile. Hilarious, right? If you want help, you better figure it out on your own or catch the clerk on their one good day of the year.

The Fucking Truth: If you're expecting helpful service, get ready to be disappointed. Most of the time, they'll treat you like an inconvenience, and you'll be lucky to get more than a grunt in response to your question.

6. "Clerks Don't Hold Grudges."

Your Lawyer's Bullshit: Of course not. The clerk would never remember that time you called them out for a mistake or dared to ask for a favor. They're way too professional for that. Right? Wrong. Cross a clerk, and you'll find your case moving slower than molasses in January.

The Fucking Truth: Clerks have long memories, and if you've pissed them off, they're not going to forget it anytime soon. Expect delays, lost paperwork, and the cold shoulder for the foreseeable future.

7. "Don't Worry, It's All in the Transcript."

Your Lawyer's Bullshit: Ah, the ultimate lie. Your lawyer will reassure you that everything important is safely tucked away in the transcript, like it's the Holy Grail of court records. But here's the thing: transcripts are only as good as the person typing them, and that person has good days, bad days, and "oh crap, I missed that" moments. Plenty of key details slip through the cracks, get twisted, or just disappear altogether. Your lawyer's acting like it's a done deal, but what they really mean is, "Let's hope we didn't miss anything too important."

The Fucking Truth: Transcripts are far from perfect. They're filled with errors, omissions, and misinterpretations. If you're relying on the transcript to save your case, you might be in for a rude awakening.

8. "Clerks Have No Influence Over Judges."

Your Lawyer's Bullshit: Oh, yeah, the clerks and judges barely know each other, and there's definitely no behind-the-scenes communication that could affect your case. Sure, if this were a courtroom fairy tale. Clerks are often the eyes and ears of the judge, and if you think their opinion doesn't matter, you're delusional.

The Fucking Truth: Clerks have the judge's ear more than you think, and if they don't like you or your lawyer, don't be surprised when the judge seems a little less inclined to hear you out.

Dirty Tactics by Clerks and Stenographers

Clerks and court reporters don't need guns or gavels to destroy defendants–they use paperwork, silence, and timing. Every "lost" motion, every "technical glitch," every "inaudible" moment in the transcript is a quiet knife in the back of anyone trying to fight the system. Clerks stall filings, misdate submissions, and play dumb when evidence vanishes; court reporters edit reality in real time, trimming the record like a bad haircut until the truth looks clean enough to convict. None of it leaves fingerprints. They don't deny justice–they just drown it in procedure. And by the time you realize what happened, your case is already dead, killed by bureaucracy wearing a polite smile.

DIRTY TACTIC #1: The Lost-In-Translation Transcript Trick

You think every word you say in court is sacred because "it's on the record," right? Cute. Now let me piss on that fantasy. Court reporters don't just transcribe–they interpret. And when that interpretation sucks, guess who pays for it? You. One missed "not," one swapped word, one subtle change in tone–and boom, your testimony just flipped from *"I didn't do it"* to *"Yeah, I guess I did."*

They'll tell you the transcript is gospel. What they won't say is the gospel got edited by a half-bored, overworked typist with earbuds in and a grudge against your lawyer. And you wanna challenge it? Good luck. It'll take a formal motion, a hearing, and probably a goddamn séance to fix one sentence. The system's built so the "official record" is whatever the court reporter decides it is–missed words, wrong words, tone stripped out like it's a damn text message. Welcome to courtroom reality: where facts are flexible, and "verbatim" is a f***ing suggestion.

Tactic #2 – The Timestamp Shuffle

"Oh look, it was filed... just not when it mattered." Ever seen a motion magically vanish from relevance? Here's how the court **kills your chances without ever denying your motion outright** – they just shuffle the goddamn timestamps.

You file something at 3:58 PM. Court closes at 5. But somehow, mysteriously, your motion is marked as **received at 5:01 PM**. Guess what? It's now "late." And because it's late, the judge doesn't even have to consider it. **Dismissed on technicality.** No ruling, no rebuttal, just vanished into the paperwork ether.

Meanwhile, the prosecutor's *mysteriously incomplete* motion that showed up at 6:45 PM the day before? Oh, that one was **"accepted nunc pro tunc."** Latin for "we're bending over backwards to make this shit count retroactively."

Clerks know exactly what they're doing – **timestamp manipulation** is one of their quietest weapons. It's not loud. It's not scandalous. But it **rearranges the battlefield** like moving chess pieces after you've already taken your hand off. This ain't just red tape. This is **time travel used as a knife**.

Tactic #3 – The "Whoops, We Never Got It" Maneuver

"Fax? Email? Courier pigeon? Nah, never showed up." This is one of their dirtiest crowd-pleasers – and it works like a charm. You or your lawyer file something airtight. Maybe it's a motion to suppress, maybe it's a last-minute affidavit that nukes the prosecution's theory. You've got the timestamp, the delivery confirmation, even the smug satisfaction of thinking you finally got ahead of the game.

Then court day rolls around. And the judge looks up with that fake confused face, glances at the clerk, and drops the hammer: **"I don't see anything in the record."** Boom – you're dead in the water. The clerk shrugs. "We never received that document." The court reporter stares blankly like a mannequin with a migraine. The judge pretends it's not their problem.

Now you're left scrambling to prove that yes, you did send it, yes, it was on time, and no, you're not full of shit. But guess what? That clock's still ticking. Hearings don't pause just because the paper trail got "accidentally" shredded by incompetence or convenience.

They don't deny your argument, they **erase its existence.** It's not sabotage if they pretend it never happened. Welcome to court: where *ghosting* is a sanctioned litigation strategy.

Tactic #4 – The Redaction Game: Black Ink, White Lies

"It's not hiding if you do it with a Sharpie." Here's how they play you like a damn fool with your own discovery: they give you the file–**but not the whole file.** Nope, you get the *special edition*, straight from the Government Censorship Department. Half the shit's blacked out like it's a CIA torture memo.

Names? Gone. Dates? Redacted. Whole paragraphs? Vanished like they were never typed. And when you ask why, they serve up that same old horseshit: **"Security reasons. Ongoing investigation. Sensitive sources."** Translation: **"We're hiding the part where we screwed you."** See, they're not just playing keep-away with the facts. They're *curating the truth.* You think you're building a defense, but you're working off a goddamn coloring book.

And your lawyer? Powerless. Judges rarely push back on redactions. They just nod and trust the prosecution like it's gospel. You could be staring at the one sentence that clears your name–and it's sitting behind a black bar thicker than your rap sheet. **They know exactly what they're doing.** They're not redacting for safety. They're redacting for control.

And by the time you finally get the "unredacted" version–if ever–it's too late. Trial's over. Damage done. Justice buried under toner ink.

Tactic #5 – The Calendar Shuffle: "Oops, Wrong Date, Guess You Lose"

They don't need to screw you with the law. They'll screw you with a calendar. You ever miss a court date you *swear* wasn't on the damn schedule? Welcome to the **Calendar Shuffle**–the legal system's version of musical chairs, except every time the music stops, **your ass lands in jail.**

Here's how it works: the clerk's office "updates" your hearing date. But somehow, your lawyer *doesn't get the notice.* Or maybe the notice goes to the wrong address. Or maybe–and this is their favorite–it gets mailed out the day after the hearing. Real slick.

Then when you don't show? Bam–**bench warrant.**
 Doesn't matter that you were never told. Doesn't matter you were ready. Doesn't matter that *they* fucked it up. You're now officially "non-compliant," "absconded," or my personal favorite: "willfully failing to appear." You go from defendant to fugitive without lifting a finger.

And good luck proving it. They'll drag out a phantom log entry, swear it was mailed, shrug their shoulders, and say, "Well, *we did our part.*" And the judge? Guess whose side they're on. (Hint: not yours. This isn't a clerical error. It's a **weaponized delay.** They control the calendar, the mail, the updates, and the recordkeeping–so they control **your freedom.** All it takes is one "mistake" and you're back in custody, starting from zero.

Tactic #6 – The Broken Copier Excuse: "We Couldn't Find That Motion..."

Your defense doesn't fail in court–it dies quietly in the copy room. Here's a dirty little secret no one tells you: **half the battle is just getting your shit into the system.** You file a motion. You think it's in. Hell, you've got a timestamp. But when you show up to court ready to argue? *Poof.* "We don't have that on file."

The excuse? "Oh, the copier was broken." Or "The system didn't scan it properly." Or—my personal favorite—"That must've been misfiled." Translation? **They threw it out.** Or better yet, *they never bothered to process it at all.*

This is the courthouse equivalent of a casino "losing" your winning ticket. Except instead of money, **what you lose is your shot at freedom.** Missed deadlines, unanswered filings, or surprise sanctions—all because some clerk couldn't be bothered to click *upload*.

It's sabotage disguised as incompetence. And don't bother complaining. They'll just point at the stack of paperwork, give you a shrug, and say, "You should've followed up." Oh, so now it's *your* job to babysit the people who control your constitutional rights?

This ain't a one-off accident. This is a **systemic stall tactic.** Delay the defense. Bury your argument. Blame the machines. Move on. Meanwhile, the prosecution's paperwork?   Flawless. Immaculate. Framed in gold.

Tactic #7 – The Mysterious Missing Transcript: "We Don't Know Where That Went"

If it helps your defense, it vanishes. If it helps the prosecution, it's laminated. So here's the setup: a witness says something wild in open court. A prosecutor screws up. A judge makes a snide, biased-ass remark that smells like grounds for appeal. You clock it. Your lawyer clocks it. Everyone in the gallery looks around like, *"Did that just happen?"*

So you do what you're supposed to do—**you request the transcript.** And what do you hear?

"Oh… that part? Yeah… we don't seem to have it." Really? That *one moment*—the one that could actually prove bias, misconduct, or straight-up perjury—**is the one part that magically didn't get recorded?** How convenient. They'll blame "technical error."They'll say "the reporter stepped out for a moment." They'll pretend it's *normal* that entire chunks of official proceedings just… *disappear.* But let's be clear—**this is a tactical redaction.** Not with a black marker, but with "oops." It's the court's unofficial edit button."Delete anything that makes us look bad."

And unless your lawyer is willing to raise hell–which they probably aren't–you're screwed. Because guess what? You can't appeal what "doesn't exist." You can't argue over a ghost.This isn't justice. This is **evidence manipulation with plausible deniability.** And once it's gone, it's gone. Forever.

Dirty Tactic #8: "Oops, the system glitched."

That's what they'll say when your motion vanishes, your exhibit file won't open, or your entire fucking transcript page goes MIA. And the best part? Nobody's liable. It's not sabotage–it's "a technical issue." Blame the software. Blame the upload. Blame Mercury in retrograde. Just don't blame the clerk, the reporter, or the IT stooge that hasn't updated the system since Obama's first term.

Paper trails get real thin when digital ghosts take over. Your lawyer filed that suppression motion? Sure they did–until the e-filing system suddenly "didn't receive it." You had a key exhibit submitted with a timestamp? Too bad, the server says otherwise. And guess who has the final say on what exists and what doesn't? The same people who just told you to "resubmit by close of business." Good luck getting the judge to believe it was ever there in the first place.

Glitch or strategy? You'll never prove it. The system is full of black holes–convenient ones. Your paperwork falls in and never comes out, and no one lifts a finger. Because once the record says "missing," you're the one left holding the bag. They'll smile, apologize, and move on with the case like nothing happened… while you scramble to redo everything under pressure.

And if you dare accuse them of pulling a fast one? That's cute. The judge will remind you that "accusations of misconduct are serious," while sipping coffee and pretending this digital black magic is just another "random error.".

Dirty Tactic #9: The Friday File Dump – Hide It in the Weekend Shitstorm

Here's how they bury you without a shovel: drop a critical motion, discovery dump, or court order late Friday afternoon–right before the courthouse turns into a damn ghost town. You blink, it's 4:59 PM, and boom–there's 300 pages of procedural horse shit sitting in your inbox with a Monday deadline. The clerks know the game. The judge knows the game. And your overworked lawyer just got kicked in the teeth by the calendar. You think this was random? Please. It's surgical. Bury your defense in weekend chaos, force a rushed response, and then act surprised when you miss something. By the time your legal team wipes the Monday morning crust from their eyes, the prosecution's already polished their "Look how sloppy the defense is" speech. Clockwork sabotage, dressed up as "routine filing procedure."

Dirty Tactic #10: The "Clerical Error" Screwjob - Oops, You Lose

Ever lose a motion because some mysterious "clerical error" just *accidentally* left it off the docket? Or found out the hearing date changed–but somehow *your* side never got the notice? Welcome to the land of procedural mugging. The beauty of a "clerical error" is no one's responsible. It's like blaming gravity when you fall off a cliff–it just *happens*. You complain? They apologize with that smug-ass tone like you're a child who spilled their juice. But the delay's done its damage. Your lawyer shows up unprepared, your argument gets tossed, or worse–they issue a bench warrant because your side "failed to appear." No conspiracy here, right? Just a little harmless "error" that conveniently fucks only *your* case.

Dirty Tactic #11: The Whisper Campaign

This one's not in the transcripts. It's in the hallways, the elevator rides, the smirks passed between prosecutors and judges when you walk in the room. Your lawyer gets labeled "difficult," "disrespectful," or worse–*"sovereign citizen adjacent."* Not because of what they filed, but because of how *they're talked about.* Quiet conversations poison your credibility behind the scenes, and you never hear a damn word of it in open court. The clerk snickers when your name pops up. The judge's tone gets colder every hearing. And suddenly, rulings start going sideways for reasons nobody wants to put in writing. That's the beauty of the whisper campaign–it's silent, invisible, and impossible to prove. Just your reputation getting slow-dripped into a septic tank.

Dirty Tactic #12: The Stack-the-Docket Maneuver

Ever feel like the court schedule was designed by a sadist? That's because it was. They'll stack deadlines like Jenga blocks with a stick of dynamite underneath. Discovery due Friday. Response to motion due Monday. Hearing Tuesday. New motion Wednesday. Repeat until your defense drowns in paperwork and panic. Meanwhile, the prosecution's got ten interns and a paralegal army proofreading their shit. You've got your lawyer, a Red Bull, and whatever's left of their sanity. It's not incompetence–it's war by scheduling. They choke your strategy with time pressure and then act shocked when your side files late. Game over, courtesy of the calendar.

Exhibit Thirteen: The Bottom Line

> *Clerks and court reporters don't wear robes, but they're every bit as dangerous—because they don't need to lie in open court. They just let your defense die in silence. No verdict. No denial. Just missing paperwork and "technical errors" that somehow always screw you and never the state.*
>
> *These aren't just support staff—they're the system's untraceable hitmen. The ones who erase your objections, bury your filings, and edit your future into a transcript that reads like a prosecutor's wet dream. And the best part? They don't have to explain a damn thing. "Clerical error" is the magic phrase that wipes away your rights like a smudge on a screen.*
>
> *So here's the truth: the court isn't fair, and it's not even honest. It's a machine. And the people keeping it running aren't in charge of justice—they're in charge of making sure you never get close to it. You're not fighting the judge. You're not fighting the prosecutor. You're fighting the motherfucker with a red stamp and a delete key.*

Next Exhibit Fourteen: How to Fight Back

Next: Exhibit Twelve – the tactical playbook. Expect step-by-step moves you can bring to counsel, templates you can use to build a paper trail, and exact phrases that force courts and clerks to act. This is where the theory becomes a dirty, usable defense.

You've seen the players. You've seen the tricks. You've watched the system turn ritual and paperwork into a trap. That's the bad news. The good news? A rigged game still has rules – and rules are exploitable. The same bureaucratic apparatus that buries you also leaves fingerprints: missed timestamps, redacted pages, unexplained "technical errors," and a paper trail that – if you build it right – becomes your weapon.

What follows isn't fantasy or moralizing. It's a practical map for making the courthouse inconvenient for the people who expect it to run smoothly for the government and quietly against you. This is about turning process into protection: forcing disclosure, preserving record, raising hell in the right places, and creating costs the prosecution and the court don't want to bear.

EXHIBIT FOURTEEN
Fighting the System
Take Control and Come Out Ahead

Because Knowing the Scam Ain't Enough. You Gotta Burn It Down. So, you made it through the first eleven exhibits. You've seen the inside of the beast – the marble façade, the rubber-stamped indictments, the whisper deals, the bullshit lawyers, the judges who play God, and the court clerks who erase your future with a shrug. Now what? What the hell do you do with all that rage, knowledge, and betrayal? This chapter isn't just a recap – it's your retaliation plan.

How to Fight Back

Each section in this exhibit hits like a counterpunch to the bullshit you already read. One by one, we revisit each part of the system that screws you – and then we show you how to screw it back. Not with idealism, not with fairy-tale legalese, but with tactical steps, psychological warfare, and the kind of paranoia that makes them nervous for a change.

This isn't "how to beat the case" – it's how to beat the process. It's about control, leverage, and making yourself unplayable in a system that banks on your passivity. This exhibit teaches you how to weaponize the paper trail, turn your silence into strategy, and hold every lying motherfucker accountable with receipts, records, and ruthless clarity.

If you made it this far, congratulations – you've earned the right to fight back. Now let's show you how to do it right.

Exhibit One: The Courthouse

You thought it was a temple of justice. Nah – it's a processing plant for human misery wrapped in marble and seal-stamped lies. The courthouse isn't here to "hear your side." It's here to grind you through a bureaucratic meat grinder that spits out convictions like a vending machine spits soda. From the moment you pass through the metal detectors and get sized up by security like cattle at an auction, your fate is already being whispered in hallways you'll never walk down.

The judge ain't blind – he's just ignoring you. The prosecutor sees your skin, your name, your zip code, and already has a plea deal drafted. And your own lawyer? They're just trying to get through the day without pissing off the people who *really* run the place. The courthouse isn't broken – it's working exactly as designed. Just not for you.

The Courthouse: How to Fightback

You want power in that building? You bring paperwork like it's a fucking weapon. You fight the courthouse with a stack of documented paranoia so thick it makes bureaucrats sweat. Every conversation you have –

follow it with an email. Every promise from a lawyer – confirm it in writing. "As discussed," "per our conversation," "as agreed." These aren't phrases. They're landmines. If your lawyer slips, you've got receipts. If the court delays, you've got a timeline. If a clerk plays dumb, you've got proof.

Create your own shadow docket. Document missed deadlines. Log every rescheduled hearing. Track how many times the prosecutor "forgot" to turn over evidence. You're not being difficult – you're building a war chest. One day, when you need to call out misconduct or incompetence, your paper trail becomes your sword.

And don't just save things. Send them. CC people. Share them. Make sure the court knows you're not just watching – you're documenting. That's when they back up. That's when your name stops meaning "easy target" and starts meaning "liability." You don't win by yelling. You win by proving, by printing, by being the motherfucker who never forgets – and never lets them forget either.

Exhibit Two: Grand Juries

Where the star chamber still lives. Secret, silent, and rigged from the jump. You don't get to see it. You don't get to fight it. You don't even get to know it happened–until it's already done. That's the grand jury. The government's secret weapon dressed up in dusty legal tradition. They sell it as a safeguard. A panel of your "peers" deciding if charges are fair. Bullshit. It's a rubber stamp with a halo.

This exhibit pulls back the curtain on the star chamber that starts it all. Grand juries are where prosecutors go to play God without having to prove a damn thing. No judge, no defense, no rules that matter. Just manipulation, omission, and a one-sided monologue designed to manufacture probable cause out of vapor.

Before they file the indictment, they run it through this quiet little factory of guilt. And once it comes out the other side? You're marked. Not just accused–*doomed*. We're going to show you how they abuse the process, who sits in those chairs, why your lawyer shrugs and says "there's nothing you can do," and why that's a goddamn lie. It all starts here. In secret. In silence. In shadows. Let's drag this dinosaur into the light.

The Grand Jury: How to Fight Back

They'll tell you there's nothing you can do about a grand jury. That's the first lie. The truth? You can't stop it—but you can fuck with its aftermath.

Start with the **transcripts**. Demand them. They won't give you much, but you're looking for sloppiness —contradictions, overreach, anything that smells like prosecutorial freelancing. If they withheld exculpatory evidence? That's your foothold. File a motion. Stir up the dirt.

Second, **weaponize the timeline**. Track when the grand jury convened, what discovery was held back, and whether your lawyer was asleep at the wheel. Prosecutors like to play hide and seek with the calendar—catch them slipping, and you can throw their whole narrative into question.

Third, **public pressure**. You want to shake the tree? Start screaming about secret courts and one-sided justice. Grand juries don't like sunlight. Media exposure, congressional complaint letters, legal blogs— use every crack in the system to shove your story into the light.

Last—**don't trust your lawyer to fight this**. Most won't. *You* need to dig. You need to question. You need to start acting like this is war—because it is. Grand juries are their ambush. You fight back by refusing to stay silent in the dark.

Exhibit Three: Indictments

So you survived the secret slaughterhouse called the grand jury – congrats, you're now the proud recipient of a federal indictment. This isn't just paperwork. This is a loaded weapon with your name on it, fired from the judge's bench and aimed straight at your future. Most people think an indictment means the government "has something." No, dumbass. It means they've got paperwork, a stamp, and a group of clueless citizens who got manipulated into saying "sure, sounds guilty."

You weren't in the room. Your lawyer wasn't in the room. Hell, your side of the story wasn't even invited. This wasn't a fair process – it was a magic trick. They said "evidence," but what they meant was "whatever the agent wrote in their report." They said "probable cause," but that just means "this sounds juicy enough to pursue." The indictment is a piece of theater, dressed up to look like justice. It's designed to feel final – like a declaration. It isn't. It's a tool, a scare tactic, and a goddamn trap.

And don't get it twisted – once that indictment drops, everything changes. Your status, your leverage, your options. You're not a suspect anymore. You're the accused. Your name's on the menu, and they're sharpening the knives. Judges will assume it's legit. Prosecutors will treat it like gospel. Your own damn lawyer might start acting like "we just have to work with this now." Like it's carved in stone. Like it's not built on smoke, bias, and bureaucratic ego. That paper ain't truth. It's strategy. And if you don't learn to treat it like war, it will eat you alive.

Indictments: how to fight back

You don't beat an indictment by crying "unfair." You beat it by dissecting it like a butcher with a grudge. Line by line. Paragraph by paragraph. You make that indictment *earn* every accusation. First move? Don't assume shit. Don't trust that what's written is even accurate. Half of it's based on agent write-ups, cut-and-pasted bullshit, and "facts" twisted just enough to sound sinister. So pick it apart. Demand the grand jury transcripts if you can. If you can't, attack the gaps. What's missing? What did they ignore? What did they twist?

Then go hunting for procedural screwups. Was proper notice given? Were discovery deadlines met? Did the indictment charge the correct statute? Most of the time, these documents are boilerplate. Sloppy. Lazy. And guess what? That laziness is your opening. File motions to dismiss, motions to strike surplus language, motions to require the government to specify what the hell they're actually accusing you of. Make them clarify. Make them sweat.

And if you can't kill the indictment? Then you make it bleed. Turn every vague allegation into a courtroom argument. Make it cost them time. Make it cost them energy. Let them know you're not here to roll over – you're here to expose every shortcut they took. Indictments only win when they go unchallenged. You want to fight back? Then you start by making the government prove they even know what the fuck they're talking about.

Exhibit Four: Arraignments

This is where they "officially" tell you what you've been charged with – as if you didn't already get the message when they kicked your door in and stuffed you in a jumpsuit. Arraignment is dressed up like due process, like your first real day in court, like some noble tradition of reading charges aloud so the accused can respond. Bullshit. This ain't Shakespeare. It's a formality. A ritual. The real decisions already happened without you – behind closed doors, during lunch breaks, in prosecutor group chats and clerk offices that smell like stale coffee and apathy.

You walk in thinking this is your moment to speak. It's not. You say "not guilty," the judge yawns, the prosecutor smirks, and your lawyer whispers something generic about "next steps." Translation? You've just been processed. Tagged like cattle. And that's it. That's all an arraignment really is – a confirmation that the machine has officially swallowed you.

And here's the real kicker – what happens right after the arraignment is what actually matters: **Pretrial Services**. That's where the government slides the shackles on without calling them shackles. Bail, ankle monitors, drug tests, check-ins, movement restrictions – the whole surveillance starter pack. And the judge? They'll act like it's all neutral. That they're just "following protocol." No. They're following the script. And that script ends with you monitored, manipulated, and halfway convicted before trial even begins.

Arraignments: How to Fight Back

You don't win at arraignment – but you damn sure can start building your defense right there. Step one: **show up ready**. You should already know your charges. You should already have your indictment. If your lawyer shows up clueless or winging it – that's a red flag. Demand they file for all discovery right then. Don't wait. Make noise early. Force the paper trail to begin on *your* terms.

Step two: **bring witnesses**. Not for the judge – for the bullshit that might go down. If the prosecutor tries to slide in new charges or play games with your conditions of release, you want someone there to see it. You're not just a defendant – you're now an investigator in your own war. Record the vibe. The facial expressions. The delays. That courtroom ain't sacred. It's a battlefield. Treat it like one.

And step three: **challenge everything**. Did they give proper notice? Are they reading the right indictment version? Are the conditions of release even justified? File early motions. Even if you lose, you're sending a message: I'm not here to beg. I'm here to *drag* this process into the sunlight and make every single person involved regret underestimating me. That starts at arraignment. You don't play defense – you show your teeth.

Exhibit Five: Pretrial Services and Bond Hearings

They call it a "hearing," but you don't get heard. They call it "pretrial," but the judgment's already made. This is the moment the system pretends to give you a chance while quietly slipping a leash around your neck.

Pretrial Services walks in with a smile and a clipboard, pretending to be your friend. They ask about your job, your family, your drug use, your mental health – like it's a goddamn therapy session. What they're really doing is building a profile that'll be used against you in court. "Unstable employment," "no fixed address," "prior convictions," "risk factors." Their report is a landmine in a business suit, and the judge reads it like gospel.

Then comes the bond hearing. Sounds hopeful, right? Like maybe you'll get to go home. What you get instead is a performance. The prosecutor paints you as a cross between Hannibal Lecter and El Chapo, regardless of what you actually did. Your lawyer mumbles something about "community ties" and "flight risk" while sweating through their cheap suit. The judge stares down from the bench like Zeus deciding whether you get struck by lightning or not.

And the decision? Already made. You either get slapped with a bond you can't afford, tossed back into custody, or "granted" release with more strings than a marionette. Home confinement. Drug testing. Curfews. GPS monitoring. Mandatory check-ins. Pretrial Services becomes your new babysitter, and every mistake is a step closer to solitary.

This isn't about justice. It's about compliance. It's about pressure. It's about making you so grateful to be out of a cage that you'll take a shitty plea just to avoid going back.

Pretrial Services and Bond Hearings: How to Fight Back

Rule number one: **stop treating Pretrial like your friend.** They're not your therapist, they're not your advocate, and they sure as hell aren't neutral. Everything you say is fuel for your cage. You need to treat every question like it's a trick – because it is.

When they ask about your job, have documentation ready. Pay stubs. Letters from employers. Proof of income. When they ask about your residence, lock down addresses, leases, bills. They want to say you're unstable – so show them a paper wall they can't knock down.

Same goes for family ties. Don't just say you have kids. Prove it. School records. Medical bills. Pictures. Letters. Make them feel like ripping you away would cause visible, undeniable harm. You're not a person to them – you're a risk assessment. So weaponize the optics. Make it _look_ like cutting you loose would cause more problems than keeping you under watch.

And when it comes to bond? **Don't let your lawyer walk in blind.** Have your shit together. A list of people willing to sign affidavits. Bank statements showing you can post. A place to stay. Transportation. You want the judge to see stability, not question marks.

Oh – and record everything you can, document every step. If Pretrial screws up, violates your rights, or plays games, **you better be ready to burn them down with receipts.**

They want you grateful for the leash. You show them you're watching the hand holding it – and you've got a knife ready if it tightens.

Exhibit Six: Public Defenders

They smile like they're your lifeline. "I'm here to help," they say, flashing a badge of overworked nobility. But let's be real – public defenders aren't the cavalry. They're the cleanup crew for a system already rigged against you. These aren't high-powered advocates digging through case law at midnight. They're triage workers with triple the caseload and half the time, juggling broken cases like hot potatoes while the prosecution preps your conviction like a roast.

You didn't choose them – they were assigned. And that's your first red flag. You're not a client, you're an obligation. One they'll skim a file ten minutes before the hearing and call it "representation." They're not fighting for you in that room. They're negotiating around you, smoothing things out for the court's convenience. Plea deals get pushed like candy – not because it's right, but because trials take time they don't have.

Sure, there are a few warriors in the public defender world. But you won't know until it's too late whether you've got a soldier or a speedbump. And the system counts on that – because if every defendant got a real defense, the whole machine would jam. The dirty truth? The government pays their check. So ask yourself – when the state charges you, and the state pays your lawyer, who the hell do you think they're really loyal to?

Public Defenders: How To Fight Back

This is where paranoia turns into preparation. First off – **stop assuming your public defender is your advocate**. Treat them like a professional you're *forced* to work with – which means you *manage* them. You don't just sit there. You don't just listen. You document.

Step one: **force accountability.** After every meeting, send a follow-up email or letter. "Per our conversation today..." becomes your new battle cry. Confirm what was said. Ask for the next steps in writing. Demand they explain strategy, discovery status, and plea offers. Force them to *be specific*. If they duck and dodge, that's your proof later.

Step two: **don't let them coast.** Public defenders get away with doing the bare minimum because most clients don't know what to ask. So *ask*. Request copies of all discovery. Demand a suppression hearing if there's anything sketchy in your arrest. Push for pretrial motions. Ask about potential defenses. If you sound like you're paying attention – like you might file a complaint – suddenly your case doesn't look like a quick file-close anymore.

Step three: **build a second record.** Parallel their file with your own. Every delay, every misstep, every ignored request – you write it down. Name, date, time. That's your insurance if they tank your case. If they screw up bad enough? That record becomes a complaint, a motion, a reason to get someone else assigned. Maybe even grounds for appeal.

And step four? **Use their fear.** Public defenders *hate* attention. CC the public defender's supervisor on your emails. Drop phrases like "I'm concerned this may rise to ineffective assistance." That's code red language. They don't want that on their radar. Use it. Because once they know *you know* the rules – the power starts to shift.

You can't fire them. But you can make them sweat. You can turn "just another file" into "a pain in the ass who might actually bite back." And in this system? That bite might be the only thing that keeps your freedom intact.

Exhibit Eight: Prosecutors

Ah, the prosecutor – the system's golden child. Suited up, smug smile, riding the high horse of "justice" while burying people for sport. Don't let the calm tone and law school diction fool you. These aren't neutral truth-seekers. These are conviction-chasers with one eye on your file and the other on their win column. Every case is a stat. Every plea deal is a shortcut to career advancement. And your life? That's just the fuel for their next promotion.

They've got all the tools: investigators, labs, confidential informants, sealed warrants, and a press machine that calls you guilty before the first hearing. And they love to pretend they're being fair – that their decisions are based on "the interests of justice." Bullshit. Their interest is power, plain and simple. They overcharge to force pleas, withhold evidence until it's convenient, and pressure witnesses behind closed doors. This isn't about truth. It's about leverage.

And the scariest part? They don't have to be right. Prosecutors can be wrong, reckless, even malicious – and they're almost never held accountable. Immunity protects them. The judge trusts them. Your lawyer fears them. And the jury assumes they wouldn't bring charges unless you were guilty. That's the real trick – they walk into court wearing a halo made of handcuffs, pretending the only goal is justice, when the real goal is a body count.

Prosecutors: How to Fight Back

You want to shake a prosecutor? Start acting like you're not afraid of them. Start acting like you know the game – and you've got receipts.

First, **don't wait for your defense lawyer to do all the work**. You research the prosecutor assigned to your case. Look at their past cases. See how many go to trial. See how many end in pleas. Track patterns. You're not being paranoid – you're profiling the enemy.

Second, **watch their tactics like a hawk**. Prosecutors will bury exculpatory evidence and pretend it's "not relevant." File motions. Demand a *Brady disclosure*. If you think they're playing games with discovery, say so – *in writing*. If they delay turning over lab results or witness statements, make it part of your case timeline. You're not just watching – you're preparing a misconduct record. Trust me, they hate that.

Third, **public pressure is leverage**. Prosecutors like to operate in the shadows – plea deals behind closed doors, threats whispered in hallway meetings. So if they get shady? Shine a light. File a complaint with the State Bar. Leak a summary of their tactics to a local reporter. Post on forums. Make noise. Make them *answer*.

Fourth, **use their fear of losing**. Nothing scares a prosecutor more than a smart, stubborn defendant who refuses to roll over. If you make them work – really work – you can force better plea deals, maybe even get the case dismissed. File every motion you can. Raise every legal issue. Bury them in paperwork like they're used to doing to others.

Finally, **don't buy their bullshit**. "This is the best offer you'll get" is a scare tactic. "If you take it to trial, we'll add more charges" is extortion dressed as procedure. Don't let their threats bend you into submission. If you've got leverage, use it. If you've got doubt in the case, hammer it.

You don't need to beat the prosecutor at their own game. You just need to show them you're not an easy win. That you've read the rules, flipped the board, and brought your own dice. In a system where they expect silence, being loud – being prepared – being dangerous to their comfort zone? That's your only shot.

Exhibit Nine: The Unholy Triangle

Welcome to the backroom handshake nobody warned you about – the unholy triangle of the courtroom: judge, prosecutor, and defense attorney. Three sides, one shape, and guess what? You ain't part of it. You're just the name on the docket getting shuffled like a manila folder while they play judicial patty-cake with your future.

This triangle doesn't argue – it choreographs. Your lawyer walks into chambers with the same prosecutor who's trying to bury you, and they both smile at the judge like it's happy hour. Deals get whispered off record. Expectations get "managed." And by the time you show up in court thinking you've got a shot, the outcome's already been soft-launched over coffee.

Don't get it twisted – this isn't some wild conspiracy theory. This is how the sausage gets made. The prosecutor wants speed, the judge wants order, and your lawyer wants peace. So they "triage" your case, which is code for rushing it through the conveyor belt. Evidence be damned. Context ignored. Because justice doesn't happen in the courtroom – it happens in chambers, where you'll never sit.

Your lawyer will tell you it's strategy. The prosecutor will call it procedure. The judge will call it efficiency. But what it really is? Collusion. A quiet agreement that you're not worth the time it would take to treat you fairly. And you'll never hear it said out loud – because it doesn't need to be. The triangle already knows the dance steps.

The Unholy Triangle: How To Fight Back

You want to disrupt the triangle? First rule: **don't play dumb**. Understand that your case is being "handled" behind your back. So start dragging everything *into the light*.

Make your lawyer uncomfortable. Ask for written updates. Demand they explain what was said in chambers. Force them to log every "sidebar" and every off-the-record conference. You're not just a client

– you're a fucking surveillance drone now. If they can't or won't give you details? That's your signal the triangle's already spinning.

Second, **get outside advice**. You're allowed to have a second opinion. You're allowed to consult another attorney, even if you're stuck with a public defender. Do it. Not to switch – but to *compare notes*. It spooks the triangle when they know you've got someone on the outside watching.

Third, **weaponize court transcripts**. Every hearing, every motion, every plea – request the damn transcripts. Read them. Compare what was said in court to what you were told behind closed doors. If there's a gap, flag it. If they're lying, document it. Nothing makes judges and lawyers sweat like knowing you're actually *paying attention*.

Fourth, **file your own motions** if your lawyer won't. Pro se filings can be a pain, but they shake the triangle's rhythm. You don't have to be a lawyer to demand discovery. You don't have to be silent just because you've got representation. One well-aimed filing can jam the gears just enough to force a real conversation.

And finally, **start recording everything they expect you to forget**. Dates, times, hallway comments, courtroom reactions – write it all down. Create a triangle map. Show how each move lines up with the others. When they see you building a narrative, they start second-guessing the one they're trying to script.

The triangle only works when you're passive – when you nod, sign, and shut up. But if you question, pressure, and expose? You break the illusion. And when you do that, the triangle doesn't just wobble – it collapses. Because the one thing that trio fears more than a complicated case… is a *complicated defendant*.

Exhibit Ten: Judges

The robe that rules the theater You walk into court thinking the judge is some wise, neutral wizard – part Solomon, part Yoda, ready to hear both sides and deliver justice. Nah. What you've actually got is a government employee in a robe, half-bored, half-annoyed, and fully invested in making the docket move like a fast-food drive-thru. They don't give a damn about your "truth." They care about calendar control, courtroom decorum, and getting to lunch on time.

Judges pretend to be referees, but they're more like rigged slot machines – spinning, blinking, and programmed to deliver the same result: conviction. They act impartial until it's your side objecting. They quote the Constitution like it's gospel until the prosecutor screws up, then suddenly "it's not prejudicial." And when your lawyer fumbles? They raise an eyebrow and ask if you want a recess – so the court can "continue efficiently." Efficient, as in: quickly sweep your ass into prison and clear the next case.

Behind the bench is a person who's seen too many lies to believe anything anymore – including the truth. They'll smile, nod, then rule based on what keeps the machine humming. They don't fear you. They don't fear your lawyer. They fear *appeals*. That's it. Which means if no one's watching, they'll rule how they damn well please – and dare you to do something about it.

You think you're walking into a courtroom. But what you're really walking into... is **their** room. Decorated with flags, old wood, and a giant fucking ego. And in their room, you're just a character in a play they've seen too many times. Spoiler: you don't get a happy ending.

Judges: How To Fight Back

You want to make a judge sweat? Don't argue. **Document.** Judges love silence – not because it's peaceful, but because silence doesn't generate appealable error. You want power? You make noise on the record. You object. You clarify. You request reasons for denials. Every time you speak, you plant a minefield in their ruling.

Second, learn **how to appeal before you ever need to.** Most people scream "I'll appeal!" without understanding that appeals only work if the judge makes a *visible* mistake – on the record. No transcript? No appeal. No objection? No error preserved. You gotta build your future appeal like it's a trap – one careless ruling at a time.

Third, watch their **patterns**. Judges are creatures of habit. They quote the same bullshit lines. Rule the same way on repeat motions. Favor certain lawyers. You're not paranoid – you're observant. Track it.

Chart it. If you see a trend, use it in your motion practice. Call it out in filings. Build a record that shows bias – not just suspicion.

Fourth, file **judicial complaints** sparingly but strategically. You only get one nuke. Use it when the judge crosses a line that's blatant and egregious. Don't whine. Don't ramble. Send cold, clinical complaints backed by receipts. It won't fix your case – but it might make the judge back off in the short run. Even kings hate audits.

And finally – **treat the judge like a hostile witness in a bad script.** Feed them lines that force them to make choices. Force rulings. Don't just sit there nodding while your lawyer mumbles. Ask to speak. Ask for clarity. Ask if they're ruling "as a matter of law" or "in the interest of judicial economy." Make them pick a lane. Then log it.

You don't beat a judge by yelling at them – you beat them by boxing them into their own rules. Because the only thing more dangerous than a pissed-off defendant… is a *documented* one.

Exhibit Eleven: Clerks And Court Reporters

The invisible hands that rig the record. You never see them coming. The clerk in the corner? The court reporter with the bored look? They're not just background noise. They're the ones holding the scissors behind the curtain, trimming your rights sentence by sentence. These aren't neutral paper-pushers. They're **gatekeepers** – and they know exactly how much power they hold. You think your battle is with the judge or the prosecutor, but these quiet assassins decide what gets filed, what gets heard, and what disappears.

Clerks can "misplace" motions, delay filings, misdate documents, or conveniently "forget" to notify you of a hearing. They can shuffle your paperwork to the bottom of the pile while smiling in your face. And guess what? There's no jury watching them. No camera pointed at their hands. They're the custodians of the process – which means they can weaponize it against you without ever raising their voice.

Then come the court reporters – the supposed record-keepers of the sacred truth. Except they don't record everything. They decide what "matters." They clean up mumbling judges. They omit off-the-record comments. They tidy up messes in the transcript so everyone looks "professional." Your lawyer got bulldozed in open court? Doesn't matter. If it ain't on the transcript, it **didn't happen**.

Together, these two groups form a shadow tier of courtroom control. And nobody tells you this. Your lawyer shrugs. The judge ignores it. Meanwhile, your case gets quietly sabotaged by the very people you didn't even think were part of the game. But trust this – they are. And they've been doing it longer than you've been alive.

Clerks And Court Reporters: How To Fight Back

Start with this: **treat every filing like it's going to war.** Triple-check your timestamps. Demand copies. Don't just "drop it off." Get a stamped confirmation. If a clerk shrugs or delays, ask – loudly and in writing – for a supervisor. You're not just submitting paperwork. You're planting legal landmines. Make them step carefully.

Next, **document interactions**. The clerk said the motion was "lost"? Email them. The clerk said the judge hasn't signed off yet? Ask for proof. Keep names, times, dates. If they lie, you escalate. If they stall, you file. Make every minor delay into a documented incident. Bureaucrats don't fear emotion – they fear exposure.

When it comes to court reporters, **get aggressive about transcripts.** Request them immediately after hearings. Compare them to your notes or your memory. Was something key "left out"? Was the judge's tone mysteriously polite in the transcript when they were actually snapping at you? File a **motion to correct the record**. Most people never do – and that's the trap.

Also: **record everything** if allowed. Some states permit it. Some don't. Either way, act like they're trying to erase your version of events – because they just might be. If you suspect foul play in the transcript, request the audio. If denied, file a motion. Create a paper trail that makes their omissions look deliberate – because often, they are.

Finally, remember: **these people aren't neutral.** They're part of the machinery. Don't treat them like friendly staff. Treat them like hostile witnesses in a slow-moving ambush. Polite? Sure. Submissive?

Never. Because in court, the truth isn't what happened. It's what got *written down*. And you better make damn sure it's accurate – or it's your ass that gets erased.

The Final Word: Burn It All Down

You've made it this far, so stop pretending you're some innocent lost in the maze. You know exactly what this system is now – a goddamn racket dressed up like a religion. The marble, the flags, the Latin on the walls – all just props for the show. You thought this was justice? No, this is organized betrayal with a filing system. Every robe, every badge, every clerk behind glass is another cog in the grinder chewing through lives to keep the machine fed.

So here's the deal – you don't reform this shit. You don't reason with it. You *wreck* it. You make them choke on their own paperwork. You weaponize every rule, every form, every line of the transcript. You drag their "clerical errors" into daylight. You bury their silence under so much documented proof they can't breathe. You stop begging to be treated fair and start making it dangerous to fuck with you.

Because justice doesn't live in their buildings anymore. It lives in your rage, your memory, and your paper trail. The courthouse, the prosecutor, the judge, the clerk – they all count on one thing: your compliance. They need you scared. Quiet. Grateful. Don't give them that satisfaction. Give them hell instead.
 This isn't about winning cases. It's about burning their playbook. You don't ask for fairness – you *force* it. You don't wait for justice – you *become* the consequence.

So go ahead. Raise your voice. File your motions. Record their bullshit. Stack your receipts like ammo. And when the machine comes for you again, don't flinch. Smile. Because now you know how to aim back.

www.ingramcontent.com/pod-product-compliance
Lightning Source LLC
Chambersburg PA
CBHW080402270326
41927CB00015B/3321